KING ICAHN

MARK STEVENS

KING ICAHN

The Biography of a Renegade Capitalist

RESEARCH BY CAROL BLOOM STEVENS

A DUTTON BOOK

DUTTON

Published by the Penguin Group
Penguin Books USA Inc., 375 Hudson Street, New York, New York 10014, U.S.A.
Penguin Books Ltd, 27 Wrights Lane, London W8 5TZ, England,
Penguin Books Australia Ltd, Ringwood, Victoria, Australia
Penguin Books Canada Ltd, 10 Alcorn Avenue, Toronto, Ontario, Canada M4V 3B2
Penguin Books (N.Z.) Ltd, 182-190 Wairau Road, Auckland 10, New Zealand

Penguin Books Ltd, Registered Offices: Harmondsworth, Middlesex, England

First published by Dutton, an imprint of New American Library, a division of Penguin
Books USA Inc. Distributed in Canada by McClelland & Stewart Inc.

First Printing, June, 1993
1 3 5 7 9 10 8 6 4 2

Library of Congress Cataloging in Publication Data:
Stevens, Mark, 1947–
King Icahn : the biography of a renegade capitalist / Mark Stevens.
p. c.m
ISBN 0-525-93613-0
1. Icahn, Carl C., 1936– . 2. Capitalists and financiers—United States—Biography. 3.
Consolidation and merger of corporations—United States—History. I. Title.
HG172.I27S74 1993
338.8'3'092—dc20
[B] 92-37592
CIP

Printed in the United States of America

Set in Bodoni Book
Designed by Steven N. Stathakis

"I create nothing, I own."

—Gordon Gekko in the film *Wall Street,* 1987

CONTENTS

PREFACE

This book—an unauthorized biography of corporate raider, CEO, and financier Carl C. Icahn—is the product of extensive research including more than one hundred and twenty interviews with individuals who have been personally involved in Icahn's life and career—some as allies, others as adversaries. The list includes corporate CEOs, investment bankers, attorneys, government officials, and investors, as well as relatives and employees of Carl Icahn, most of whom have spoken for attribution; others cooperated on the grounds that they would remain anonymous.

The author has also had virtually unlimited access to Icahn himself, who was interviewed at length and who has made his aides and associates available to the author, all, including Icahn, without limitations on the subject matter or control over the book.

Although this is a biography, the goal is not to cover every incident or transaction in Icahn's life but instead to reveal the forces that shaped the man and to explore how and why he would have a stunning impact on the nation's business community during a tumultuous and controversial decade. In doing so, the goal is to learn something about the corporate establishment, as well as the man who would learn to manipulate it, amassing one of the great fortunes in America.

THE BILLION DOLLAR EPIPHANY

"I was once the rich uncle. Now he's the rich nephew."
—ELLIOT SCHNALL

In the summer of 1979, Carl Icahn, then a relatively obscure Wall Street figure with a hole-in-the-wall brokerage firm and a knack for making money in the options business, traveled to Miami to visit his mother Bella and his uncle, Elliot Schnall. In the course of a dinner with Uncle Elliot, a successful businessman who had been an Icahn role model all of his life, Carl made a startling announcement: He was going to start a new business: investing in, and taking over, undervalued companies.

To Schnall, a dashing social butterfly who had parlayed the sale of a looseleaf company into an idle-rich lifestyle with homes in Palm Beach and Southampton, the idea of young Carl running off half-cocked into a risky new adventure was positively frightening.

"When Carl told me he was going after undervalued compa-

nies, I said, 'What! Why the hell don't you stick to Wall Street—
stick to what you know? You don't want to get involved in
running companies. I've been involved in running two companies, and I can tell you you don't need that headache.' "

To Schnall, and to almost everyone else in America in the
relatively innocent 1970s, the reason you bought a company was
to run it and build it and someday will it to your heirs. So when
Carl asked Schnall to invest in his first move on an undervalued
company—the Ohio-based Tappan Company—the same uncle
who had earlier loaned Carl $400,000 for a seat on the New York
Stock Exchange, balked. Schnall rejected Carl's overtures, saying, "To hell with that. I'm not moving to Ohio." The way
Schnall saw it, "If you went after a company, you had to live
there."

Undaunted, Icahn pressed on, repeating what would
become one of the key buzzwords of the 1980s: "Undervalued.
Undervalued. Undervalued." Still he made no headway with his
prospective backer, who could only view a takeover in terms of
traditional corporate ownership.

"I said to Carl, 'What the hell are you going to do with
Tappan anyway? You don't know a damn thing about stoves. In
fact, I know more than you because I owned one and those
Tappan stoves are lousy.'

"When Carl said I was 'missing it,' I fired right back at him
saying, 'I'm not. Tappan's just a lousy stove.'

"But to Carl, what the company made was basically irrelevant. I didn't understand that at the time."

Determined to get another perspective on the matter,
Schnall contacted a friend who had played a key role in creating
acquisition strategies for the high-flying conglomerate Litton
Industries. Recalling that Litton had considered buying Tappan,
Elliot recognized that the company's due diligence could now
prove invaluable to Carl. As it turned out, the former Litton
executive had some pointed advice for the budding takeover
artist.

"Tappan's a lousy company," he told Schnall. "Tell your
nephew to stick to Wall Street or he'll lose his shirt."

When the dutiful uncle delivered what he hoped and believed would be the coup de grace to Carl's wild scheme, he found instead that the warning carried no weight at all. Carl's response to the Litton caveat: "What the hell do they know?"

As it turned out, not very much. Soon after, Icahn would launch a battle for control of Tappan, intimidating management to the point that a white knight would be called in to rescue the beleaguered appliance maker from the clutches of a hostile take-over. But Carl would prove to be the big winner, netting a $2.7 million profit as Tappan's shares were acquired for a premium over Icahn's purchase price.

For Uncle Elliot, it was a lesson he would never forget.

"Carl was still a young man, and in a single deal that took place over a period of months, he was able to make about $3 million." Schnall says, "At the time, all I could think of was that it takes smart guys twelve lifetimes to make that kind of money.

"I was awed by it."

But to Icahn, the Tappan experience simply validated his theory about corporate management. Soon after, he would see an even more desperate management give him his first taste of greenmail. At the time, Icahn had built a position in a company, then traded over-the-counter, to the point that he owned a substantial block of the outstanding stock. As a major shareholder concerned with his investment, Icahn informed management that he wanted to see significant changes in the way the company did business. In response, senior management agreed, reluctantly, to grant Icahn an audience.

On the appointed day, Icahn appeared at the company's executive offices, where he was promptly ushered into a meeting with the CEO and his top lieutenants. In this closed-door session, Icahn presented his litany of complaints about how the company was run along with a punchlist of improvements he believed would spike up sales and profits. Although Icahn never said so directly (at this stage of the game he was still testing his limited power), there was a veiled threat that if changes weren't made, the company's most outspoken shareholder would seek a controlling interest.

Listening to Icahn's monologue in utter silence, the CEO and his team allowed the brash gadfly to make his galling presentation, and then asked him to wait in a reception area while management conferred with an investment banker who had sat in on the session at the company's request. Convinced that he had made a forceful case for reconfiguring the business, Icahn paced like an expectant father, waiting for what he hoped would be a favorable response to his plan. When the investment banker returned, Carl greeted him enthusiastically. "What do they think? What do they think?"

What Icahn was about to hear shocked him. The conversation went like this:

Investment banker: "You know, Carl, they don't like you at all."

Icahn: "That's funny, I thought I was making some headway."

Investment banker: "No, you're a bad judge of character. They just don't like you, Carl. Let me tell you what we're going to do to you. We know you're a tough guy and what have you, but here's what we're going to do to you.

"I don't like to threaten you, but we are going to begin by smearing your name. We've got three PR firms. We've got the best three PR firms in New York. Starting tomorrow, we are going to start smearing your name . . . and we know you may not be scared of that. But you know they are going to start calling you a racketeer, and maybe your wife doesn't like being with a racketeer when she goes out to a restaurant. It's not well thought of. Maybe your friends will sort of smirk, so think about that one. But after you are smeared in all the newspapers, think about the next step. If you keep buying stock, then we are going to dilute the hell out of you. That is what we plan to do. We are going to issue an awful lot of stock here to all the people, all our friends, and you keep buying stock but it's like we're printing up stock in the basement.

"It's like the old days with the robber barons, you know. Vanderbilt was buying stock with the other guys in the basement printing it up. Fisk or Gould was printing it up and selling it to him. That's what we are going to do. We are just going to print up stock and we are going to give it out all over the place . . . Now that's what we're going to do and we have a few other things we haven't told you about."

Just as Icahn thought he had run headlong into an unyielding adversary, a carrot replaced the stick.

"Now on the other side of the coin," the investment banker continued, "here is what we are willing to offer you: a $10 million profit if you will go away. And I'll tell you another thing. I've got a list of ten other companies in my pocket that I suggest you go after. That's my offer."

Then he said, "Hey, look, Carl, do you want twenty-four hours?"

For an options trader who had learned full well the importance of taking profits when they materialized before his eyes, there was little to think about.

Icahn said, "I don't want twenty-four hours, I'll take the deal right now . . ."

This was more than a financial coup for a bright and ambitious young man. It was a lesson, an epiphany, that would enable Icahn to terrorize America's corporate establishment for a decade, amassing one of the nation's great fortunes in the process.

Today, Icahn Enterprises—encompassing securities brokerage, rail car leasing, real estate, interests in an airline, junk-bond trading, and thoroughbred breeding—is headquartered in a compound of modern, low-rise buildings in Mt. Kisco, New York, just minutes from the chairman's 120-acre estate. His personal office, a replica of an English duke's drawing room enlarged to the size of a cricket field, is adorned with exquisite oriental rugs and a rich inventory of antiques. Everything about the setting smacks of wealth and power. A stairway leads to a book-lined balcony that wraps around the office and a personal elevator to the side of Icahn's massive desk whisks the king to his private dining room one level below. Here he dines majestically, overlooking an environment of ponds and rock gardens created to please his eye and soothe his mind.

An elegant conference room, where Icahn is known to preside over marathon negotiating sessions that stretch deep into the night, reeks of subdued power. Twelve beige tufted-leather chairs surround a large conference table. At the boss's end, a telephone console is at his fingertips, as is a remote-control wand for opening and closing the power window shades that lie behind long green drapes. Inset in a mahogany-paneled wall is an oil portrait of *Bold Ruler: Horse of the Year 1957*. Icahn, himself a horse breeder through his company FoxField Thoroughbreds, is the proud owner of Meadow Star, a champion filly.

At his first sight of Icahn's headquarters, which Icahn built to house his collection of companies including TWA, ACF, and Icahn & Company, a senior executive with Drexel Burnham Lambert, once Icahn's takeover financiers, quipped to his associates, "My God, we're making too much money for this guy. Get back to your desk and figure out a way to raise his fees."

Icahn is a creature of the telephone, speaking on one line while a control panel's blinking red lights remind him of the lawyers, investment bankers, and assorted seekers of his time who are lined up in holding patterns waiting to give him news of ailing airlines, casinos that can be bought on the cheap, undervalued companies waiting to be picked off like so many fish in a barrel.

He talks in a rambling, New York street style, heaped with schmaltz and laced with heavy doses of "screw them," "fuck him," and "tell them to go to hell." Eyes closed, one hand snaking through his thinning hair, he is completely absorbed in the conversation, planning and strategizing as he engages in the intellectual wrestling match that is his forte. Totally self-reliant, he is a master negotiator. He believes no one, expects the worst of people, distrusts his allies and adversaries alike, and makes no pretense at intimacy.

"If you want a friend on Wall Street," he has said, "get a dog."

Although he is surrounded by high-priced executives and sycophants, only one person—long-time deal analyst and alter ego Alfred Kingsley—truly has Icahn's ear. From the earliest days of the Icahn juggernaut, Kingsley has been by his side, identifying takeover patsys, planning tactics, presenting the opportunities and the caveats for the boss's review. Blessed with a brilliant financial mind and a gift for seeing through corporate financial statements to find diamonds in the rough, he is a backroom numbers cruncher whose insights come to full flower in Icahn's skillful hands.

"Carl and Kingsley operate like a couple of rag merchants," said Joseph Corr, former president of TWA, the airline controlled by Icahn. "Carl is always yelling at Kingsley, but it all bounces off Al. Al has a great mind. He puts things in a language Carl can relate to. I used to explain things from a cash-flow standpoint but Kingsley would recast it into a 'Put up your money and here's what you get for it' approach. Carl likes it that way."

Many who have observed the men in action over the years insist that Kingsley has earned hundreds of millions of dollars for Icahn. Still, he has never been annointed a partner. In Carl Icahn's kingdom, there is no place for partners. Virtually all of the equity and all of the power rest with the king.

"Carl is a very tough guy with everyone," remarked attorney Marvin Olshan, who represented Icahn in his early takeover transactions. "He plays a certain game that's very hard and very tough.

"No one has been nurtured by Carl. Guys who worked around Bass, Milken, Perelman, all got rich in their own right. Not with Carl. If Kingsley made any money it's because he was there and because he knew how to make investments himself. Carl doesn't share his success with anyone."

Icahn's steely assessment of his own financial tactics can be summed up by an exchange he had with federal judge Gerald L. Goettel in the course of a 1984 legal proceeding over alleged improprieties over the purchase and sale of Saxon Industries stock. Explaining his stock market philosophy, Icahn said: "If the price is right, we are going to sell. I think that's true of everything you have, except maybe your kids and possibly your wife."

When a shocked judge responded by asking "Possibly?" Icahn confirmed that he had heard right. "Possibly," Icahn repeated, adding the caveat, "Don't tell my wife."

At six feet three inches, gawky and pigeon-toed, Icahn wears his height poorly. One could easily take him for an elongated clone of Mel Brooks. Dressed in a poorly fitted blue suit that looks as if it were bought off the rack at Robert Hall's "going out of business sale," he is hardly the vision of a Forbes 400 capitalist with a fortune estimated at from $650 million to more than $1 billion.

"There was always something quirky about Icahn," says a former Drexel Burnham investment banker who advised Icahn in his 1985 takeover battle with Phillips Petroleum. "On several occasions, I would be talking with Carl in his office when he would abruptly excuse himself, announcing, of all things, that he was going to change his socks. Change his socks! Why would he need to do that in the middle of the day. Not once but several times! I never asked—some things you don't ask a client—but I always felt this guy was slightly strange."

Although he can, and generally does, focus on his myriad business deals with extraordinary intensity, at times he can drift off on a perplexing tangent. In a typical episode, Icahn—deep into a strategy session with a lawyer from a prominent Manhattan firm—suddenly stared at a Bic pen he was holding in his hand. Mumbling to himself about his low opinion of Bics, he called out to his long-time administrative assistant Gail Golden, making the announcement that he hates this brand of pens and why do they have them in the office and what the hell can be done to get better pens. For fifteen minutes, Icahn stayed on the Bic tirade until, his point made, he returned to the intricacies of the deal at hand without missing a beat.

Observing him in person—the cheap suit, the gawky gait, the sudden tangents—you can find yourself wondering if this is really the formidable raider and financial tactician Carl Icahn, or if a poor schnook from Brooklyn is minding the store in his absence.

But in time, you realize that this is, of course, the genuine article and that he has few peers in a real life monopoly game where intellect, creativity and brute force triumph over sartorial splendor every time, no matter what the "dress for success" gurus have to say. It is in this real-life game that Icahn has proven himself a master, transforming a middle-class nerd from Queens into a powerful manipulator of the capitalist system. In little more than a decade, he has combined an extraordinary intellect with a battering-ram personality to exploit a glaring weakness in the American corporate establishment, earning enormous sums as he attacked the likes of Tappan, Marshall Field, American Can, Simplicity Pattern, Phillips Petroleum, Chesebrough Pond's, Owens Illinois, ACF Industries, TWA, Texaco, and USX.

"Observing Carl over the years, I have come to think of him as a bull, snorting and pacing in front of a barbwire fence," said Gail Golden, Icahn's executive assistant since 1978. "He is always looking for a way to get through that fence to strike a deal. Although it looks to everyone else as if there's no way out, Carl finds a way."

As much as he relishes the macho image of the fearsome raider who makes CEOs quiver, he is and always has been an intellect who delights in tinkering with ideas and concepts, arranging and rearranging the pieces into innovative forms. Seated behind his sprawling desk, he is often wielding his favorite weapon, scissors, clipping charts, graphs, articles, stock tables, and spreading them in a collage on his blotter. When working at home he will listen to music—Tchaikovsky's *Violin Concerto in D* and *Rigolletto* are favorites. He is always looking for ways to synthesize information and to arrive at original concepts others are blind to. Relying only marginally on the advice and counsel of the lawyers and investment bankers that are at his beck and call, Icahn—who has a deep-seated disdain for self-proclaimed experts—prefers to do his own thinking and his own negotiating.

"Carl is the kind of person who follows his own instincts and formulates his own ideas," remarked attorney Theodore Altman, who represented Icahn in his raids on Dan River, Phillips Petroleum, and Simplicity Pattern. "We could line up all the recognized experts in the world on how to do something and Carl will say, 'Let's look at it a different way.'

"He is determined to pursue his own instincts."

So extraordinary are those instincts that investment banker Brian Freeman once said: "If he lives long enough, Carl will have all the money in the world."

In recent years, however, even Icahn supporters have come to believe that his determination to squeeze his adversaries beyond ordinary limits will blow up in his face, leading ultimately to his undoing.

FROM
BAYSWATER TO
PRINCETON

"The Empiricist Criterion of Meaning"

"In his Princeton yearbook, Carl said his goals in life were medical school, marriage and children.
"If ever a person didn't do what he set out to do."
—A PRINCETON ADMINISTRATOR

As a child in the 1940s, Carl Celian Icahn was one among many bright Jewish boys coming of age in the tidy middle-class community of Bayswater, New York. Located at the eastern tip of the borough of Queens, Bayswater was a demographic midway point between the wealthy Five Town communities of Lawrence, Woodmere, Cedarhurst, Hewlett, and Inwood and the working class enclave of Far Rockaway.

Where one lived within this economic archipelago was determined by income and occupation. Park Avenue surgeons, Seventh Avenue schmata makers and Wall Street investment bankers inhabited the imposing brick, Tudor-style miniestates that made the Five Towns a *House & Garden* showcase. General practitioners, self-employed lawyers and mom-and-pop shop-owners lived in the cookie-cutter capes that lined Bayswater's well-swept streets, such as the Icahn home at 2408 Healey Avenue. Waiters, civil servants, and assorted schleppers were relegated to the rental apartments and tiny cottages of downscale Far Rockaway.

From this vantage point young Carl, who had been born in Brooklyn on February 16, 1936, and moved to Bayswater the following year, witnessed New York's economic strata in microcosm.

The Long Island Rail Road tracks divided Far Rockaway into two parts, Bayswater and Wave Crest. Wave Crest had a lower-middle-class look about it. The homes were tiny, the landscaping was sparse and amateurish and the roads were cracked.

"Bayswater, on the other side of the tracks, was a notch up," recalled Maurice Singer, an Icahn contemporary who grew up in Wave Crest and went on to become a TWA pilot. "Although the homes were modest, they were well maintained and professionally landscaped. But if that made the Bayswater residents feel as if they had arrived, a drive through the Five Towns would put them in their place. That's where the captains of industry, men who owned Bulova Watch and Van Heusen shirts, held forth on two-acre estates. It was a real order of magnitude up."

Throughout Bayswater, the dream was to move over the Queens border and into the promised land. For the most part, Bayswater's inhabitants were first- and second-generation Americans—hardworking, ambitious, and obsessed with climbing the economic ladder. They dreamed of homes with Wagner swimming pools, Coupe de Villes in the driveway, wrists and necks adorned with Tiffany jewelry.

Marching to a decidedly different drummer, Michael and Bella Icahn were repelled by the excess, the wealth, the elitism the Five Towns represented. For Bella, a strict, strong-minded teacher at a Bayswater public school, the aversion to upper-class privilege stemmed from an egalitarian philosophy.

"I always hated the way the Five Towns people talked about their servants," Bella recalled. "They'd say, 'Can you believe it?

You have to lock the refrigerator door or they'll steal your food.'
I found it repulsive to talk of people that way or to treat them as
second-class citizens.

"Through the years I was teaching, we had a housekeeper,
Henrietta, who looked after Carl from the time he was three
months of age until he reached fifteen. I paid her $45 a month.
The neighbors were furious because that was $10 more than the
going rate. But I didn't care what they said or thought. I saw it
as the right thing to do."

To Bella, the Five Towns mentality—preoccupied with con-
spicuous consumption—blinded the social climbers to the best
things in life. "My husband's brother was a wealthy doctor. Did
that mean he was well off and we weren't? People may have
thought that, but it wasn't so. My husband used to say to his
brother, 'Lou, you are rich, but we live rich.'

"The fact is, we lived modestly and we liked it that way."

A gifted pianist as a girl, Bella had abandoned the dream of
a concert career to pacify her mother, who preferred the "security" of a teaching position. As she grew older, she satisfied her
love of music by developing a passion for the theater.

"In those days you could live nicely on a teacher's salary,"
Bella says. "If I wanted to take my family to the theater, I had
the money for that. And if I wanted to buy myself a mink coat,
I could do that too. But nothing was ever done to impress others.
Nothing was showy. I drove the same shabby Chevrolet for
twelve years."

Compared to her husband, Bella was a free-market reaction-
ary. A ferocious critic of laissez-faire capitalism, and of the vast
disparity of incomes and lifestyles that it spawned, Michael Icahn
railed endlessly at the wealthy "robber barons" comfortably
ensconced in the sprawling estates of Lawrence and Woodmere,
Greenwich and Scarsdale.

"When Carl used to visit me in Scarsdale, he'd get a look
at the affluent life," said his uncle Elliot, Bella's kid brother, who
married into money and was installed by his father-in-law as
president of the Cole Steel Co. "It was Carl's first exposure to
living on a high scale, and he was taken immediately by the
gracious living, the beautiful home, and cars and servants.

"But Carl's father never liked the way I lived. He looked askance at it. His attitude was: 'How can you have all of this—the pool, the maids—when there are children starving.' "

For Michael Icahn, this was representative of a fundamentalist philosophy that viewed everything in the world as black and white, good and evil.

"My father was a very opinionated man," Carl recalled. "He had set opinions on everything, and his strongest opinion was that there was something wrong about great wealth. To describe his feelings about this as an opinion is really an understatement. Wealthy people outraged him. The social juxtaposition of a tiny group of people living in great splendor and many more living in abject poverty was anathema to him."

Michael was cold and aloof to his only son. "He never played ball or anything with me, so when I was eight or nine we'd just sit home for hours at a time and talk. He'd read Schopenhauer to me. Or we'd argue. Almost as two adults. He was very dogmatic and expressed his beliefs with a kind of fury."

The source of Michael's incessant rage stemmed largely from failed hopes. Much like his wife, Michael had dreamed of a career in music, singing the role of Pagliacci on the great stage of New York's Metropolitan Opera. But unlike Bella, who was blocked from fulfilling her musical ambitions by an insecure mother, Michael had to face the painful truth that he lacked the talent for a career in opera.

"That doesn't mean he ever got the dream out of his system," said Schnall, a Jew turned Unitarian who changed his name from Melvin to Elliot. "Although he earned a law degree at Fordham University, it was really a waste because he never practiced law. Instead, he would seize every opportunity to sing, Metropolitan Opera or not. One time he took a job singing Irish songs on the radio. I remember coming home from Brooklyn's Erasmus Hall High School on a St. Patrick's Day and hearing Michael on the radio singing 'Danny Boy.' "

Strange work for a man who would be appointed to the revered post of cantor at Cedarhurst's Temple Beth-El. Or was it? Although born a Jew, Michael Icahn had become a confirmed atheist, disavowing all forms of organized religion. Serving as a cantor was not as much a career in Judaism as it was in music.

"The leaders of the temple used to refer to my husband as their goyish cantor," Bella recalled. "They knew where he stood on religion—Michael was never one to keep his thoughts to himself—but they put up with all of that because he sang so beautifully.

"Not that Michael didn't make some compromises. When Carl came of age, we had him bar-mitzvahed at Beth-El. Not because we felt deeply for the tradition, because it wouldn't look very good if the cantor's son was exempt."

An intense man with a searing intellect, Michael felt compelled to use his intelligence to challenge and incite, bullying those who came into his little orbit. Family members were subject to his constant quizzing. "What's the biggest planet? How close is the nearest star?" He would even goad the Beth-El rabbis, declaring that Unitarianism was the best religion and demanding that they defend Judaic principles.

Much of his time, however, Michael isolated himself from the world. For hours on end, he would sit in his room, listening to music, alone in a semihypnotic state. Anyone who dared to speak received a tongue lashing.

One time a visitor to the Icahn house was chatting with Carl's mother, boasting of her daughter's impending marriage. Hearing this, Michael rose with a fury, dashing to the woman's side and pressing his face within inches of hers.

"You fool," Michael shouted. "Do you think anyone cares about your daughter's marriage? How can you talk of such drivel when Schubert is playing? What is wrong with you? How dare you do that?"

Carl was a bright child. His fascination with books, his inquisitive nature and his facility with mathematics were sure signs of his budding intellect. When he was still in grade school, he was offered a scholarship to Woodmere Academy. But the Icahns' populism rose like a brick wall between Carl and the private school world of saddle shoes and navy blazers.

"One of the officers at Temple Beth-El was influential at the

Academy, and he was eager to have Carl enroll there," Bella recalled. "They were aware of Carl's scholastic abilities, and they hoped that by recruiting him, along with other bright children from the public schools, they could raise the Academy's academic standards."

His parents mulled over the offer. They visited the school and spoke to the teachers. In the end though, they decided against sending Carl to Woodmere. "Something about the atmosphere, and the values Carl would be exposed to, bothered us," noted Bella. "Maybe it was the spoiled kids bragging about the fact that 'My mommy just got a brand-new white Cadillac.' That lifestyle was anathema to us, so we kept Carl in Bayswater."

Somehow, it is fitting that Carl spent his formative years in the New York City schools, because the qualities he would display as a ferocious takeover artist have much to do with his being born in Brooklyn and raised in Queens. He is a product of the city of New York, a genuine street fighter.

In the subways and schoolyards and kosher butcher shops that sold live chickens in and around Rockaway, the young man learned to seize the advantage before someone else seized it. He learned to trust no one—and to trust them less when they swore they were telling the truth. And he learned that in a city of eight million people, someone is always looking to sell a bill of goods. Growing up in New York gave him a hard-boiled skepticism they didn't teach anywhere else in the world. And Carl Icahn learned the lesson well.

Bella was the strongest influence while Carl was growing up. An archetypical Jewish mother, she was forceful, demanding, kveching, prodding—a tidal wave of love and pressure, of guidance and guilt, that would wash over him and leave him suffocating under its weight. But she was also a positive influence, prodding Carl to set the highest goals for himself and then achieve them.

"If my mother had a theme, or a philosophy, that she instilled in me, it was that nothing was ever good enough. You could always do more. You could always do better."

Carl would never hear the familiar parental refrain: "Do whatever you like, just do it well." As far as his mother was concerned, the only acceptable option was for young Carl to distinguish himself in the practice of medicine. Before her son knew the difference between stickball rules and the periodic table of elements, she had decided that he would attend medical school.

To New York Jewish families of the era, medicine was as noble a calling as the priesthood to the city's working-class Irish. The dream of "my son the doctor"—deeply ingrained in middle-class Jews—stemmed from a respect for learned professions and from the promise of a guaranteed, Depression-proof affluence.

From Bella's perspective, the promise of economic security was critical. "My mother always worried about security," Icahn said. "She always worried, 'They're going to take everything away.' She believed if you were Jewish, middle-class and had hardly any money, you had three strikes against you."

In spite of his intellectual capacity, those who observed Carl Icahn as a young man could not have guessed that this gangly bookworm would emerge as a giant of the financial community. Through all of his years in Bayswater, Icahn was just another grind who blended into the woodwork.

"I attended Far Rockaway High the same time as Carl, and my sister taught there during that period, but neither one of us has any remembrance of Icahn in those days," said former schoolmate Maurice Singer. "Actually, people who know Carl today don't find that surprising. One time when I was flying an L-1011, [former TWA executive] Joe Corr came into the cockpit to watch the landing from the flight deck. When I mentioned that I grew up with Carl but didn't remember him from high school, Joe said, 'That sounds like Carl. He wouldn't be a cheerleader. He'd be the quiet guy on the chess team.' "

During his junior year at Far Rockaway, Carl decided that he would apply to Ivy League colleges, picking Princeton as the top choice, with Harvard a close second. For a straight-A student at Woodmere Academy, this evolution from prep school to the academic elite would have been a natural progression. But for a middle-class Jew from Queens, applying to Princeton was a so-cial-class hurdle. Icahn's peers, and his academic advisers, were certain he would fail.

"Most of us who went to Far Rockaway High applied to the city colleges," Singer recalled. "Harvard and Princeton were the furthest things from our minds. They just seemed unattainable."

Although Princeton had never accepted a Far Rockaway student, Carl was determined to be the first, compounding the challenge by seeking a full scholarship. In doing so, he was displaying early flashes of the iconoclasm and compul-sion to challenge the establishment that would become Icahn trademarks.

"Carl liked the sound of Princeton," Bella remembered. "He read books about it. Because he graduated number two in his high school class—a girl beat him by a fraction of a percent-age point—he believed he had the right to get the best education America could provide. But when he went to see a member of the faculty—this thin-lipped, anti-Semitic witch—she noticed that the Princeton application was at the top of Carl's pile.

" 'No, no,' she said, 'Princeton doesn't even read our applications.'

"Carl answered, 'I already put the stamp on it and I don't want to waste it.' "

He didn't. In the spring, Carl was accepted.

Arriving at Princeton in the fall of 1953, Icahn entered a world that was alien to him. In the space of a three-hour drive, he left the schoolyards and stickball courts of New York for the bucolic campus of a venerable institution—one that had served as the nation's capital for five months in 1783 and that counted among its illustrious alumni James Madison, Aaron Burr, Woodrow Wilson, and John Foster Dulles.

More than any other Ivy League school, Princeton nurtured an elitist culture. "The Princeton of the 1950s had a southern character about it," recalled Dr. Peter Liebert, Carl's senior-year roommate, now a physician in Harrison, New York. "Although the school was considered part of the Eastern establishment, it recruited a great deal of its undergraduates from the South. So much so that some people said Princeton was 'the northernmost of the southern schools.' "

Princeton's all-male undergraduates, most of whom had attended prep schools as part of the grooming process for the privileged class, viewed themselves as "gentlemen." Those who had clawed their way up from public schools were regarded as "mutts and geeks," grossly inferior in intellect and breeding.

Princeton social life revolved around its eating clubs, an institution in which undergraduates, many still in their teens, discussed campus politics as salaried waiters in starched white jackets served their meals and occasionally passed out Cuban cigars. In this rarified version of fraternity row, the clubs competed with one another to recruit the most desirable freshmen, defined by their wealth, social standing, wardrobe, and athletic prowess. In the midst of this Brahmin selectivity, one club defied the social conventions, establishing itself as a refuge for all who failed to make the grade at the top-drawer clubs. It was at this safe harbor, the Prospect Club, where Carl Icahn was introduced to Princeton social life.

"There were no fraternities at Princeton, so if you didn't belong to a club you were socially isolated," said Dr. John Whetten, a former president of the Prospect Club (now an Associate Director of the Los Alamos National Laboratory). "The way it worked was really insensitive. We'd have these 'bicker periods,' similar to fraternity rushes, when the clubs would recruit their candidates and all of this picking and choosing would go on. But when the music stopped, there was always a group of guys who found themselves without a chair. Needless to say, that was humiliating."

More often than not, those left out in the cold were Jews, the only minority group attending Princeton in any significant numbers. Appalled by this blatant prejudice, Whetten declared an open-admissions policy during his tenure as Prospect's president. In this environment, Prospect attracted Jews (many, like Carl, were premed students), a clique of pre-sixties rebels who rejected the rigid Princeton caste system, as well as stray "mutts and geeks" who found all the other doors slammed in their faces.

Although Carl's religion posed a barrier for entry into the premier clubs, former classmates agree that had he made a concerted effort, he would have found a home among the elite. But Carl preferred the Prospect. With its eclectic mix of social and religious outcasts, Prospect was closer to Carl's roots than the traditional WASP clubs, where the members looked alike and dressed alike and had prominent families in prominent positions. The genteel nature of the mainstream clubs violated Icahn's sensibilities. A lifelong "outsider," he was determined to pre-empt the "insiders," rejecting them before they could reject him.

Icahn's Princeton years were intensely cerebral. No one would ever mistake him for an Ivy League preppie caught up in a whirlwind of campus politics and debutante balls. A philosophy major, Carl spent much of his time in his room at 621 Cuyler immersed in Socrates, Plato, Machiavelli, Nietzsche, and Schopenhauer. In his free time, he played an occasional game of basketball, joined his fellow Prospect Club members in volleyball matches, and worked diligently on his chess game, which had become one of the best on campus.

"When I think of Carl in his Princeton days, I think of a brilliant thinker, one with a strong analytical mind, poring over his philosophy books and wrestling with the concepts they espoused," Liebert said. "He was pleasant, easygoing, definitely not the kind of guy you'd pick to set the world on fire.

"The only career choice he ever talked about was medicine. If he went that route, I thought he'd more likely wind up as a member of a med school faculty than a private practice physician. That's because he appeared to be more of a thinker than a doer."

Like many students struggling to find themselves in the never-never land of academia, Carl was uncertain of what he would do with his life. At one point, he said, "I thought of becoming a chess master, but I dismissed that when I realized there was no way to make a living at it." Although still unfocused, Icahn was nevertheless driven to excel. He made a pledge to himself: Whatever he chose to do, he would be the best at it. He would make a name for himself.

This determination found its first clear expression in Carl's senior year, which at Princeton is devoted primarily to independent research culminating in a thesis related to the student's major course of study. Traditionally, the top-ranking students compete for the highly coveted prize of the best senior thesis, an honor Icahn was determined to claim.

He chose a complex and intriguing subject: The Problem of Formulating an Adequate Explication of the Empiricist Criterion of Meaning. The paper reveals an introspective mind and a keen intellect obsessed with testing the validity of what is accepted as. fact. On every page, there is evidence of a young academic engrossed in intricate thought processes.

"Another failing of the verifiability criterion is that sentences containing meaningless disjuncts will still be found meaningful providing that one of the disjuncts is meaningful. For example, let N designate the sentence, 'The absolute is perfect.' There is no finite class of observation sentences conceivable from which this sentence might logically be inferred, and this sentence is not analytic. Therefore, the verifiability criterion finds this sentence both cognitively and empirically meaningless."

"He would go into the library for hours and hours without coming out for fresh air," Bella remembers. "It seemed that he could think of nothing else. He was always adding, changing and refining his thoughts. Near the end of the term he brought the thesis home so that he could put finishing touches on it, improving, improving up to the last minute. Just knowing that the document he had labored over for so long was off campus left me feeling edgy. I said, 'My God, Carl, you're going to lose it on the train and you won't be able to graduate.' "

In the end, "An Explication of the Empiricist Criterion of Meaning," which Icahn dedicated "To my parents to whom I am eternally indebted for my education," took first prize, giving Carl the crowning achievement of his Princeton years and affording him the first taste of success in "doing something better than everyone else." But more than that, what Carl had discov-

ered in researching and writing his thesis gave him a philosophi-
cal framework for applying his considerable intellect to real-life
challenges.

"Empiricism says knowledge is based on observation and
experience, not feelings," Icahn said. "In a funny way, studying
twentieth-century philosophy trains your mind for takeovers.
. . . There's a strategy behind everything. Everything fits. Thinking this way taught me to compete in many things, not only
takeovers but chess and arbitrage."

This philosphical framework would ultimately prove to be
Icahn's greatest weapon as a businessman. Although Wall Street
has an abundance of gifted number-crunchers and savvy traders
with keen instincts for the market, few make an intellectual tour
de force of their work. In time Icahn's intellectual powers, his
determination to see "the strategy behind everything" and to
decipher how the pieces of that strategy fit together logically,
would make him the terror of the corporate world. The epiphany
gained in the study of empiricism must be viewed as a watershed
in the evolution of Carl Icahn.

In hindsight, Princeton provided the ideal academic environment for a young man with Icahn's temperament and intellect. A bastion of liberal arts education, the school exposes
students to an eclectic mix of human knowledge, teaching undergraduates how to think and explore and question rather than
preparing them for specific careers. Based on this philosophy,
the undergraduate curriculum is devoid of traditional business-
management courses. Princeton believes that the best thinkers—
those exposed to the most eclectic range of knowledge—will rise
to the top of their chosen careers precisely because they have not
limited themselves to narrow courses of study. That concept can
be backed by hard figures. In a 1990 survey of 1,500 current and
former Fortune 500 CEOs, thirty-two were Princeton graduates,
second only to Yale graduates.

During Carl's Princeton years, Bella kept pushing him toward
medicine. Just as her mother had prodded her toward the secu-

rity of a teaching career, Bella found the same Jewish angst prompting her to drive her son toward medicine. That Carl was a bright boy was a given; that he was good at chemistry and math and the other prerequisites of a med school education was a given. And in Bella's view it was a given that he should use those gifts to win a medical degree. That Carl had not the slightest interest in probing for tumors or listening for arrhythmias was immaterial. Bella was convinced that she knew best, and that someday Carl would come to thank her for it.

"My mother has always had a tough, challenging personality," Icahn says. "And she used everything she had to press me to go to medical school. She thought that was the best career for a bright kid. She used to say, 'You'll go to work for Pfizer and they'll pay you $70,000 a year. And there'll be no risk.'

"The way she put it, there was no room for discussion. It was decided. Period."

Looking back, Bella explained her insistence on medicine.

"Considering that his parents couldn't give him a business, medicine was the best choice for a boy like Carl. Of course, there were other professions, like the practice of law, but Carl's dad urged him not to be an attorney. One of Michael's professors at Fordham once told him, 'Look at all of those men walking on Wall Street. Nine out of ten of them are lawyers. They're a dime a dozen.' "

Facing what appeared to be the inevitable, Carl reported to New York University Medical School in September 1957. For Bella it was a glorious day, but for her son, the reluctant medical student, it was the beginning of a painful ordeal that left him torn between a longing to please his mother and a personal distaste for the career she had pushed him toward.

"I was pretty good at the academic part—the chemistry courses and the like," Icahn recalled. "I could see what elements you needed to make the formulas react, and that if you put one element together with another what compound you would get. But that didn't disguise the fact that I hated medical school.

"For that reason I started to slack off. Whoever wanted to go out to a bar, I would go with them. Then medical school got so bad that I kept wanting to leave, and I even did leave a few times, but I came back because I knew how badly my mother wanted me to get that MD degree."

Were medical school solely an intellectual exercise, Icahn would likely have muddled through NYU, driven by his compulsion to succeed. But once he was required to leave the classroom for hands-on experience in a clinical setting, Carl the loner found the experience intolerable. Sickened by the sight of blood, and convinced that he had contracted every disease he came in contact with in the sprawling hospital wards, he was unable to complete his rounds. The breaking point came on a tour of the tuberculosis ward.

"The resident said, 'Give me a differential diagnosis on that guy,' " Carl recalled. "I said, 'What do you mean? It's up there on the wall. This is the tuberculosis ward.'

"Well, I went over finally and I tapped the guy on the chest and he coughed all over me. I said, 'Christ, I have TB. I'm getting out of here.' "

Determined to escape, Icahn walked out of NYU, never to return. For Bella, a lifelong dream had come to an end. "When Carl finally left medical school," she said, "we were distraught."

But for Carl, it was a liberating experience. For the first time he felt in control of his own destiny. Looking back on his medical school experience more than thirty years after he left NYU, Icahn told CNN: "One of the greatest things I did for the human race was not to become a doctor."

MY SON, THE OPTIONS BROKER

3

"If you can dream—and not make dreams your master;
　If you can think—and not make thoughts your aim;
If you can meet with Triumph and Disaster
　And treat those two imposters just the same;
If you can bear to hear the truth you've spoken
　Twisted by knaves to make a trap for fools,
Or watch the things you gave your life to broken,
　And stoop and build 'em up with worn out tools:

If you can make one heap of all your winnings
　And risk it on one turn of pitch-and-toss,
And lose, and start again at your beginnings
　And never breathe a word about your loss;
If you can force your heart and nerve and sinew
　To serve your turn long after they are gone,
And so hold on when there is nothing in you
　Except the Will which says to them "hold on!""

If you can talk with crowds and keep your virtue,
  Or walk with Kings—nor lose the common touch,
If neither foes nor loving friends can hurt you,
  If all men count with you but none too much;
If you can fill the unforgiving minute
  With sixty seconds worth of distance run,
Yours is the Earth and everything that's in it,
And—which is more—you'll be a Man, my son!"

> —RUDYARD KIPLING, "Brother Square-Toes"
> —*Rewards and Fairies,*
>   a verse Icahn says has influenced
>   his business career from the earliest days.

In the spring of 1960, Carl Icahn was an unemployed Princeton graduate and med school dropout with no family money, no career ambitions, and no marketable skills. Although deliriously happy to be free of Bella's doctor fixation, he hadn't a clue what he would do with the rest of his life.

Determined to bide time until he could set his priorities in order, Icahn enlisted in the army reserves in April 1960. "One of the reasons I went into the service is that once you joined, you couldn't get out," Carl said. "That meant my mother couldn't come after me telling me to go back to medical school. From that standpoint, it was the safest place I could be."

Not surprisingly for an intellectual loner with a love of reading and chess, Icahn's army stint was hardly the fodder for an Audie Murphy sequel. Going through the motions, Carl endured two months of basic training at New Jersey's Fort Dix before being transferred to Fort Sam Houston in San Antonio for advanced training as a medical specialist. The only thing notable to come from Icahn's army stint was a growing fascination with poker, which he played for hours on end in the Texas barracks. Having a keen mind for numbers and an instinctive skill for leveraging a good hand and bluffing his way to the pot even when the cards were running against him, Icahn built a profitable sideline as the unit's card shark. After four months in the Lone Star state, Icahn was released from active duty on October 9, 1960. For the next five and a half years he would remain a reservist, assigned to Company A of the 302 Medical Battalion based in the wilds of Manhattan at 529 West 42nd Street.

Once back in New York, Icahn decided he wanted to make money like his Uncle Elliot, but just how he would earn his fortune remained a question mark.

"Then it came into my head that I should get involved in marketing," Icahn recalled. "Don't ask me why, it just seemed like a good place to start. So I took a job as a management trainee at Macy's. It was during the Christmas rush and I was paid $100 a week.

"I knew I wasn't going to get rich quickly at that rate, so I started playing around in the stock market, using a stake of more than $4,000 I had made playing poker in the army. A friend of the family was a securities analyst and I would read his research, talk over opportunities with him, and buy fifty shares of this and a hundred shares of that. I'd check the papers every day to see how my picks were doing and sure enough, I seemed to be picking winners.

"So I said to myself, 'If you're good enough to do this on the side, why not go to Wall Street?' "

For a bright young man with strong mathematical skills and a growing interest in stocks and bonds, Wall Street had a magnetic appeal. But given the stock market's boom-and-bust cycles, it was the last place Bella Icahn wanted her son to launch his career.

"Maybe I'm a dimestore psychiatrist, but I think that after medical school, and our emphasis on security, Carl wanted to go out and prove that he could be a success on his own in a field with very little security," she said.

Icahn's first contact with Wall Street was arranged by Uncle Elliot, who called a friend, then a partner at Dreyfus & Co., and set up Carl's first interview on the Street. This turned promptly into a job as a $100-a-week broker trainee.

Icahn reported to Dreyfus in 1961, just as the Street was in the midst of a roaring bull market that saw the Dow soar nearly 200 points to 730. It was the kind of "another-day-another-record high-close" upswing in the cycle that created euphoria in

the houses of Merrill and Hutton and Dean Witter, and that
made every broker believe he was a genius on the verge of a
windfall that would set him up for life.

Twenty-four-year-old Carl Icahn was no exception.

"I was a good salesman and so I had the ability to get clients
to buy on my recommendations," Icahn recalled. "And I was
moving fast, telling customers to buy this and buy that and sell
the other. Because everything was going up at the time, I felt like
a seer and I started to look like one."

With his career in finance starting to take off, Icahn was
truly happy for the first time in his life.

"I was never a well-adjusted kid—never really happy,"
Icahn said. "I think that's true of most successful people. They
have conflicts that have to be resolved—pressures they have to
learn to deal with. When I was finally doing something I liked,
and the money started rolling in, I felt free and independent for
the first time. I knew the yoke of medical school was off for good,
and that had a liberating effect."

Celebrating his newfound independence, Icahn moved out
of his parents' home to a rental apartment at Lexington Avenue
and 37th Street. A tiny space with a window that looked out on
a soot-stained brick wall, and furnished with odds and ends
handed down by family members, it was nevertheless Tara to the
med school defector turned East Side man-about-town. At that
point, young Carl seemed to have everything: pocket money,
freedom, and a promising career.

And then the bubble burst. In 1962, the market broke.
When the Dow fell to 535 in June, the advances of a two-year
rally were erased.

"When the market went into its nosedive, I lost all that I
had made, about $50,000 to $100,000. Things got so bad that I
had to sell my white convertible Ford Galaxie for $2,500 so that
I could have enough money to eat."

Worse yet, Icahn could no longer afford to pay his rent. For
a terrifying moment he envisioned moving back to Bayswater.
"My mother said the only way I could go home was if I went to
medical school again." Dreading that fate, Carl cut a deal with

a middle-aged acquaintance in search of a discreet setting for romantic liaisons. In return for rent "subsidies," Carl had to abandon the apartment for hours at a time while his boarder of sorts entertained women in the dingy flat.

"Sometimes the guy would use the place for these marathon poker games as well," Icahn recalls. "When I returned after these sessions, the place reeked so badly of cigarette smoke that I had to keep the windows open for three days at a time to get the stench out. It was a hell of a way to live, but my 'partner' paid half the rent and because that meant I could stay there, it was a price well worth paying."

Icahn's first experience with a Wall Street boom-to-bust cycle was certainly a disappointment, but it also taught him two lessons he never forgot. First, no one makes money playing the market. A small investor dabbling in stocks is always vulnerable to bigger, more powerful forces that time after time will wipe him out.

Second, if he was going to emerge as a dominant force, he needed more than a broker's training. He had to gain expertise in a market niche overlooked by the hordes of brokers content to sit by the phone and take orders. His study of empiricism had taught him that "there is a strategy behind everything," and now he had to determine what that strategy was. Unlike his peers, who viewed the peaks and valleys of the stock market as an inevitable part of the business, Icahn the empiricist, Icahn the chess player, was determined to outsmart the system or at least to find a void he could exploit.

That the stock market had bested him, would prove for Icahn to be a blessing in disguise. The swiftness of his gains and losses made him realize that this was a business of enormous complexity and equally enormous rewards for those who could decipher the codes. To succeed required patience, intelligence, determination, and the ability to concoct shrewd strategies involving intricate and interrelated moves—precisely the kind of process that had always appealed to Carl Icahn.

With this in mind, he recognized that the options business—not the traditional brokering of stocks and bonds—was

the ideal place to launch his career. Two critical factors figured
into his thinking. Because options trading occupied a niche market, it was free of the pervasive competition in traditional brokerage. What's more, as complex instruments, options allowed for
a wide range of creative techniques and strategies. Rather than
simply picking stocks, Icahn, the options specialist, could delve
deeper into the intricacies of the market.

After launching into options trading at Dreyfus, Icahn took
his book of business to a smaller company, Tessel Paturick &
Company, where he teamed up with two fellow brokers Joseph
(Jerry) Freilich and Daniel Kaminer. When the opportunity
arose to build an options department at Gruntal & Co., Icahn,
who was starting to make a name for himself in the field, moved
again, taking Freilich and Kaminer with him.

"In those days there was some fear of working with the
smaller firms like Tessel Paturick," said Freilich. "Rumors of
financial weakness were all over the Street. For years Tessel
Paturick had cleared its trades through a larger firm, but when
managing partner Arthur Paturick decided to start clearing for
himself, we decided it would be best to move on."

In short order Icahn built Gruntal's options business into
one of the firm's biggest revenue producers, doing so at a time
when options were traded in a wild and wooly market dominated
by a handful of trading firms that earned rich spreads at the
expense of their clients.

"When Carl got into options, there was no such thing as a
central forum for buying and selling options, like the Chicago
Board Options Exchange, which was yet to be established," said
Robert Lange, a senior vice president with Lindner Management,
a St. Louis–based investment firm. "All you had was a fairly
liquid, over-the-counter market. If you wanted to sell, you had to
go out and find a buyer through one of the few firms that did a
significant business in options. Those firms did very well because
they had the market pretty much to themselves.

"When Carl established his options business, he joined that
select group. To me, that showed where Carl's head was at from
the beginning. He had finely tuned antennae for finding where
the money was and partaking of it.

"Think about it: By going into the options business, Carl was injecting himself in what amounted to an oligopoly."

To distinguish himself from the competition, and to build a national following based on price appeal, Icahn published a newsletter, the "Midweek Option Report," which served as a rudimentary over-the-counter market for options. Reflecting on those early years, Icahn remembered: "When I went into the options business, it was tightly controlled by a small group of men. They did nothing criminal, but they charged huge markups for buying and selling options. . . .

"I felt there was a need for something whereby option investors across the country would know what prices they should be getting for their options. In other words, a guy would sell an IBM option or he would sell a call in those days, and perhaps one of these put-and-call dealers would call a broker, who really didn't know very much, and say, 'Look, try to get me these calls.' And he'd pay him $400 and the call really should be worth $550 or something.

"So my idea was to come up with the 'Midweek Option Report' and in that scrupulously tell people what these things were trading for and what they should be getting, and I built a good business . . . .

"What I would do is—there was a guy in Kansas, for instance, and he told me he wanted to sell calls on Ford Motor . . . So I would get a bid from a put-and-call dealer for $400. And very often the guy in Kansas would say, 'Well, go ahead and do them. That's pretty good.'

"I would go back to the dealer and would fight with the dealer to get $500, because I knew it should be $500. Even though I could have done them for $400, and the dealer would be a little beholden to me, I would wait and hold out for two or three hours, sometimes lose the trade, but I would go back to the guy and say, 'Look, instead of $400, I got you $500.' Well, obviously, the guy loved me. Here's a guy in New York he didn't even know getting him another thousand dollars."

Icahn's tactics so infuriated the old-line options dealers that a secret plan was hatched to blackball him. The way the scheme was planned, all of the options houses would refuse to buy or sell with Icahn. But, in what would prove to be another important lesson for Carl, the plan fell apart when the conspirators put their own interests before the group's.

"Each of the option brokers who were party to the 'secret' deal called me on the sly. Real hush-hush they said, 'Look, Carl, the other guys don't want to do business with you. But I think you're a great guy so I'm going to break ranks. You'll have my business—just don't tell the others.' It was comical."

In those days Icahn was obsessed with building his business, hunting down every lead, every prospect, no matter how remote. One day he received a letter, scrawled in barely legible handwriting, from one H. B. Jones (fictitious name used to disguise customer's identity). Mr. Jones, a resident of the Southwest, was in need of an options broker. Following up, Icahn called more than a half dozen times, only to be told on each occasion: "H.B. can't come to the phone now, he's in the fields." Speaking in a deep southern drawl, the party on the other end failed to elaborate further.

After the tenth call, hearing once again that H.B. was "in the fields," Icahn asked the question that had been bugging him for weeks. "What kind of fields is he in?"

For a moment there was silence. "Why, the oil fields, of course," the party answered.

"Of course, the oil fields," Carl answered. "The oil fields."

Sensing opportunity in this mystery man, Icahn called two more times, finally landing H.B. on the phone.

"Mr. Icahn," H.B. said in a drawl so thick it could be sliced with a Bowie knife, "I like the company Phillips Petroleum. I want you to sell me options on that stock."

H.B.'s initial order, for $100,000 worth of Phillips options, was a major transaction for Carl Icahn in the 1960s. He executed the order promptly and called H.B., asking him to forward a $50,000 check for the margin payment. That's when Icahn's elation over his new client turned to gloom.

"I'm sorry, Mr. Icahn, but I only pay 30 percent down," H.B. said. Although Icahn insisted that the margin requirements called for 50 percent, H.B. refused to budge, adding, "I have my brokerage account at DuPont, and you can check my credit with them."

Still on the phone with H.B., Icahn whispered for an assistant to call DuPont to confirm H.B.'s standing at the brokerage house. As Carl continued to press his customer for the payment, the assistant motioned wildly for a "time out." When Icahn excused himself for a moment, putting the receiver to his chest, the assistant blurted out, "I checked with Du Pont. Your guy's their single biggest account." Without missing a beat, Icahn said to his client, "H.B., 30 percent will be just fine. Just fine."

Months later, as his account with Icahn grew into millions of dollars, H.B. invited Carl to meet with him in his hometown. Landing at a small airport, Icahn found the unlikely oil man waiting behind the wheel of a battered, rusted ten-year-old Chrysler, the engine running. Motioning for Icahn to jump in, H.B. shifted into first and headed north toward his home. The odd couple—Carl in his suit, H.B. in soiled dungarees and a tattered shirt—bumped along dusty roads, passing oil rig after oil rig. After what seemed like an interminable ride, Icahn asked H.B. when they would be getting to his place. "We've been on it for half an hour," H.B. replied.

When Icahn volunteered to take his client to lunch, H.B. pulled up to a diner on the only street in a local town. When Carl suggested that they opt for something less spartan, H.B. insisted, "This will be fine. Just fine."

Determined to foot the bill, Icahn rushed ahead of H.B. as they loaded their trays, cafeteria style. When they reached the cashier, the New York options broker found himself paying the tab for the cheapest business lunch of his life: $2.69 for two plates of beef and string beans.

After talking stocks over lunch, Carl and H.B. left the restaurant, where they were greeted in the street by a tall, handsome gentleman dressed in a western style suit. Quickly he rushed up to greet H.B. "H.B., H.B., how are you? How come you haven't returned my calls?"

Apparently peeved with the man, H.B. made no attempt at conversation, shrugging off all questions with no more than a wave of his hand. When the man left, clearly deflated, Icahn asked H.B. who that was.

"The governor," H.B. said.

Shocked, Icahn asked, "The governor of what?"

"The governor of the state," H.B. drawled.

"Why did you give him the cold shoulder?" Icahn asked.

"Let me put it this way," H.B. said. "Next November, he's up for reelection and he's going to lose. You know why? I'll tell you why. Because a few months ago he lied to me."

"I get the message, H.B.," Carl said.

"I like you, Mr. Icahn. I like you."

Although Icahn was prospering as an options broker, his operation was still a Wall Street sideshow and his quest "to do something better than anyone else" still a distant dream. With this in mind, Icahn decided to take a major step designed to catapult his career. He would buy a seat on the New York Stock Exchange.

At this point Uncle Elliot served in another critical capacity—this time as a money man.

The timing was perfect. "In 1967, the Dictaphone Corporation approached me about buying American Looseleaf, a Clifton, New Jersey, company I'd purchased after my divorce in 1965," Schnall remembered. "At the time I was making lots of money, running the company was fun, and I had no interest in selling. But then things changed. Around 1967, I started having union troubles, and that led to one headache after another. I guess Dictaphone got wind of it, because they came knocking at my door again, and this time I was ready."

Flush with his windfall, Schnall was having a grand time, doing Manhattan "the right way." During this euphoric period, he was dining one evening with Carl at the 21 Club when Icahn blurted out that he wanted to buy a seat on the stock exchange and furthermore that he wanted his rich uncle to finance the purchase. The request took Schnall by surprise.

"Carl said, 'You've got all that money now, what the hell are you going to do with it?' Well, he knew what I was doing with it, because he had it in an account for me at Gruntal. Then Carl said, 'I want to buy a seat on the exchange.' When I asked Carl how much it would cost, he said, 'Anywhere from $300,000 to $500,000.' "

In return, Icahn offered Schnall 8 percent on his money, plus an additional $20,000 a year as well as equity in the new business he would form, Icahn & Company. Although Elliot had never loaned money to anyone before ("I was very WASPy about lending," he recalled), the deal Carl was proposing seemed fair. And because Icahn had already made money for Schnall trading options on his behalf, the confidence was there. Before leaving for Palm Beach to spend spring vacation at the Breakers with his children, Elliot handed Carl a blank check. According to their agreement, Icahn would bid on the seat and then fill in the amount. To this day, Schnall remembers his nephew calling him at the Breakers telling him he had the seat and the price was $400,000. He still has the cancelled check.

With his own seat on the exchange, Icahn launched his lilliputian brokerage firm at 42 Broadway. Joining Carl as minority partners were his colleagues Freilich and Kaminer, followed soon after by another Gruntal broker, Jerry Goldsmith. All took equity positions in the company, basing their investments on the conviction that they were hitching their fate to a brilliant financial mind who was destined for success.

They quickly learned, however, that being partners with Icahn, rewarding though it might be, often proved arduous. Bullheaded, egotistical, determined to call all of the shots, Icahn was, in every sense, the absolute ruler.

"Carl was brilliant, excitable, opinionated—anyone like that is difficult to work with," Goldsmith said. "His opinions would have to win out almost all the time. No one can be right all the time, but he was the boss. There was only so much air in a room and Carl had big lungs.

"But if you look at the tenure of the people who were with Carl in those days, most stayed for a long time. Carl was a brilliant teacher and the overall experience was more rewarding than it was difficult."

Joining Icahn & Company in 1968 was another former Gruntal employee, Alfred Kingsley. Seven years Icahn's junior,

Kingsley was overweight, unkempt, poorly dressed and financially brilliant. A Wharton School graduate, Kingsley had gone on to earn a masters in tax at New York University. It was during his NYU days that he first started working part time for Gruntal. Immediately, Icahn was impressed with Kingsley's ability to quickly decipher complex financial transactions and to bring extraordinary creativity to securities trading. By the time Kingsley joined him full-time, Icahn was thinking of expanding beyond his options brokerage to another area of securities trading.

"We were busy doing puts and calls when Carl said to me one day, 'What do you know about arbitrage, Kingsley?' I said, 'Not a thing,' " Kingsley recalled. "But I could tell Carl was intrigued. He said, 'I hear people are making a lot of money at it.' "

Determined to learn more, testing the waters as they went, Icahn and Kingsley engaged in classic arbitrage, buying securities of such companies as LTV and American Motors, taking positions in the companies' stocks, bonds, warrants, and convertible debentures, often buying one and shorting the other, and using this approach to hedge their bets.

"Depending on our perspective on the stock of the companies we were trading, we would short all or part of our positions," Kingsley said. "If we were bearish on the stock, we would short a small part of the position, collect the bond interest and perhaps make a bit on the short sale. If we were bullish on the stock, we would short less of the shares."

By focusing on niche markets, Icahn parlayed his success in options and arbitrage into an income exceeding $350,000 in the late 1960s. Reflecting his new prosperity, Icahn moved from his tiny flat to an uptown apartment at Third Avenue and 63rd Street and then to the more affluent environs of Sutton Place, where he took a two-bedroom apartment at the foot of the East River.

Well before the public had ever heard of him, Icahn had become a successful entrepreneur, options trader, and Wall Street operator. Clearly, he had made a quantum leap from

Bayswater's middle class bric-a-brac to Manhattan's silk stocking district.

"People often think Carl grew up with the 1980s crop of raiders," Lange said. "But Carl was making smart, successful moves as early as the mid-1960s. There is a lot more to Icahn than simply picking off companies. Before he even started that, he had a good grounding in the stock market. The qualities that made him successful in his early years would make him a great deal more successful later on."

It was at this early stage of Icahn's ascent that a poignant scene took place between Carl and his father. Convinced that Carl would starve were he to forgo medical school, Michael had warned his son many times that he lacked the personal qualities to make it in business. Proven wrong, the senior Icahn found himself perplexed, especially by how a young man could earn so much at this bewildering process of "arbitrage."

Approaching his son during a visit to his Sutton Place apartment, his manner atypically sheepish, Michael placed a pad and pencil before him. "Show me, Carl," he said, "how do you do it?"

Although Icahn likes to recount how he worked around the clock during these up-from-the-bootstraps years, as the money started rolling in and he started to savor success, he began to make the rounds at the Manhattan hot spots, weekend in the Hamptons, and date a succession of attractive women. In this realm Schnall remained his mentor, introducing Icahn to a hedonism that as a loner and an egghead he had never known. Although he was intoxicated by the change of lifestyle, he could never cross the threshold into the New York fast track. An introspective streak still dominated his personality.

"I was making lots of money, living marvelously in a gorgeous penthouse at 730 Fifth Avenue," Schnall reminisced. "On many nights I would meet Carl for dinner and drinks at the 21 Club. We double dated often, and Carl always brought along beautiful women. Oh, we had marvelous times.

Even though we were fifteen years apart, Carl and I were great buddies."

In those years, Schnall owned a big Dutch Colonial a few blocks from the beach in Southampton. When Carl would come up in the spring to look for a summer place to share with close friends, Elliot would make the rounds with him, visiting real estate agents and inspecting the properties for rent. One of Carl's first summer homes was a modest place in Amagansett that cost about $1,000 for the summer.

"Carl always loved the beach, but he was never much for the Hamptons' party scene," Schnall said. "I remember taking him once to a big cocktail party hosted by Jerry Finklestein at this fabulous house by the ocean. I worked the party, making my way through the house, talking with everyone who was anyone. But Carl found someone to talk to and just stood there. He was never one to work the crowd. That wasn't Carl."

Although Icahn was building an increasingly successful brokerage business, he made little attempt to change or camouflage his quirky, go-it-alone personality. Even when it threatened to thwart his ambitions. This was evident in a botched attempt to publicize a discount brokerage service Icahn launched in the mid-1970s. Advised to hire a public relations firm to generate media coverage for his new venture, Icahn—at this point unfamiliar and uncomfortable with the press—proved to be his own worst enemy.

"Someone probably told Carl to court the press, but to say he had no flair for it would be generous," said a partner with a major New York PR agency that briefly represented Icahn & Company in the mid-1970s. "He related to numbers, not to people. Reporters—he had no patience for them.

"One day I set up an interview for Carl with a prominent *Business Week* editor. The idea was to talk about discount brokerage and some of the other activities Carl was active in.

"We met in Icahn's office, with Carl sitting on one side of me and the reporter on the other. At one end of the office, a window overlooked the trading floor, where computer screens were flashing stock quotes. When the reporter broke the ice by asking a question, Carl remained silent. So the reporter repeated his question. Still Carl remained stone faced.

"At this point, I said, 'Carl, would you answer the question, please?' I'm terribly embarrassed because Carl's eyes look like they're glazed over. He's fixated on the computer screens. As far as the reporter and I can tell, Icahn hasn't the slightest interest in the interview. He looks as if he's either disinterested, dead, or out to lunch.

"Just when I thought things couldn't get worse, Icahn suddenly snapped to attention, announced that he wouldn't respond to the reporter's questions because 'I have something more important to do' and then cavalierly walked out of the room. No apology, nothing."

On another occasion, the PR man—having been assured that Icahn had changed his ways—arranged an interview with a *Barron's* writer. But things went from bad to worse. This time Icahn fell asleep right in the midst of the interview. "When I asked the reporter if he wanted to reschedule, he just about laughed in my face," the publicist recalled. "You have to understand that Carl was a relative pisher at the time. The press wasn't willing to put up with him."

Even Icahn's break with the PR firm revealed a strange, intensely private side of his personality. "I was in Carl's office when I noticed a picture of an attractive young woman that was in a silver frame behind his desk," says the public relations executive. "The woman looked familiar, but from where I was sitting, I couldn't be sure. So when Carl left the office for a few moments, I walked over and took a good look. It was then that I recognized the woman as a Russian emigrée, a former ballerina, who had served as my secretary a few months before.

"When Carl returned to the office, I pointed to the picture, asking, 'Isn't that Victoria?' Well, Carl absolutely blanched. He asked how I knew her, and when I told him she had worked for me, he seemed terribly uncomfortable. As if there were something embarrassing about he and I knowing the same woman. I couldn't tell if his feelings were of arrogance or jealousy.

"Anyway, about a week after the incident, Carl sent me a

letter cancelling our work for him. I always regretted saying anything about that young woman."

At the time, Icahn & Company was still a gnat by Wall Street standards. Its bargain basement offices at 25 Broadway, where the company moved in May 1972, looked like a boilerroom operation strewn with piles of paperwork and cramped with battered steel desks. Carl split his time in the makeshift trading room, where he bought and sold options, and in a small private office, where he tended to paperwork. Clearly he was more of a trader, a strategist, and a gambler than a professional manager.

This led to a run-in with the New York Stock Exchange, the first of a series of bouts with market regulators that would escalate in tandem with his rise as a Wall Street force.

In October 1974, the NYSE found Icahn & Company in violation of section 10(b) and 10(b)4 of the Securities Act of 1934 (in regards to the short tendering of securities) and in violation of exchange rule 342(a) (for failing to place its business activities under proper supervision and control). The Big Board also found Carl Icahn in personal violation of 342(a) for allegedly failing "to reasonably discharge his duties and obligations in connection with supervision and control of the activities of employees of Icahn & Co., Inc." and "failed to establish proper control and guidelines in the supervision of employees of Icahn & Co . . . and also failed to establish a system of follow-up and review at Icahn & Co." The transgressions were minor, owing mostly to Icahn's preference for making deals rather than for building an air-tight organization replete with all the requisite checks and balances designed to monitor trading activities.

When action was taken, the NYSE's hearing panel imposed penalties of censure (basically a reprimand) and a $25,000 fine for Icahn & Company as well as a censure and a $10,000 fine for Carl Icahn.

To the world Icahn & Company appeared to be just another shoestring brokerage house trying to make it at the epicenter of capitalism. But a major change was about to take place. As Icahn reflected on the world beyond Wall Street, he recognized that a confluence of powerful forces sweeping through the economic arena was creating an unusual window of opportunity for a businessman with the vision to see it and the tenacity to exploit it. Rather than continuing in classic arbitrage, Icahn recognized the time was right to pursue a bold gambit that could leapfrog the slow and steady wealth-building process.

It all began when Kingsley, who had left Icahn & Company in 1973, returned to work for Carl in 1975. Although word has it that Kingsley left in disgust after Icahn refused to make him a partner, according to Kingsley it was boredom that drove him from Icahn & Co.

"Right before I left, I was doing classic arbitrage centered around about twenty or so securities issued by IT&T," Kingsley said. "They had a virtual alphabet of preferred stocks, bonds, convertible stocks. I used to trade a basket of these securities, and much of the day I would be wired into the exchange floor asking, 'How's the alphabet doing?' It was boring as shit.

"To make matters worse, IT&T was involved in some kind of scandal in Chile, and all day long I would have to monitor news reports on what was going on there. I'd sit at my desk with this plug in my ear listening to news reports and trading on what I was hearing. One minute I would have to sell, another I'd buy, and then I'd sell again. After a while I just couldn't take it anymore, I needed a break badly. So I went to F.L. Salomon, a little brokerage house specializing in new issues. I just needed a change of pace."

When Kingsley returned to Icahn, the Lone Ranger and Tonto—as Icahn would call them—began exploring "undervalued opportunities," securities trading below their asset values. At first the duo invested in closed-end mutual funds selling for prices substantially below the collective value of the securities in the fund portfolios.

In those days Icahn and Kingsley lunched together in a basement cafeteria (they nicknamed it "the dungeon") at 26 Broadway, giving shape to their emerging strategies. Soon they realized that they could pursue a much broader and more profitable approach—one that could have a profound impact on the American corporate establishment.

Kingsley recalled, "We asked ourselves, 'If we can be activists in an undervalued closed-end mutual fund, why can't we be activists in a corporation with undervalued assets?' Just what Icahn and Kingsley were formulating is best described in a memo distributed to prospective investors in the first partnership designed to put their plan into action:

"It is our opinion that the elements in today's economic environment have combined in a unique way to create large profit-making opportunities with relatively little risk. Our nation's huge need for energy has resulted in a massive flow of dollars abroad. This, coupled with huge deficit spending and decreasing productivity, has caused a high inflation rate and a sharply declining dollar. As a result, the value of gold and goods in general have skyrocketed. An obvious corollary to this is that the real or liquidating value of many American companies has increased markedly in the last few years; however, interestingly, this has not at all been reflected in the market value of their common stocks. Thus we are faced with a unique set of circumstances that, if dealt with correctly, can lead to large profits, as follows:

"A great deal of unwanted dollars have and continue to accumulate in foreign hands. The United States remains one of the few safe political havens that can accommodate this massive dollar accumulation. As the tangible asset value of American companies continue to markedly appreciate in value, they become more attractive—not only to foreign dollars, but also to the vast amounts of cash that has been accumulating in the treasuries of other large American enterprises.

"However, the management of these asset-rich target companies generally own very little stock themselves and, therefore, usually have no interest in being acquired. They jealously guard their prerogatives by building 'Chinese walls' around their enterprises that hopefully will repel the invasion of domestic and foreign dollars. Although these 'walls' are penetrable, most domestic companies and almost all foreign companies are loathe to launch an 'unfriendly' takeover attempt against a target company. *However, whenever a fight for control is initiated, it generally leads to windfall profits for shareholders.* Often the target company, if seriously threatened, will seek another, more friendly enterprise, generally known as a 'white knight' to make a higher bid, thereby starting a bidding war. Another gambit occasionally used by the target company is to attempt to purchase the acquirers' stock or, if all else fails, the target may offer to liquidate.

"It is our contention that *sizeable profits can be earned by taking large positions in 'undervalued' stocks and then attempting to control the destinies of the companies in question* by:

a) trying to convince management to liquidate or sell the company to a 'white knight'; b) waging a proxy contest; c) making a tender offer and/or; d) selling back our position to the company."

With this "Icahn Manifesto," the one-time bookworm from Queens had found a way to intimidate corporate America, driving the CEOs of the Fortune 500 into a corner, using his opponents' own greed and imperiousness to defeat themselves.

Interestingly, the roots of Icahn's theory can be found in the conclusion of his Princeton thesis.

"It seems to me that the quest for an explication of the empiricist meaning criterion, as it has progressed, may be likened to the tale of the city that suddenly finds itself in possession of a great homogeneous mixture of gold and sand. If the gold could be separated from the sand it would prove a great deal more valuable to the inhabitants. The wise men of the city diligently search for a method of separation. By so doing they not only vastly increase their insight into the nature of gold, sand, homogeneous mixtures, etc., but also produce a series of increasingly potent methods of separating the chaff from the gold, the meaningless from the significant."

The nation's chief executives, and their sycophants on the boards of directors, held the power, the money and the weight of the corporate establishment on their side. But Icahn had the strategy, and the chutzpah, to threaten the CEOs and the thrones they so jealously guarded. It was a role he would relish on a personal level. For all of his life, Icahn had been an outsider challenging the establishment. Told that the Ivy League would not accept a Bayswater Jew, he applied and won a scholarship to Princeton. Invited to seek membership in a mainstream eating club, he opted instead for the Prospect Club's counterculture environment. Immersing himself in the options business, he would make a name for himself by confronting the established powers and rewriting the rules for options brokerage. Always, there was great satisfaction in defeating those who had dismissed or underestimated him, and who had been cocksure of their place in the pantheon of power.

Now in seeking to "control the destinies" of his target companies, as his battle plan suggested, Icahn would be acting in a ruthless, self-interested manner devoid of any concern for corporate history, tradition or the fate of the employees. A student of Machiavelli, Icahn believed with absolute certainty that "the ends justify the means" as long as the means enriched Icahn himself.

Although the fraternity of chief executives would come to detest Icahn, the fact is they had created an environment in which he—as well as Boone Pickens, Saul Steinberg, James Goldsmith and their fellow raiders—thrived in the America of the 1980s.

All across the Fortune 100, CEOs were ensconced in an opulent lifestyle that perpetuated itself without regard for corporate performance. What's more, as the corporate giants had grown ever larger, and further removed from their shareholders, the CEOs began to regard themselves as the "owners" of their companies, placing their interests (power, position, and money) before those of the stockholders (who sought maximum return on their investments). Because corporate management was inclined to repel takeover attempts regardless of the positive impact they might have on shareholder values, Icahn was betting that the barons of the executive suites would prove to be his reluctant allies. Threaten their privileged lifestyles and they would use the shareholders' money to buy him off, either by paying greenmail (which is a premium for a raider's shares over the current market value) or by finding white knights to acquire their companies by making above-market price bids for the out-standing stock. Either way the would-be raider would walk away with a quick and handsome profit.

Icahn had detected a weak link in the capitalist system, and he would exploit it with enormous success over the course of a tumultuous decade in American business.

FIRST

STRIKES

"Controlling the Destiny of Companies"

"In a fight, I go over a certain line and I become very tough. I even surprise myself. I reach a certain point in a fight where there is no turning back."

—CARL ICAHN

By 1977, Carl Icahn was ready to move out of the shadows and onto Wall Street's center stage. Two decades of thinking and observing had come together in a cohesive vision. He would make his mark, and his fortune, by controlling "the destinies of companies"—a feat he would accomplish not with brute force or financial might (neither of which he possessed at the time), but instead by putting a new spin on a time-tested Wall Street battle tactic, the proxy contest.

For years, proxy battles had been waged by corporate gadflies and assorted power brokers seeking to enlist the support of shareholders to oust incumbent management and replace them in the executive suite. These battles resembled political contests, with both sides claiming they were better suited to run the companies profitably, and in turn to meet the universal litmus test of increasing shareholder value.

Icahn recognized that while a proxy contest could be used to gain control of a company (and ultimately to build it into a more profitable enterprise), much faster profits could be earned by simply appearing to seek control. By acquiring big stakes in companies whose asset values substantially exceeded their share prices and then launching proxy battles, Icahn would be calling attention to the gap between market and inherent values. This gap existed in hundreds of public companies because Wall Street tends to rate stocks on the basis of earning potential, as well as on asset values. From Icahn's perspective, blame for the gap rested with management, which, through incompetence or arrogance, failed to maximize the companies' financial performance.

If all went according to plan, cash-rich vultures would recognize the inherent value in the Icahn targets and would engage in bidding wars for them, rapidly inflating the value of Icahn's holdings. In another, equally attractive scenario, frightened management would offer to buy out Icahn at a substantial profit over his per share cost. Either way, Icahn the catalyst would walk away with millions of dollars in proxy spoils.

With this idea Icahn launched his first major move to control corporate destinies, and in turn, to earn the kind of windfall profits he believed were awaiting those gifted strategists who saw the opportunities in the system and had the gumption to exploit them. Standing at the vanguard of a new form of financial engineering that would have a cataclysmic impact on American capitalism, Icahn would fire his opening salvos at Baird & Warner, a slumping real estate investment trust (REIT), and a sleepy, Mansfield, Ohio-based range and oven maker, the Tappan Company.

When Icahn launched his offensive against Baird & Warner Mortgage & Realty Investors, the Chicago-based REIT was run by John Baird, a prominent figure in the local business community. For generations the Baird name had been one of the most respected in Chicago, lauded for the family's business acumen as well as for their extensive involvement in civic and charitable institutions. In this tradition, John Baird was widely acknowledged as a gentleman and an asset to the community.

None of this meant a thing to Carl Icahn.

Like scores of REITs created in the 1960s and early 70s to make investments in portfolios of office buildings and shopping centers, Baird & Warner rode high at the outset, its stock soaring. But as the real estate market took a drubbing in 1975, REIT stock prices tumbled. When Icahn started accumulating Baird & Warner's stock in May 1978, it was selling for $8.50 a share.

Icahn was not the only one to see that REIT purchases made for good bottom fishing. With the real estate sector apparently on the verge of a sharp recovery, buying REIT shares while their prices were still depressed promised substantial profits over a narrow time frame. Considering the significant spread between book value and stock prices, investors saw minimal downside risk. Theoretically, all they had to do was wait for the gap to close and cash in their chips.

"As an expert on REITs I was buying stock in a number of them," said attorney Marvin Olshan. "At one point, I placed an order with Icahn & Company. Because it was a small outfit, and I felt somewhat insecure about that, I asked to have the stock certificates delivered to me.

"Well, four months and several phone calls went by and still no stock. So I called Carl himself to get the certificates. We got engaged in conversation, one thing led to another, and he asked me why I bought the REIT. He said he was thinking of investing in Baird & Warner and he wanted my opinion on it.

"A research report had said that Baird & Warner was worth about $15 a share, but I told Carl that if it were liquidated, it could yield as much as $22 a share. I don't know how much I had to do with it, but he proceeded to buy the stock and he asked me to represent him as his lawyer."

If the stock price capped at Baird & Warner's book value of $14 a share, Icahn would earn a tidy $5.50 per share, or about 65 percent on his investment.

"A REIT was like a closed-end fund in real estate," Kingsley said. "Because the Baird & Warner REIT was undervalued, it was a natural. We were confident we could profit on it."

But Icahn had another motive. By attacking Baird & Warner, and liquidating its more than $80 million in assets— including real properties and construction loans that could be sold to financial institutions—the raider could generate substantial capital for use as a takeover war chest.

Indicating at first that he was in the stock just for the ride, Icahn began to show signs of a greater ambition, building his position to the point that he could play an activist role. In what would become his trademark modus operandi, Icahn's strategy was to tweak shareholders' emotions, turning them against management and using the proxy vote as a catalyst for change. In this case, "change" meant selling the REIT for a sum at or near its book value.

When Icahn had bought 20 percent of the REIT's stock, he petitioned for a seat on the board. From this insider's position he could serve as a catalyst for actively seeking a buyer or dismantling the REIT and selling off its assets. But the REIT's board, which had no desire to change the status quo, twice blackballed Icahn's petition to serve as a director.

"The first time I met Icahn, he showed up in my office saying he wanted a seat on our board," recalled John Baird. "Well, I'd never even heard of the guy until he started buying our stock, and I don't even recall if he had an appointment to visit with me. So his demand for a seat didn't make me want to turn right around and accommodate him.

"Instead, I asked him what kind of experience he had that would enable him to contribute to the board. Of course, his answer was unsatisfactory because the truth is he didn't know beans about real estate. All he kept saying was that he had the stock and that entitled him to a seat."

This chilly reception hardly came as a surprise to Icahn, who had already formed a view of management as a spoiled elitist group insulated from the company's ups and downs by the generous terms of their compensation packages. And he was fully prepared to act against them. In the Baird & Warner case, he did so by identifying an apparent weakness in the REIT's management, using this vulnerability to rally the shareholders to his side.

Carl claimed that the company's financial performance was hampered by an all-too cozy relationship whereby Baird & Warner Mortgage & Realty (the REIT) was paying substantial management fees to Baird & Warner, Inc., a privately owned real estate company that had founded the REIT. Related to this, a number of the REIT's construction loans were apparently made to clients of Baird & Warner, Inc., with the latter collecting brokerage fees for engineering the loans. Compounding the problem, about a third of the REIT's loans were seriously in arrears.

Under financial pressure, management made what may have been a disastrous mistake: It skipped a dividend payment. Because REIT investors expected a steady flow of income, this created a sense of uneasiness and ill-will among the shareholders. Icahn, always searching for leverage, jumped on it.

"Given the difficult times we were operating in, many REITs were skipping dividend payments," Baird said. "But the shareholders didn't take any comfort in that, and Icahn used the opportunity to build his case with our investors. The knowledge that we were vulnerable at the time drew him to us, and he used that vulnerability to further his own interests."

The picture that Icahn painted for his fellow shareholders was that of a REIT functioning primarily for the greedy self-interest of its board, depriving the true owners of the company of a satisfactory return on their investment. But as Icahn was poised to launch a proxy battle to install himself and his own slate of directors on the board, the REIT went on the offensive, seeking to preempt Carl by voting to liquidate the trust at $19 per share.

On the surface, this seemed to be an ideal turn of events for Icahn, who would be turning a substantial profit on his Baird & Warner shares. But the manner in which the liquidation would take place made Icahn furious. According to the plan, it would be a three-year process. Were Carl to let this drawn-out liquidation go unchallenged, his money would be tied up for thirty-six months. Compounding matters, his investment would be at the mercy of the board, which, because it owned only 2 percent of the REIT's stock, had no vested interest in ensuring that the liquidation proceeded in the shareholders' best interests. In fact, the process could be used to retaliate against Icahn by delaying and otherwise thwarting an orderly liquidation.

Rather than rejoicing, Carl the street-smart skeptic asked, "What if they try to get $19 and fail? What if they simply try to screw me? What if my investment goes sour while the board is taking three years to do what can be done in a matter of months?"

Motivated by this worst-case scenario and by a built-in distrust of his adversaries, Icahn was determined to quash the board's liquidation plan, to get his own slate on the board and to quickly close the spread between Baird & Warner's book and market values. To this end, Icahn and an investment group he had assembled stepped up their purchases of the REIT, acquiring 34 percent of the shares—enough to block the board's liquidation plan, which required approval by two-thirds of the shareholders.

On a second front, Icahn launched a proxy battle, this time to replace the entire board with his own slate of candidates. In campaigning for this sweeping change, he formed a shareholders' committee and touted himself as the living embodiment of all that is pure and moral.

"If the Committee's slate is elected," Icahn declared, *"neither my firm, Icahn & Co, Inc., nor I (as a director or an officer) will take any salary, advising fees or director's fees from the Trust. My only interest is to increase the value of the shares of the Trust."*

In the heat of battle, Icahn, his executive assistant, Gail Golden, and others in the fledgling company called shareholders directly, making the pitch that they were the real owners of the company and that they should insist on a management that performed on their behalf. This commitment to spend the time building his case with the shareholders, calling them at work and at home and walking them through the issues, would become a hallmark of Icahn's proxy battles. Although Icahn has never been a "people person," when his interests are at stake he can be an effective salesman.

"We talked about corporate democracy, something the smaller shareholders hadn't given much thought to before, and they responded well to this," Golden said. "Oh, sure, some told us to bug off and leave management to do as they saw fit, but in most cases we got a fair and positive hearing."

When the vote was taken on May 22, 1979, Icahn emerged victorious, knocking out the incumbents and taking control of the REIT. The victory proved especially sweet to Icahn, who says Baird dismissed him at the outset, responding to his announcement that he'd filed a 13-d (a document investors accumulating more than 5 percent of a public company must file with the SEC) by saying, "What's that?"

By training a spotlight on the incumbents' mediocre performance, by revealing that the trustees had approved $1.5 million in fees to Baird & Warner, Inc., a firm that employed four of the trustees, at a time when the REIT was losing money and by proving that his presence could raise the price of the REIT's shares (which had already climbed to about $14 a share), Icahn convinced the shareholders to support him.

On June 1, Icahn was elected chairman of the board of trustees, and the REIT's name was changed from Baird & Warner Mortgage and Realty Investors to Bayswater Realty and Investment Trust, a reference to Carl's childhood community. By the end of the year, Icahn would reveal a master plan, approved by the shareholders, to revoke Bayswater's status as a REIT and merge it into a subsidiary, Bayswater Realty & Capital Corp. This made the business eligible for a wider range of investment activities, including the opportunity to invest in marketable securities. Trading through brokerage accounts at Icahn & Company, Bayswater would become a conduit for Carl's accelerating activity as a takeover artist.

"As soon as Icahn took over the REIT, he started liquidating the assets and turning them into cash," Baird said. "That fit perfectly with his strategy, one I'm certain guided him from the day he started buying our stock. He would use the funds he realized from the liquidation to fund his takeovers."

Another component of the Icahn master plan was in place.

In late 1977, Icahn began buying Tappan stock at about $7.50 a share. His timing was impeccable. A sturdy enterprise, still run by a member of the Tappan family nearly a century after the company's founding, the business was suffering from a poorly conceived acquisition in the heating and cooling market and from a slump in home building. As a result, Tappan posted its first loss in about forty years, which sent the stock reeling.

With its limited product line, Tappan was a relatively minor force in the appliance industry, surrounded on all flanks by such diversified giants as General Electric and Westinghouse. But management's goal—to establish a profitable niche in cooking appliances much as Maytag had with washers and dryers—offered promise for a strong return to profitability, especially after the cyclically depressed housing market rebounded.

Icahn choose Tappan as an early target for two critical reasons: First, he believed that a turnaround was in the offing and the company's stock price failed to reflect this potential. Second, Tappan's book value of roughly $20 a share was more than two times the price of its stock. This spread between book and market value was where Icahn saw his ultimate profit. By flushing out a buyer willing to acquire the company or its assets at a price somewhere between the price Icahn paid for his shares and the book value per share, he was assured of a substantial return on his investment. As Icahn's war-room tactician, Kingsley drafted the takeover strategies built around the Tappan raid.

"At the time we took our position in Tappan, everyone else was hot on Magic Chef," Kingsley recalled. "But I said, 'The multiples on Magic Chef are too high. Where is it going to go from here? Magic Chef was at the top of its cycle and Tappan was at the bottom. That's where I preferred to stake our claim."

This reflected Kingsley's preference for stocks with minimal downside exposure. By and large, shares selling for high multiples of earnings were too rich for his taste. Instead, he gravitated toward out-of-favor stocks, such as Tappan, that had already been discounted by the market.

In what would come to be characteristic of his modus operandi, Icahn couched his first contact with Tappan in the guise of a friendly telephone call. On the morning of January 5, 1978, he and Kingsley called Tappan president Donald Blasius to report that Icahn had purchased 10,000 to 15,000 Tappan shares and that he was exploring the possibility of making a "substantial additional investment," both for Icahn's account as well as for large clients of Icahn & Company.

Throughout the brief conversation Icahn was appearing to be syrupy-sweet and naive. At one point he asked Blasius for general information about Tappan, including innocuous details about its products and manufacturing facilities. This was Icahn's attempt to lull the unsuspecting corporate executive into a false sense of security. To know Icahn is to know full well that he would not have invested a dime in Tappan before Kingsley the numbers-crunching analyst put the company under a microscope. What's more, the idea of Icahn the born skeptic putting a penny's worth of faith in management's assertions is laughable.

At this point his prey had yet to figure out that it was under seige. As Blasius noted in a memo to Chairman W. R. Tappan, Icahn "seemed pleased that we took the time to talk to them about the company."

Icahn had yet to become a feared corporate raider, and the Blasius memo speaks volumes about corporate management's naivete concerning his intentions. Carl Icahn "pleased" that executives of a company in which he held a major investment would take the time to talk to him? Nonsense. As a shareholder, Icahn believed that Tappan and Blasius worked for him, that they continued in their capacity at the pleasure of the shareholders and that they were obligated to be responsive to him. But for now he was content to play Mr. Humble, probing, sensing, taking the lay of the land before moving his next pawn into place.

Although Blasius saw no cause for alarm, he did inform Dick Tappan that one of his staffers had done some "quiet" checking on Icahn & Company and "while I see no problem, I think we should try to maintain some view as to what their future purchase status would be."

This would come into sharper focus when Icahn and Kingsley called Blasius again on February 22. By this point Icahn had increased his stake to more than 70,000 Tappan shares, and for the first time he slipped the word "takeover" into the conversation, noting, rather nonchalantly, that he had purchased the stock partially for its appeal as a takeover target. He told Blasius that Icahn & Company "had made a lot of money in buying low-priced stocks that were in the process of turnaround. In some cases, the turnaround improved the value of the stock, but in other cases a buy-out was completed which approximately doubled their stock price." A Blasius memo on the talk with Icahn and Kingsley noted: "They consider us a good possibility for this occurring, which is an added incentive for their investment." But when Tappan's president asked point blank if a takeover was going to be part of Icahn's strategy, "they said absolutely not—that they are not in that kind of business and do not want to be."

According to Blasius, Icahn assured him that his purchases of Tappan stock were for investment purposes only. Carl then promptly increased his stake to $3 million worth of Tappan shares. Knowing that his purchases would fuel speculation of an imminent takeover, Icahn believed he was setting off a chain reaction. On one hand, arbitrageurs would bid up Tappan shares, hoping to get a piece of the action before a takeover was announced. On the other, investment bankers from one side of Wall Street to another would be feverishly pitching their clients to make a bid for Tappan, thus assuring the bankers of a seven-figure fee. In what would prove to be a pattern for the 1980s, simply indicating that a company was a takeover target would be a self-fulfilling prophesy, leading ultimately to an acquisition by the original suitor, another hostile challenger or a white knight.

At the time he was pursuing Tappan, though, the mergers and acquisitions boom had not yet built the head of steam that would drive it like a runaway locomotive throughout the following decade. If Icahn expected a stampede of prospective buyers to engage in a bidding war for Tappan, he would be sadly disappointed. After he had held the stock for about nine months, nary a bidder appeared. With most of the speculation focused on Magic Chef, few saw the value in Tappan that Kingsley had identified.

Icahn's strength, even at this nascent point in his career as a takeover bully, was to function—in fact, to thrive—in adversity. It is precisely the specter of challenge that sends Icahn into intellectual high gear, searching for a new tact or a missing puzzle piece that will help to secure his objective. Undoubtedly, Icahn is blessed with a superior mind, but it is his determination to play an activist role in his business deals, to keep finding solutions to a maze of problems, that separates him from the run-of-the-mill Wall Street opportunists who are quick to write off problem deals and move on to the next. Starting with his earliest campaigns, Icahn would build his reputation, and his all-important credibility, by refusing to retreat no matter how bleak the picture or how much the deck was stacked against him.

In an attempt to light a spark under his Tappan investment, Icahn hosted an early May luncheon meeting in New York with Blasius, Tappan V.P. William Block, and Fred Sullivan, chairman of the conglomerate Walter Kidde & Co., which had purchased a 20 percent equity stake in Icahn & Company. Carl's unwritten agenda called for interesting Sullivan in acquiring Tappan to complement Kidde's Farberware division, a maker of cooking products. In effect, the arbitrageur turned fledging takeover artist would be acting as an investment banker.

When Blasius arrived in New York on the morning of May 9, 1978, he called Icahn to confirm the meeting plans. Only then did he learn that Sullivan would be joining them for lunch. Icahn said that Sullivan was a large Tappan shareholder and that he was interested in talking to the company.

From Icahn's perspective, the meeting started swimmingly. Sullivan talked at length about Farberware and expressed interest in acquiring Tappan. But just as Icahn's deal-making adrenaline began to rise, Blasius gave a chilly reply. The last-minute news that Sullivan would be attending the meeting could only mean that Icahn was engineering an acquisition without having discussed his intentions with Tappan, and Blasius was fuming.

Although he made the obligatory statements that Tappan was a public company and the management would of course review any offers with the board, the bottom line was that the company was not for sale.

Compounding Icahn's problem, Sullivan responded that Kidde was unalterably opposed to hostile takeovers, going so far as to admit that the company's only unfriendly transaction, its acquisition of U.S. Lines, was probably a mistake and that the line had already been sold. Hearing this, Blasius breathed easier. As the Tappan president noted in a post-luncheon memo, Sullivan "understood that we were not for sale and, therefore, would not go any further. Then he added without any suggestion on my part, 'If anyone comes along that you are not interested in, or you would like to come to a friendly port, we would be very happy to talk to you.' "

If Blasius hoped to leave the meeting free of the Icahn threat, he was mistaken. In style, if not in substance, Icahn is much like the old Peter Falk television detective Colombo. Just when you think he is off the case, when you are certain you have heard the last of him, he returns with a new round of penetrating questions, speculations, and veiled threats. True to form, as the New York meeting was about to conclude, Icahn indicated that he planned to buy more Tappan stock, up to and including enough to trigger a 13-d filing. Once again Carl assured Blasius that his action was all in the realm of pure investment.

As Blasius noted in his minutes of the meeting: "He repeated that this was not an attempt to accomplish, or the beginning of a buy-out—that they felt the stock was undervalued at approximately $8 and had good growth potential. He also indicated that we should not be worried if a 13-d were filed as it would not be intended as the beginning of a takeover attempt."

Although Blasius summed up his impressions by noting that the meeting had been cordial, and that an unfriendly offer did not seem to be in the works, he did wave a red flag, noting, "We obviously have no guarantee of what will happen."

.   .   .

Soon after the meeting, Icahn redoubled his efforts to find a buyer. Calling around the Street, he tried to pique the interest of investment bankers, wealthy investors, and corporate clients, declaring to one and all the exceptional value in buying undervalued Tappan. In a call to Blasius on May 26, he opened the possibility of a Japanese connection, saying that he had learned from his sources that certain Japanese producers of microwave ovens were exploring the purchase of a range manufacturer in order to broaden their product lines and to add clout to their marketing capabilities. With this, Carl clearly hoped to whet Tappan's appetite for a rich buy-out, but Blasius pooh-poohed the idea on the grounds that a number of Japanese companies were already in the range and microwave businesses and that for Tappan a strategic union with a microwave manufacturer "would not make a great deal of difference as far as our long-term need is concerned."

With Blasius clearly cool to the prospect of a Japanese connection, and with Carl unable to find a Japanese company willing to pursue Tappan unilaterally, the prospect short-circuited there.

Throughout the summer and early fall of 1978, Icahn continued to shop the company, working the phones, meeting with clients, employing the market-making skills he had developed in the options business. But for all of his beating the bushes, he was hard pressed to flush out a single qualified buyer with an interest in acquiring Tappan. No one else, it seemed, saw the value in the company that Icahn (with Tonto behind him) kept insisting was there.

Still, Icahn was not to be stopped. Maintaining the Chinese water torture tactic that has come to be his trademark, he kept the pressure on Tappan by purchasing an additional 40,000 of the company's shares on November 3, 1978, and by telling Blasius that he was considering buying more. As Icahn knew full well, building his stake in the range maker increased his leverage by raising the specter of an Icahn takeover, thus forcing management to buy him out or to accept a third-party acquisition (which would also take Carl out for a handsome gain).

From Icahn's perspective, the additional purchases were equivalent to buying a low-risk option on Tappan shares. With the stock price still hovering at about half of Tappan's book value, Icahn saw little downside threat. One scenario—a takeover and ultimate breakup of the company's assets—would provide a tidy return. Icahn could also benefit more from a turnaround in Tappan's performance (thus boosting its share value) or from the buy-out he was still determined to engineer. At this juncture he was sending Tappan's management a dual message: As an aggressive buyer of shares, he was a clear threat to control the destiny of the company. On the other hand, he was still disavowing any immediate goal to take over the business. To the unsuspecting, this appeared to be the flip-flopping of an indecisive raider. But in fact it was an integral component of Icahn's attack strategy, designed to keep his adversaries off-balance, wondering where the next strike would come.

In a memo concerning a November 3 conversation with Icahn over continued stock purchases, Blasius noted: "In response to a direct question, he said that he was buying for Carl Icahn, not for anybody else. He said, 'You can relax and enjoy your weekend—it is not a buy-out or tender offer.' " But to make certain Blasius didn't relax too much, Icahn added that he would likely buy more Tappan stock and "would, of course, then have to file under 13-d."

Although Blasius still seemed inclined to believe Icahn's claim that he intended to remain a passive investor, the warning light started blinking brighter and faster.

"At this point, I can detect nothing other than a straight investment plan," Blasius noted. "We should keep in mind, however, that he is the one that tried to promote a buy-out by a third party once before, and would, undoubtedly, not be unhappy if a tender offer did come in with a substantial increase over his investment base of between $7 and $8."

On November 16, two phone calls—one from the *Wall Street Journal* and another from a shareholder—alerted Tappan management that an Icahn 13-d was imminent. Seeking to confirm what was still just a rumor, Blasius called Icahn a day later, informing him of the phone calls and of a related report that

Icahn's most recent 40,000 share block had been purchased from Walter Kidde & Co.

When Blasius sought to pin down Icahn's intentions concerning the SEC filing, he ran smack into Carl's double-talk, another component of the Icahn modus. As he rambles on, apparently confused by the events and the details before him, he draws his opponents into a labyrinth of thoughts and speculations that leaves them as confused as Icahn appears to be. What his adversaries fail to detect, until they are well into the game, is that he has personally created the labyrinth and has carefully plotted every route of escape.

Sitting across the table from Icahn, Blasius could not have known this. His memo concerning a November 17 conversation offers a clear insight into Icahn at work, weaving his web.

"He said he was confused by the whole situation—they had not filed a 13-d because his attorneys had not come back to him yet. He did indicate, however, that probably would still be doing so and, also, might buy some more stock, but would call us as he had indicated before he would, if and when such a filing were made."

In the course of the conversation with Blasius, Icahn began to hit his stride as a master strategist, throwing open the possibility of his moving in every direction at once. He might buy more stock, but then again he might not. He might file with the SEC, but then again he might not have to. He planned to remain more or less a passive investor, but he was on the verge of buying even more stock. He would like to interest a third party in acquiring Tappan, but he suggested a preference for a management-led buy-out.

"He asked a number of questions regarding the possibility of the officers buying out the company—said you could become a millionaire very quickly," Blasius recalled. " 'Why don't you borrow the money on the assets and buy out the company?' "

In spraying the negotiations with a thousand possibilities, Icahn creates a complex environment in which he can camouflage his strategy. What does Carl really want? Which direction is he headed in? By tossing out dozens of variables, he leaves everyone guessing. The more his adversaries try to figure him out, the more he opens new channels: some deadends, others viable options. It is in this context, where less accomplished negotiators look for symmetry and consistency, that Icahn thrives.

Although Icahn promised to inform Tappan of any move to file a 13-d, the company asked its Washington lawyers, the prominent firm of Jones, Day, Reavis & Pogue, to keep a watchful eye at the SEC. They more or less expected Carl to file. The only questions were when and, more important, what would follow. Those questions seemed to be answered on November 27, when Tappan received a copy of the 13-d, followed ten minutes later by a phone call from Icahn, who insisted that he was still in the stock as a "good investment and a cheap buy."

In the waning days of 1978, Icahn purchased another 44,000 shares at \$8⅝. Speculation about a Tappan takeover made the rounds on Wall Street—possible buyers ranged from Icahn himself to Rockwell International—but all such rumors were rejected by management, which sought and received Carl's assurances that he was not plotting a takeover. In fact, on January 2, 1979, Icahn told Blasius that if the shares, then buoyed by the takeover rumors, were to rise two or three more points, "we probably would not see him anymore."

If an increasingly wary Tappan management team thought this, they would be sorely disappointed. Throughout January, Icahn teased the company with word that an anonymous corporate buyer had approached him about acquiring his shares in the \$15 to \$17 range. According to Icahn, the buyer had recently failed in its attempt to take over another company and this time it was determined to line up major shareholders before proceeding with its Tappan strategy. Later Icahn reminded Blasius that the Rockwell rumors were rampant and that Walter Kidde might still be willing to serve as a white knight if an unfriendly offer surfaced. In the process, he was planting ideas, options, fears.

Stage two of the Icahn offensive was launched at 5:10 on February 20, when in the course of a phone conversation, Icahn asked Blasius if he would consider adding a tenth member to the board.

Not surprisingly, Icahn was nominating himself. Equally predictably, Blasius rejected the idea.

In a memo to Tappan executives, Blasius noted: "I explained that our board was limited to nine members with only two being representatives of management and that the number had been fixed by the board either last year or the year before.

"I also gave him an outline of our board strength that I felt was represented and that I really believe we have an efficient board match—independent, very capable and doing a good job and that I, personally, saw no need or desire to add a tenth member."

Ever since Icahn began to reach out to control corporate destinies, he pictured himself a positive force shaking up an entrenched and close-minded management. The Tappan company's knee-jerk rejection of his bid to join the board gave credence to this. Why not add a smart, savvy financial man to the ranks of the company's directors? With Icahn's knowledge of Wall Street and his ability to serve as a catalyst for raising shareholder value, wouldn't his counsel benefit Tappan?

Instead, management viewed him as a threat. In boosting the company's performance for its shareholders, Icahn might well tamper with the status quo, perhaps arranging a merger or a buy-out that, for one reason or another, failed to win management's support. In corporate America, that was, and is, considered unacceptable.

Much as they deny it, CEOs and their boards of directors come to view the companies they run as their own. Should an outsider threaten their prerogatives, they will do everything in their power to repel him. This insiders vs. outsiders mindset violates both the spirit of the corporate democracy and the fiduciary responsibility boards of directors owe to a company's shareholders. Although the idea of having a gadfly on the board—one who would seek acquisitions or lobby for buy-outs—is considered to be heresy among the corporate establishment, viewed from the standpoint of the shareholders' interests, it makes all the sense in the world. In all likelihood, it is the gadfly alone who will uncover opportunities to maximize shareholder values through unconventional means, including mergers and break-ups, that may reward everyone but the handful of overpaid executives living high off the corporate fat.

This is not to say that Carl Icahn is the champion of stock-holder rights he claims to be. Icahn has always sought a profit, first and foremost. What motivates Icahn, however, is not as important as the fact that his quest for ever greater wealth in some cases benefits shareholders as well as himself. As would happen as the Tappan deal unfolded.

Within weeks after launching his trial balloon for a place on the Tappan board, Icahn got word of the company's plan to issue serially preferred stock. Icahn also feared that Tappan would use the preferred shares to go on the offensive by making an acquisition of its own. Because this would cloud the picture surrounding Tappan's financial position, the company's share price would almost definitely drop, giving Icahn a paper loss and, more detrimental to his master plan, would scare off potential acquirers. This would put Icahn in a terribly weak position. With the threat of a tender offer greatly diminished, and with the likelihood of a Tappan buyer coming forward a long shot at best, Icahn would be left without a gun to hold to management's head.

Determined to prevent that, Icahn took the offensive.

"We first learned of the serially preferred tactic through a proxy statement that came in the mail," Kingsley said. "As soon as I saw it I said, 'If we are going to do something, Carl, we had better do it now.' "

Since Tappan was scheduling a shareholders' vote on the plan to issue the new preferred, Icahn swung into action. Accusing management of using the preferred to protect their self-interests, he sent Blasius a registered letter demanding a list of Tappan's shareholders. With exactly a month to go before the company presented its preferred plan at the annual meeting, scheduled for April 23, 1979, Icahn had a narrow window to present his case against the preferred to his fellow shareholders.

At first Tappan management tried to convince Icahn that the preferred was no threat to his interests on the grounds that the company had no "intent" to use the new security to block a tender offer. But Carl, whose Queens radar goes on high alert when adversaries volunteer to protect his interests, answered, "If you killed thirty people, you might say it was not your intent to do that, but the result was still the same."

From the earliest days of his career Icahn viewed trust as a weak and dangerous concession that had no place in business negotiations. Viewing the world through skeptical eyes that see every man out for himself regardless of his assertions to the contrary, Icahn prefers to confront transactions with a worst-case mentality. Before making a move, he surveys the chess board, asking himself, "What is the worst thing my adversaries can do to me, and how can I protect myself on all flanks?" In planning his strategies, Icahn looks to three checkpoints simultaneously: his goals, weak points, and his leverage.

As Carl checked his position in the spring of 1979, his goal—to collect substantial profits by engineering an acquisition of Tappan—remained constant. So did his leverage as a major owner of the company's shares and as a determined catalyst for change. But if the serially preferred shares were issued, his leverage would diminish and his downside risk would grow. Rather than placing his trust in management's intentions, Icahn was determined to bolster his leverage by winning a place on the board and using that position both to defeat the plan to issue preferred and to mount a more aggressive campaign to sell Tappan for a substantial premium over its market price.

He was promptly rewarded for his determination. Just the specter of Icahn launching an all-out campaign for board membership was enough to win a major concession from management, which agreed to withdraw its proposal for the preferred shares. However, if Tappan and Blasius thought this would dissuade Icahn from seeking a place on the board, they were mistaken. It is precisely this scenario, when his opponents are retreating, which emboldens Icahn and prompts him to go for the jugular.

As Blasius noted in a memo regarding a March 30 conversation with Icahn, "Relating to the board-seat matter, he said he thought he had already gone too far and would probably want to continue. Said he felt someone with the number of shares he controlled should be represented on the board and thought he could be helpful to us. . . . Said he couldn't understand why he was not entitled to a board seat and hoped we would not fight the issue—said he had enough shares to 'win one or two seats.' In general I tried to discourage a proxy fight but do not believe I was successful."

He wasn't. In a letter to Tappan shareholders dated April 11, 1979, Icahn pressed his case for board membership and ultimately for the sale of the company:

"I am writing this letter to ask you to elect me to the Board of Directors at the Annual Meeting of Shareholders on April 23, 1979. As the largest shareholder of Tappan, I would like to see our company acquired or tendered for at a price close to its December 31, 1978, book value of $20.18."

In an effort to play on the emotions of the shareholders by presenting a picture of an ineffective, self-indulgent management team, Icahn trained a spotlight on the company's financial records.

"During the past five years Tappan, under its current management, has lost $3.3 million on sales of $1.3 billion and during the same period W.R. Tappan and D.C. Blasius, Tappan's Chairman of the Board and President, respectively, received salaries and bonuses totaling $1,213,710."

A chart built into the text of the letter drove home the disparity between corporate performance and management compensation. Breaking down earnings and salaries on an annual basis, the analysis revealed that in the same year, 1974, that the company had lost more than $7 million, Dick Tappan and Blasius collected salaries and bonuses of $83,096 and $131,806 respectively.

Using figures like these as the setup, Icahn then delivered the clincher: "If I *personally* owned a business with these operating results and which had substantial net worth, I would certainly seek to sell that business. I believe this same logic should apply in the case of Tappan."

Icahn went on to note that management had withdrawn the proposal to issue the new preferred, but warned that such a proposal would likely surface again in the future. Declaring that management itself had admitted such a preferred issue "might have the effect of discouraging some future attempt to take over the company by a cash tender offer or otherwise," Icahn promised that if elected to the board he would "discourage any such future proposals in their embryonic stages."

Appealing to the shareholders' primary goal of profiting on their investment in the company, Icahn pledged: "As a director of Tappan my first act will be to recommend that we retain an investment banking firm (unaffiliated with me) to solicit proposals from third parties to acquire our company at a price near its book value, which at December 31, 1978, was $20.18.

"Although management has stated to me that they do not desire the acquisition of Tappan by another company, I assure you that, if I am elected, I will inform would-be suitors that at least one member of the Board does not share management's views with respect to the acquisition of Tappan by another company. I will attempt to see to it that shareholders are made aware of any indications of interest or actual offers to acquire our company, which are received from third parties."

Icahn ended his letter with a plea for support, asking the shareholders to send their proxy cards to him or his proxy solicitor, the Carter Organization, before the date of the annual meeting.

When the dust cleared, Icahn had won his place on the board.

Seated as a director, Icahn wasted no time in trying to goad his peers to put Tappan assets on the auction block. At his first board meeting, Icahn pressed for a sale of the company's Canadian subsidiary, Tappan-Gurney, an anemic money loser that owned valuable real estate in downtown Montreal. Icahn's pitch: liquidate the subsidiary and turn the property into cash. In a similar vein, Icahn noted that Tappan's Anaheim, California, plant was a big employer of Mexican factory workers. Given the value of the plant, and the ready pool of Mexican laborers south of the border, Icahn called for selling this property and relocating the manufacturing operation to Mexico.

On another front, Icahn pressed his case to find a third party to buy out Tappan. But with the balance of the board set against him, the fox in the chicken coop was unable to convince any of the other directors to second his proposal. Faced with this show of solidarity, meant to intimidate the Wall Streeter, and to demonstrate that he would carry a small stick on the board, Icahn resorted to another of his now-classic moves: He found a way to carry a bigger stick. In this case, that took the form of a threat that if no progress were made in the search for a buyer, he would consider running another candidate for the board the following year. Based on his successful effort to inject himself into Tappan's inner sanctum, the threat had to be taken seriously.

For the time being, however, Icahn continued to stir the pot, shopping Tappan to an eclectic mix of prospective suitors including leveraged buy-out investors, private investment groups, and major corporations in the United States, Europe, and Japan. Throughout the process he filled the air with possibilities, referring to any number of potential investors and buyers, most of whom would have to remain anonymous. In July 1979, Icahn told Blasius that he had been approached by a party interested in a leverage buy-out. In August, he revealed that he was holding talks with the president of a major company. Always a veil of secrecy was wrapped around the negotiations.

As Blasius recalled the August conversation, Icahn said the president "is very interested in buying the Tappan Company . . . Carl would not identify the man or the company at this time because he had been asked not to. I told him I felt I should know at least the name of the company with whom I was going to speak, if a meeting were arranged. He said he would ask the man's permission to give me the name."

Through all of this hinting, Icahn was preparing management for the fact that a buyer could emerge at any time and that he himself had no intention of abandoning his efforts until his mission was accomplished. Management faced two major options: to fairly appraise friendly offers that came Tappan's way (or risk facing a hostile takeover) and/or to search for a friendly buyer on their own.

Once management recognized this, which it did with great reluctance, Icahn had won. Regardless of which option management chose, they were playing into Icahn's hand.

Preferring to see the company sold to a white knight than

to allow Icahn to liquidate it, Tappan and Blasius flew to Sweden for secret talks with AB Electrolux, the huge European appliance maker. The two companies had been discussing a joint venture arrangement whereby Tappan would enter the recreational vehicle market, making the vehicles' ranges and cooling systems and Electrolux would provide the refrigerators. But with the lone wolf of Wall Street at Tappan's door, the company's senior executives posed a new idea to Electrolux managing director Hans Werthen: Would the Swedish giant be interested in buying Tappan?

In short order a deal was struck whereby Electrolux agreed to acquire Tappan for $18 a share, giving Icahn a $2.7 million profit on his holdings of 321,500 shares.

Icahn's profit on the Tappan deal was minuscule compared to the huge gains he would earn in the eighties, but his philosophy about corporate values had been proven correct. Clearly a glaring disparity had existed between intrinsic value and stock market value. A catalyst for change had successfully narrowed that gap, producing rapid gains for himself and, incidentally, for all of the shareholders.

The Icahn/Kingsley theory had been proven in the crucible of the real world: Focus the market's attention on the disparity in values, and someone—most likely management or a white knight—will buy you out. It was one of those elegant ideas that is at once simple and powerful.

Even Dick Tappan became a true believer. "We held a final board meeting, at which time the directors approved the company's sale to Electrolux," Tappan recalls. "Icahn attended that meeting and sometime during the course of the evening I said, 'Icahn has done us a favor. We got a 50 percent premium over the company's market value, and Electrolux is going to make capital investments in Tappan.' "

Knowing a good idea when he saw it, Tappan glanced across the table at Icahn, passing along a hint he hoped the raider would pick up on.

"I said, 'If you have any deals you want to cut me in on—'

That's when Icahn said, 'Yes, I have one going on now.' " With that, Tappan would become a limited partner of his former adversary, placing $100,000 with the Icahn juggernaut. Quickly he would recoup his investment plus a healthy profit and would proceed to invest in a series of Icahn deals.

To date, his only regret is that he withdrew the original stake once he earned it back. "I did well with Icahn, but if I had let that first $100,000 ride, I would have made a lot more money."

Tappan was one of Icahn's first big payoffs, but Icahn took no time out to celebrate. In a pattern that would repeat itself through all of his conquests, he proceeded to his next deal without as much as a victory toast.

"I used to think we should have a party, even just a small one, to commemorate our success, but that just didn't interest Carl," Golden said. "Carl was never the kind to say, 'I've had great success. I'm taking the next two weeks off.' "

Although it could not be detected in his marathon work habits, a major change had occurred in Icahn's life. He had become a family man. After a brief courtship with Liba Trejbal, a Czechoslovakian ballerina who had emigrated to the U.S. in 1968, Icahn married her in 1978. The couple had met at a Hamptons' party a year earlier. At the time, Liba, a thirty-year-old beauty with a delicately chiseled face and understated sensuality, was working as an interior designer with the Hoffstratra Co. The wedding ceremony, held at a friend's Manhattan apartment, was celebrated at the 21 Club, the party attended by close friends and family.

With no time in workaholic Icahn's schedule for a honeymoon, Carl returned to work the next day.

Pressed to explain his single-minded focus on work, and on creating ever greater personal wealth, Icahn's face twists up in a question mark, as if he is at a loss to explain his own compulsion. But then he refers to an essay, "The Special Dangers of High Commercial Developments," written more than a century ago by Walter Bagehot, former editor of the *Economist* magazine:

"We often talk as if the haste to be rich, the mere desire of wealth, were the only motive power in these great speculative transactions which, when they fail, cause so much misery and so much scandal. But no mistake can be greater. We do not for a moment mean that the desire to be rich, the passion for making wealth, is not far too great—and in a considerable measure the cause of the speculative rashness we see. But it is not by any means the sole cause, hardly, perhaps, even the chief cause.

"We find as a rule that the men who can handle large armies well are apt to favour war when any international question arises which involves war; and if this be so, how much more natural it is that those who can handle, or who think they can handle, great commercial combinations well, and who of course anticipate from them, not the misery which war always causes even to the victor, but the satisfaction and employment which useful commercial enterprises bring, should feel a bias of which they are unconscious in favour of the exercise of their faculty, and against the timid counsels which would have them keep within the strictest limits of prudence."

Clearly, Icahn believes that his capabilities as "a man of commerce" are too great to be restricted by pedestrian concerns, or by "timid counsels," meaning anyone who fails to see the grand scheme of his work. Including, perhaps, his wife.

"Sometimes, I feel there is no reason he really should work anymore, but then where is he going to go from here," Liba said. "In regular families, the husband works and there is always something financially to look forward to. They are building, building.

"But here, how much more money he makes is not going to make any difference. The point is that he doesn't need any more money.

"But it's the game, as he says."

Even at this early point in his career, Icahn began to demonstrate traits that would distinguish him from the pack of takeover bullies who would come to prominence in the 1980s. Unlike his peers—men who would pursue corporate prey without apologies to anyone—Carl Icahn found a need to justify his actions. Repeatedly he would tell the press that his cause was more than the accumulation of personal wealth. It was also, he claimed, a campaign to remove the insulation surrounding corporate management and to make America's CEOs and their boards accountable to the shareholders whose companies they had come to treat as private treasuries.

"I feel strongly about corporate democracy, about shareholders having more say in what they want from their investments," Icahn told *Business Week* in June 1979. "When a company's performance is poor, something should happen to that management to ensure a return for the shareholders."

Icahn's need to couch his motives in the framework of "shareholder rights" can be traced to two factors. First, Michael Icahn's constant railing against robber barons, against the gross imbalance between the haves and the have-nots, had instilled a genuine sense of outrage in his son. From Carl's perspective, the real parasites were not the takeover bullies but instead the corporate CEOs. That this dovetailed nicely with his personal financial interests made it all the better. No matter how wealthy he would become, he would regard himself as a Robin Hood rather than as a robber baron.

Related to this, Icahn was convinced that the corporate establishment was distorting and therefore endangering America's capitalist system. If boards of directors deferred to CEOs, and CEOs pursued their own self-interests above all else, America's shareholders were no better off than the early colonists who were forced to endure taxation without representation. Unless those shareholders were given a practical voice in the disposition of their companies, corporate democracy in the U.S. was a sham.

Icahn held up the role he was now playing as the ideal solution to the problem. "A guy who owns a 30 percent stake in a public company and then plays a role in maximizing that company's return to the shareholders plays a vital role in the system," he said. "Because unlike the CEOs, he's not in it for the Gulfstream jets and the country clubs. He's not in it to see how many people, how many legions, he can have reporting to him. He's in it to protect that 30 percent investment and to make it grow. That's why he is so valuable a force to the company. Because if he doesn't like what's going on—if earnings are down or something else is wrong—he's going to come into that company and make certain that whatever is broken gets fixed. And because his presence is felt, the CEO isn't going to be able to go fishing or to the golf club or to take his spouse on a jaunt to Paris. He's not going to be able to do that because unless things are going gangbusters, the guy with the 30 percent is going to say, 'Hey, what the hell are you doing? Why aren't you here?'

"For business to function properly, you need that accountability. But too often in today's big publicly held corporations, management just does what it wants. There is little or no accountability to the shareholders and that's why the economic machine isn't working."

Based in part on his obsessive pursuit of wealth, and in part on a genuine belief in corporate democracy, Icahn would accelerate his attack on the business establishment, resulting in vicious confrontations with CEOs of the largest and most powerful corporations in the world.

TALK LIKE A POPULIST, ACT LIKE A RAIDER

"At times I guess I would plead guilty to being a bully if you call a bully a guy who says, 'Look, I have your stock and I'm going to do this, and I'm coming in, so why don't you sell me the company?' "

—CARL ICAHN

For all of his adult life, Carl Icahn has seen the world as a battle zone. On a visceral level he associates with brawn, machismo, brute power. Reflective of this, a bronze sculpture of an Indian warrior, displayed at his former offices at 25 Broadway, carried a plaque reading "Apache Renegade."

It was with this warlike mentality that Icahn mounted his next attack, putting the screws to Saxon Industries, a New York–based marketer of paper and copying machines. Beginning in July 1979, Icahn started accumulating Saxon stock, ultimately building a block of more than 750,000 shares. Ostensibly, his goal was to gain control of Saxon and find a buyer willing to pay a price reflecting the company's true value and to pocket the profits. This formula had worked so well at Tappan that Dick Tappan now joined Icahn as an investor in the Saxon raid, as did attorney Marvin Olshan.

Asked why, Olshan said, "Because I was always asking Carl Icahn in various conversations what he's buying, in a manner similar to E.F. Hutton, where the guy says, 'My broker is E.F. Hutton.' I'm one of the guys on the outside who's got big ears, and I try to find out what Carl Icahn is buying so that I can buy the stock too."

In late November 1979, an Icahn-led investment group filed a 13-d with the SEC indicating that they had accumulated more than 5 percent of the company's stock. On that day, Icahn called Saxon president Stanley Lurie to request a meeting. Because CEOs track big movements of their companies' stock, and generally learn from their investment bankers who is behind the purchases, Icahn was stunned when Lurie claimed he'd never heard of him.

"He said, 'Icahn, how do you spell it?' " Carl recalled. "I thought, Is this guy playing a game with me or is he for real?"

If Lurie really didn't know of Icahn, he would be the last CEO to ask Carl to spell his name.

The next day, Lurie, Saxon senior vice president Bruce Tobin and general counsel Walter Feldesman met with Icahn and Kingsley at Carl's request. This tense session, held at Saxon headquarters at 1230 Avenue of the Americas, began with some small talk that included Carl's fatherly cooing over the recent birth of his son Brett (daughter Michelle would be born three years later) and his lambasting of Jimmy Carter for his "inept" handling of the Iranian crisis.

Soon Icahn moved to his primary agenda, to intimidate Lurie, in part by confronting him with figures—such as Saxon's 7 percent return on assets—that reflected the company's poor financial performance. Both sides were testy, playing their cards close to the vest. Questioned by Lurie about his intentions, Carl refused to be more specific than to say that he was after a good return on his investment. According to Icahn's recollection,

Lurie said, "You know, what happened at Tappan could never happen here."

Turning the tables, and at the same time using the opportunity to put the fear of God in Lurie, Icahn asked if the CEO had "ever thought of selling the company in as much as the shareholders might prefer it." Lurie countered that he would be willing to listen to any offer and insisted that the shareholders' interests remained uppermost in his mind. As the conversation began to drift, Icahn and Kingsley tested the waters on various proposals to sell Saxon's assets, such as the company's copier group, which they suggested would be a plum catch for a Japanese manufacturer.

When Kingsley went a step further, suggesting that a paper company might acquire all of Saxon, Lurie raised the specter of antitrust obstacles relating to Saxon's distribution and manufacturing operations. Icahn agreed with this point, but speculated that "foreign money" could be a good bet to buy pieces of the distribution business, which could be sold in segments.

Only after Icahn had successfully engaged Lurie in the discussion of asset sales did he lower the boom, asking for a seat on Saxon's board. The way Carl posed it, this was not just a request, but an expression of his rights as a major shareholder. A Saxon executive participating in the discussions remembered Carl putting it this way: "He said that since he now owns more stock, four to five times than all the current directors, that maybe he should be on the board. He said he had no intention of participating in the management of the company and was not an operations man at all, but it might be useful to all parties if he had a seat on the board."

With this approach Icahn was once again appearing as a passive investor. But were his intentions really that benign? Under questioning by an SEC attorney looking into Icahn's takeover practices in October 1980, Carl indicated that he had hoped to take a more active role.

SEC: Did you consider any alternatives with respect to Saxon, such as merger, acquisition, liquidation?

Icahn: We had no formulation or plan of what we could do

with Saxon. They had a staggered board, after all, and there was very little influence I could—I mean even if I got on the board, I really couldn't make decisions of that type. *But I hoped that being on the board, I might be able to influence certain decisions.*

SEC: What types of decisions did you hope to influence?

Icahn: *Well, basically, the way the business was being run.* (italics added)

Responding to Icahn's bombshell that he wanted a seat on the board, Lurie countered that Saxon's board was fine just as it was, but he agreed to inform the directors of Icahn's request at their next meeting, scheduled for January 1980. During the course of his meeting with Lurie, Icahn never asked for greenmail. But his talk of board seats and asset sales was likely his way of preparing the calf for slaughter.

"Icahn didn't say, 'Either pay me or get out of my way,' " Feldesman recalled. "I think he was too smart to do that. I believe that his technique was to threaten to buy a company with the implication that he could be stopped by buying him out. But at this point, there was no bold-faced threat."

From their first meeting, Lurie tried to intimidate Icahn in return, boasting that Saxon was represented by the legal overlords of mergers and acquisitions, Joe Flom, patriarch of the firm of Skadden, Arps, Slate, Meager & Flom, and the firm generally on the other side of the table from Flom—Wachtell, Lipton.

If that wasn't sufficient to give Icahn pause, Lurie dropped the name of Jerome Kohlberg, a founding partner of Kohlberg, Kravis & Roberts, the firm that would dominate leveraged buyouts in the 1980s. But Icahn was not frightened. Recalling the conversation with Lurie, Icahn said, "Then he told me that Kohlberg . . . is a very good friend of his. . . .

"He is in the newspapers all the time now, and he is on his board and he would put in a great amount of money. He said, 'I can always print up stock and give it to this fellow, Kohlberg. . . . He's very happy to buy my stock, and that, of course, will dilute your position.' "

From all accounts, the picture of Lurie trying to intimidate

Icahn was comical. A short, plumpish man given to conservative black suits and blue ties, Lurie had begun his relationship with Saxon as the company's outside auditor, serving as a CPA with the firm of Westheimer, Fine, Berger & Co. Asked by management to join Saxon in 1968 as senior vice president for operations and administration, he made the transition from public practice to industry, rising to president when former chairman Myron Berman had died in a car crash in 1977. Even as president, Lurie lived modestly, his home a two-bedroom apartment in a respectable but lackluster Manhattan building at 400 E. 56th Street. A chauffeur-driven limousine was his only indulgence.

Considerate, soft-spoken, gentlemanly, Lurie was well liked—and viewed by most everyone who knew him as a pussycat. In dealing with Icahn, he was pitted against an unrelenting foe who looked upon Lurie's benign style as a weakness to be exploited.

"Icahn against Lurie was like a barracuda against a goldfish," said Marvin Olshan. "Carl was real rough. Never one you would call smooth or diplomatic in any sense. And he just didn't like these guys who ran companies. If the CEO showed up with a Lincoln and a driver, Carl would think, 'Why the hell does he need a driver?' And if the guy came back with a Lincoln and no driver, Carl would think, 'Why the hell don't you drive a Volkswagen?'

"Carl was always that way. He had no patience for Lurie, his lawyers or his accountants."

Just what happened after the veiled Kohlberg threat is a matter of debate. According to the company, Icahn presented Saxon's CEO with an ultimatum: Unless the company purchased his group's shares for a handsome profit, he would wage a proxy fight for the four board seats to be voted on at the next annual meeting.

Icahn asserted that he had reason to believe that his investment in Saxon was at risk, and on that basis he asked Lurie to buy him out without a word of a threat.

He recalled talking to a former Saxon employee who "told me that he felt there were certain things that weren't completely above board that went on there; that there were certain sweet-heart deals and that certain of the values might not really be what they are purported to be. That got me a little nervous . . . .

"I talked to some people that knew more about business machines involved with Saxon, and I got the feeling they were having a lot more troubles than it appeared in that area. . . . At any rate, after thinking about all this . . . it started to have the effect on me that you know maybe I'd be better off getting done with the situation rather than going ahead and really trying to get involved."

Icahn then told Lurie that he had heard, through a New York investment banker, that Saxon wanted to buy him out. When Lurie confirmed this, Icahn teased the CEO, saying he would rather acquire his shares than give him a seat on the board.

"He said, 'No, no. I like you and I think you're a very bright guy,' " Icahn recalled. "He shook my hand when telling me this— 'Whether I buy you out or not, I want you on the board anyway.' . . . and I said, 'Well, Stan, I'd like to be on it anyway, because I like you.' But I said to myself . . . this is a lot of bull, but okay.

"I remember his words that day, because I thought this old guy is still trying to be an actor. You know, maybe that's how he got to be at the top of the company."

Lurie could tell Icahn he loved him and that he wanted to name a building after him, but all Carl heard was that Saxon wanted to buy his stock. Whether the offer was in response to Icahn's threat to move against the company or was management's way of preempting an attack, Icahn didn't care. All that mattered was that he was soon seated at the negotiating table working out the details of a greenmail settlement that was all but certain to make him a wealthier man. That this would come at the expense of the shareholders, whose interests he declared were dear to his heart, revealed the hypocrisy that would weaken Icahn's soap-box oratory on corporate democracy.

As Icahn remembered the greenmail episode, Lurie opened the bidding with a low-ball offer: "What do you want?"

Icahn said, "No, no, you make me an offer."

"Well, maybe I could pay you 8½, 9, something like that."

"No, that's way too low."

"What do you want?"

"Oh, around 11."

"Well, I think that's doable . . . but I have to talk to my board. This is not for disclosure, because this is not a deal and we're just negotiating."

Soon the discussions stalled with Carl waiting for a formal offer that was not forthcoming. According to Icahn, he then contacted Lurie, saying, "Stan, you have to tell me one way or another because I have bought a block of stock. In my opinion, you've got me stymied here."

Although Saxon claims Icahn threatened a proxy fight, Icahn counters that Lurie first raised the issue of a proxy battle in an effort to flex his corporate muscles. Icahn recalls the confrontation—which sounds like a couple of adolescents challenging each other at the schoolyard—this way:

Lurie said, "You know, you'd never win in a proxy fight anyway."

"Stan, who is talking about a proxy fight? But I would beat you in a proxy fight; there's no question I would."

"No, you wouldn't."

At this point Icahn said Lurie reminded him that he had the Doberman pinschers Flom and Wachtell, Lipton on his side. Then the schoolyard bravado began anew.

Icahn countered, "Stan, you can go through all that you want, but you're not going to be able to beat me in a proxy fight. But who is talking about a proxy fight anyway? I mean, you told me you wanted to put me on the board anyway, so what's the whole deal?"

"Oh, no, no, we're just talking generally. I want you to know that I'm not afraid of you."

"Well, Stan, I'm going to buy more stock unless you tell me one way or another. Are we putting this to bed or not?"

This favored Icahn threat ("I'm going to buy more stock. . . .") was enough to make Lurie cave in. According to Icahn, Lurie replied:

"Look, of course we're doing it, but I can't announce it because I haven't talked to this guy and I haven't talked to that guy. But wait one week, and Feldesman [Saxon's attorney] is coming back and we're going to have a meeting with you and I and Feldesman. . . ."

In January 1980, Icahn—pushing Lurie to make a decision on the possible buy-out of his Saxon shares—arranged a dinner at New York's Boardroom restaurant. Also attending were Saxon's attorneys from Baskin and Sears, Jerome Tarnoff, Robert Millstone, and Feldesman and their counterparts Marvin Olshan and Morris Owens from Icahn's firm of Olshan, Grundman & Frome.

The mood was icy. Icahn, who had come expecting to nail down a price, was shocked to find Saxon's lawyers appearing to play the role of deal busters. According to Carl, Feldesman took the lead, saying first that Saxon wasn't interested in buying his stock and then taking issue with the $11 per share price Carl was asking for. The more the lawyer talked, the angrier Icahn became.

"I tried to be cordial and I was always trying to be very nice with Lurie, and I always tried to sort of hold back when he puffed a little bit, but I wasn't about to take this guy coming on the way he was. I said to myself, 'I don't have to listen to this; I don't need them to buy my stock.'

"I said, 'Look, Mr. Feldesman'—and I got very irate with him—'I don't want to listen to this . . . bull that you're giving out. . . . I'm not interested. Let's just forget the whole deal."

The ill will between Icahn and Feldesman extended to Icahn's lawyer Marvin Olshan. Asked to recall the events of a meeting with Feldesman, Olshan said, "I purposely and intentionally daydream when people bore me, and he was boring me."

The obvious friction between Icahn and Saxon's lawyers was to be expected when a takeover artist makes a play for a client company. But in this case the specter of Saxon paying greenmail threw fuel on the fire. Specifically, a disagreement flared over the propriety of a public company paying a premium to buy out a shareholder.

Lurie raised the issue in a meeting with Icahn on January 16. In response, Carl had sent a newspaper clip detailing a similar purchase by the Morrison Knudsen Company of nearly 300,000 shares from the Crane Co. Although Icahn intended for the clip to demonstrate a precedent for such a purchase, Feldesman raised the red flag that the Morrison Knudsen matter was in litigation, thus underlining the dangers of such a buy-out.

But Icahn's lawyers countered that it would be relatively easy to justify the buy-out under Delaware law.

After listening impatiently as the lawyers muddied the waters with case precedents and related legal gibberish, Icahn decided to take the matter into his own hands. If the chatter didn't stop, he threatened, he would force the issue by buying more of Saxon's stock.

"I said to myself, The hell with it . . . if they don't put me on the board, I'm going to have a proxy fight with them, and the hell with selling the stock . . ." Icahn recalled. "I'm going to go out and buy more stock and finish it off. That's how I felt."

The attempt to intimidate and confuse Icahn with a legal offensive had clearly backfired. With both sides poised at the brink, eyeball to eyeball, someone had to blink. Finally Saxon agreed to ask their Delaware lawyers to bless the proposed buy-out.

What makes this extraordinary is that at this point in his career, Icahn would have been hard pressed to take over Saxon. With limited capital and a band of edgy investors supporting him for the promise of rapid gains, he could only hope that his tough-guy act would keep the confrontation from reaching a showdown.

There was eleventh-hour negotiating to be done, once again over the price of the shares, and again Icahn proved intractable. Invited to Feldesman's office for a last-minute meeting, Icahn and Olshan arrived at the session expecting to close the deal, only to find that Saxon was not yet ready to sign. Sensing a stall tactic concocted by Saxon's lawyers, Carl blew up, spewing forth a masterful mix of threats that made clear he was not about to water down his demands.

Icahn recalled the events this way: "Feldesman started all over again with this whole bit, 'This deal can't be done for this price.'

"I said, 'Well, then, forget it . . . forget the whole thing.' He

said, 'Well, you know, we can do a deal and I think we could pay
you 9½.'

"I looked at him and I said, 'You know, Mr. Feldesman, I'm
not going to tell you that I'm the President of the United States,
and I'm not going to tell you that I can't take off a few minutes
to come up here, but I really don't like you and I don't understand why you called me up from my office on Wall Street, where
I have things to do, to insult me with 9½, when I've told you all
along—I mean, do you like me enough just to want to see me
again? I mean, isn't this an insult? You know I'm not going to
take 9½.' "

Sensing what he was up against, Feldesman asked Olshan to
join him outside the office to discuss the matter briefly. Shortly
thereafter, the lawyers returned and Olshan asked Icahn to step
outside, where he told Carl that Saxon was offering $10 a share
and that he could take the time to think it over. But from Icahn's
perspective, accepting a break in the negotiations would make
him appear weak.

As he recalled, "I walked back in the office about twenty
seconds later. I remember Feldesman said, 'You didn't take very
much time to think.' I said, 'There's nothing to think about.
. . . You're not going to intimidate me, Mr. Feldesman. I don't
like you. I don't like your kind of lawyer. . . . Let's just forget
this deal.' "

"You know," Feldesman said, "you're a very obstinate
young man; very obstinate."

"I'm not asking for a psychological picture of myself."

"Well, you can bend just a little just to help us, can't you?"

"Yes, I can bend a little. I'll tell you what I'll do; I'll bend
a little—10¾. That's my final offer. Yes or no?"

"We have so many legal problems."

"Forget it, that's it," Icahn snapped.

Just as he was set to leave, Lurie took control of the negotiations, suggesting that Icahn join him for lunch the next day, this
time without lawyers. As Icahn recalls it, Lurie opened the
dialogue:

"You don't want to fight me."

"I don't want to fight you."

"You said you'd take 10¾. I'm having a lot of trouble. . . . If you said you'd take 10¾, you can live with 10½."

For Icahn, 10½ was close enough to ice the deal. On February 7, Saxon issued a press release announcing its board had authorized an agreement in principle to acquire Icahn's holdings of 766,700 shares for $10.50 per share. This gave Carl and his investors a profit of about $2 million on a transaction consummated in less than ninety days.

At the time, no one besides Lurie and a handful of his associates knew that from the beginning, Lurie had a secret motive for keeping Icahn from seizing Saxon: Lurie was cooking the books, reporting phantom earnings that existed on paper only. Were Icahn to gain control and bring his auditors in, Lurie knew that his scam would be detected. His choice was to pay greenmail or to blow his cover.

"Of course, I had no idea that Saxon was awash in fraud when we were buying the stock," Kingsley says. "When you read the reports of a NYSE-listed company, you don't expect that pervasive fraud lies behind the numbers.

"But after leaving the first meeting with Saxon, I was rushing to catch an F train when Carl asked me, 'What do you think?' I said, 'That guy's going to buy you out.' When Carl asked me why I felt that way, I said, 'I don't know, but all I can tell you is that he's going to buy you out.'"

In playing hardball, Feldesman, who was on the Saxon board but was not aware of the book cooking, was following Lurie's orders to keep down the cost of a greenmail settlement. Knowing better than anyone else that the company could not afford a rich ransom, Lurie was hoping to get out of the Icahn mess with minimal damage.

"At the meetings between Carl and Lurie—where Icahn was trying to get more for his stock than Lurie wanted to give—Carl kept saying the company was worth a lot of money and Lurie kept saying it wasn't," Olshan said. "It's incredibly funny when you think about it now. Carl thought Lurie was just negotiating, but the fact is he was telling the truth. He knew the damn company wasn't worth what the numbers said it was worth."

Behind the scenes, Lurie had been working to restructure Saxon's financing, with the idea of covering his tracks. Because financing sources would freeze at any hint of takeover, Icahn's threatening actions would do irreparable damage to Lurie's plan. Although Icahn claims he was seeing warning flares all around Saxon, indicating that something was foul, he had no hint of the extent of the book cooking, of the refinancing plans or of the impact a takeover move would have had on Lurie.

"A threatened takeover or adversarial action of any kind could have jeopardized Lurie's plans," Feldesman said. "I imagine Lurie was very anxious about that. I would say that was added pressure on Lurie to be more responsive to Icahn than he might have been otherwise."

Saving himself from Icahn was not enough to save Lurie from the law. In June 1982, Saxon filed for bankruptcy; three months later Lurie would be removed as chairman. Ultimately, he would plead guilty to a host of crimes including mail and securities fraud and would be sentenced in Manhattan's U.S. District Court to a five-year prison term.

As it turned out, had Icahn taken over Saxon, as he had with Baird & Warner, he would have walked into a booby trap, overpaying for a company he was certain was sitting on a rich lode of hidden value.

"When I heard what was really going on at Saxon, I had only one response," Kingsley said. "Whew!"

At the time of Saxon's bankruptcy, the company's creditors collected one-third of the $300 million owed to them. And shareholders who had purchased the company's stock for as high as $40 walked away with slightly more than $1 a share.

"Just think about it—if Carl had gone through with the Saxon deal, he would have been finished right then and there," said a former Icahn adviser familiar with the transaction. "Don't forget, he wasn't *the* Carl Icahn yet. He was just another guy with an idea for making money. Into only his third raid, he was on the verge of making a tremendous blunder. Had he done that, he would have looked like the world's biggest schmuck."

Once again the investors riding Icahn's coattails found they had made more money, and made it faster, than they had ever dreamed possible. From Icahn's perspective, the Saxon deal was further confirmation that he could force poorly performing companies to enhance shareholder values. In this case, however, the only shareholders benefitting were Icahn and his clique of investors. Apparently, the self-proclaimed guardian of shareholder rights felt no compunction about enriching himself at the expense of his fellow stockholders. In spite of his proclamations heralding the glories of corporate democracy, in practice Icahn's real world persona was that of a shrewd arbitrageur who had found a weak link in the corporate system and was determined to exploit it for personal gain.

Icahn has sought to justify his greenmail profits by insisting that the CEOs he has confronted come away from the bruising and in some cases humiliating battles determined to improve their companies' performance in order to keep other raiders from launching successful attacks. When pressed, however, Icahn admits what is abundantly clear to the rest of the world: He would have mounted his raids and taken his profits whether he left his prey on the verge of turnaround or the verge of destruction. For Icahn, personal gain has always been the key motivating factor, outrage or no outrage.

A class-action suit filed on behalf of Saxon shareholders against the Icahn group charged: "Upon the sudden announcement by Saxon that it had purchased defendants' stock, the market price of Saxon's stock rapidly deteriorated. The public had purchased approximately 2,600,000 shares during the defendants' manipulation at inflated prices. Thus the public (which is the class in this action) suffered losses from said unlawful inflation in amounts ranging from about $1 per share to about $4 per share. The total loss of the class from defendants' unlawful activities is estimated to be of the order of $8,000,000."

The suit goes to the heart of the case against greenmail, citing the inequity of corporate management cutting an exclusive deal with a greenmailer. When this happens, the greenmailer walking away with the profits appears to be the sole villain. But is that fair? Although he has clearly demonstrated a willingness to profit at the expense of his fellow shareholders, the greenmailer could not write his own check on the company's funds. Only management has that authority, and in its rush to do so, the powers that be are also guilty of an outrageous act.

In paying Icahn to go away, Saxon appeared to legitimize his charge that corporate management is often insulated, self-centered, more concerned with retaining its power than protecting the interests of the shareholders. In an opinion intended to justify the company's purchase of Icahn's shares, Saxon's Delaware law firm—Richards, Layton & Finger—seemed to underline the fact that a gadfly need only make waves and management can use the power of the checkbook to be free of him.

"It is established Delaware law," the opinion noted, "that a corporation may purchase its own shares from a dissident minority shareholder or group of shareholders, in order to end dissidence, dissent, and disputation, and that the corporation may use its own funds and may pay a reasonable premium to accomplish this legitimate corporate objective."

But why not allow a dissident to have a seat on a corporate board? If management were truly interested in maximizing shareholder value, one would think that a man of Icahn's talents and temperament would be invited to serve as a director. That the idea was noxious—to the extent that the company would prefer to pay greenmail rather than tolerate dissent—gives credence to Icahn's charge that America's corporate suites are packed with an old-boy network whose primary purpose is to protect the members' mediocrity.

"In many big corporations, the person who makes waves, who gives criticism, who does things to rock the boat—hell, he's persona non grata," Icahn said. "The guys above him who are worrying about their jets and their other perks see to it that he's kept down in the ranks. That he doesn't make trouble.

"In most cases, boards don't rock the boat either. They just come to get their paychecks. They don't rock the boat because they are members of each other's boards, and each other's compensation committees. Everyone is watching out for everyone else.

"You have to understand how the system is structured. The guy who gets to the top of the big corporations is, with notable exceptions, a political animal. He's a survivor. He knows how to watch his back. That means hiring a number two guy that's not as smart as him. That works for the CEO because he's never threatened by his second in command.

"But think what that does to our corporate establishment. If the number two guy is always a little worse than the number one guy, sooner or later you're going to have a country run by a bunch of morons. In American business we have a reverse Darwinism that provides for the survival of the unfittest."

"FEAR OF GOD" GAMBIT MEETS THE "STIFF-ARM DEFENSE"

"I'm like a gunfighter you hire to save the town. That gunfighter is there to do good. He knows he's on the right side, and he's proud of it, but he'll only do what he does if he knows he'll get paid for it."

—CARL ICAHN

With the Tappan, Baird & Warner and Saxon deals under his belt, Icahn's strategy of identifying undervalued companies, acquiring big stock positions and then employing a series of tactics to enrich himself by playing off the gap between book and market values, was proving to be formidable—if not foolproof. Regardless of what corporate America threw at Icahn, he would throw it back, often with deadly accuracy. As his adversaries were quickly learning, he could not be frightened, worn out or distracted. Once he homed in on a target, he proved relentless.

In the course of researching the move on Saxon, Icahn

became intrigued by the paper industry, specifically the fact that major assets including plant, timberland, and huge inventories of product were often carried on the books well below market value.

The opportunity to profit from these undervalued assets turned Icahn's attention to Erie, Pennsylvania–based Hammermill, a $1 billion a year paper giant run by CEO Albert Duval. It all started when Al Kingsley, who spent the great bulk of his time sifting through corporate data, spotted a Value Line report touting Hammermill's stock as a buying opportunity, in part because of its appeal as a takeover candidate.

"A lot of timber and paper companies had already been acquired by others, and it seemed this naturally might be the type of company that someone else might want to buy. . . . " Kingsley recalled. "Cash flow was very high, the earnings were in an uptrend, the industry was good and so it seemed like a very good one."

Based on Kingsley's recommendation, Icahn began to accumulate Hammermill stock.

Referring specifically to Hammermill, Kingsley said:

"I might present ten companies to Carl. . . . I might buy some myself, but if I think it's going to be a big one, one that really has a lot of potential. . . . I will discuss it with Carl generally before we do anything, and this was one of them. He thought it looked good on the few papers I had given to him, and I don't remember if we did it right away or waited a little while and bought 4,000 or 5,000 shares. Then we kept getting deeper and deeper into it. . . . Exactly why we kept buying it I can't answer the question because there were many other companies we were looking at at the time that also looked good."

By the time the Icahn group filed a 13-d in February 1980, they held nearly 10 percent of Hammermill's stock. The shares were owned by Icahn & Co. and a series of investment entities including C.C.I. (Carl C. Icahn), Brett Investment Corp., Liba Partners and Bayswater Realty and Investment Trust.

At this stage of his career, Icahn was operating with lofty ambitions but limited assets. Lacking sufficient capital to fund all of his proposed transactions with personal resources, he had assembled a group of limited partners who funnelled money into C.C.I., backing the increasingly successful takeover bully and profiting along with him.

The C.C.I. partnership agreement spelled out the Icahn manifesto in language his investors could relate to. The partnership would be "taking large positions in 'undervalued' stocks and then attempting to control the destinies of the companies in question by: (a) trying to convince management to liquidate or sell the company to a 'white knight'; (b) waging a proxy contest, or; (c) making a tender offer and/or (d) selling back our position to the company."

In a "Summarization of Important Points Concerning the C.C.I. Partnership Agreement," it was noted that the partnership would concentrate its investments and possibly use these investments to "gain control." The document went on to illustrate the impact of takeover attempts by various raiders on share values:

STOCK PRICES DURING UNFRIENDLY MANEUVERS

TARGET COMPANY	3 MONTHS PRIOR TO ATTEMPT AT TARGET	HIGH AFTER ATTEMPT
Warner Swasey	29	80
National Airlines	15	50
Wylain	13	28½
Flintkote	30	55
Fairchild Camera	29	66
Tappan	8	18

As Icahn structured C.C.I., which served in effect as a war chest for his takeover campaigns, units in the limited partnership were sold at $100,000 each. Initial investors—some of whom purchased multiple units—included a clique of friends and business associates. Among them were Samuel Sax (chairman of Chicago's United of America Bank and treasurer of Bayswater); attorney Allen Barry Witz, a Bayswater director; and Stanley Nortman (president of a Great Neck, New York, metals brokerage firm, Nortman Metals).

Icahn's charter investors, all experienced businessmen, recognized that their point man's strategy for intimidating corporate management and for playing the spread between asset and market values, offered enormous opportunity for rapid gains. With a short but impressive track record already established, Carl was emerging as a phenomenon. That he was incurring the wrath of corporate management was a positive sign—the best evidence that he was breaking the rules of corporate etiquette and profiting from it. This was an image that suited Icahn's predator personality, his competitive temperament, and his lingering sense of outrage at the corporate establishment. He wore the bully label as a badge of pride.

In a letter handwritten to a prospective C.C.I. investor at the time of the Hammermill assault, Icahn boasted, "I also enclose an article in *Barrons* where they call me a monkey. I hope we get many bananas on this one."

The C.C.I. summarization letter held out Carl's completed deals as teasers for what was yet to come:

- In December 1979, the Tappan Company was sold for $18 per share. Since the stock was purchased at 8½ on 50 percent margin, Icahn's return on capital was approximately 250 percent.
- More recently, after acquiring almost 10 percent of the outstanding shares of Saxon Industries at an average price of 7⅛, Icahn accepted Saxon's offer to buy back the shares at 10½. Since the stock was purchased over a six-month period on margin, this represents a return on investment of approximately 200 percent.

The letter also noted that an $80,000 investment in Icahn & Company at the time of the firm's founding in 1968 had grown in value to $7 million.

Although Icahn preferred to function without assistance from anyone, enlisting limited partners gave him the financial wherewithal to take big stock positions, which increased his credibility with his fellow shareholders and, in turn, maximized his leverage with corporate management. Considering that Icahn's positions were purchased on margin, which allowed him to buy shares with only 50 percent cash down, every $100,000 raised for C.C.I. translated into a $200,000 block of stock. What's more, the way the limited partnership was structured, general partner Icahn & Company was entitled to 20 percent of C.C.I.'s realized profits. So the more stock Carl bought with his partners' money, the greater his potential for profit.

In an effort to widen his search for capital, Icahn enlisted Uncle Elliot to beat the bushes for new prospects. "As Carl was preparing for Hammermill, he came to Palm Beach to visit me," Schnall remembered. "He had prepared a prospectus on the deal and asked me to take it to wealthy friends with the idea of selling them limited partner stakes with a minimum investment of $250,000. He said, 'Come on, you know all these rich guys. Take this prospectus around to them, show them what I've done to date and if you sell them, you get a piece of the action.'

"Well, I didn't like the idea of going around hawking deals, but I tried it with three or four wealthy guys I knew in Palm Beach. They all said it looked interesting but that turned out to be a diplomatic way of saying 'no' because they all declined to participate.

"When I told Carl I wasn't going to demean myself by continuing to look for investors, he said, 'Fine, go back to your parties with your old broads.' "

In the text of its 13-d Hammermill filing, the Icahn group declared that it was considering whether to solicit proxies to nominate a slate of directors and was also considering "whether a sale of certain or substantially all of the Issuer's [Hammermill] assets, a merger of the Issuer with a third party or a purchase by a third party of the shares of the Issuer might represent the best course of action for the benefit of the Issuer's stockholders (including Bayswater), and in this regard it reserves the right to recommend such actions or other courses of action to management and to the stockholders of the Issuer."

This "fear of God gambit"—almost identical to Icahn's

moves to shake up his earlier victims—played differently at
Hammermill, where CEO Duval was determined to keep the
paper company independent regardless of Icahn's threats. This
stiff-arm defense took shape with the filing of the 13-d. Notified
of the filing during a visit to New York for the annual meeting
of the American Paper Institute, Duval issued a terse statement
denying any previous knowledge of Icahn or of his intentions
regarding Hammermill. If he feared an Icahn attack, he wasn't
about to let the takeover bully—or the wider financial community—know about it.

Interestingly, Saxon Paper's CEO Stan Lurie contacted
Duval soon after the report on Icahn's Hammermill stake became public, offering to share some of his war stories with Carl's
latest target. When Duval took him up on the offer, the portrait
Lurie painted of Icahn was that of a quick-buck artist who would
seek to force Hammermill into making the Hobson's choice of
facing a disruptive proxy contest or agreeing to buy Icahn out for
a short-term profit.

"I called Mr. Lurie," Duval recalled. "I found him very
anxious to talk to me. . . . He described a mode of operation that
seemed to fit with what we had read . . . and he gave me specific
details of his relationships with Mr. Icahn, of the piracy involved
there and the short-term gains desired there and the pressure
brought upon him—as he referred to it—blackmail."

If Duval had not decided to stand tough against Icahn at the
beginning, his conversation with Lurie may have been a turning
point.

"Mr. Lurie indicated that Mr. Icahn had been very difficult
to deal with, was a very unreasonable person and was out to
wreck Saxon if he couldn't get his way. Saxon at that time was
involved in a major refinancing effort, and they were ready to
sign the documents. Mr. Icahn somehow or other found this out,
brought pressure to bear on Mr. Lurie. Mr. Lurie told me he gave
in to that pressure, and it was the damnedest thing he'd ever
done in his whole life."

At a meeting with Duval on March 28, 1980, held at a
Hammermill sales office in New York's Pan Am Building, Icahn
asked directly for two seats on the Hammermill board. The CEO,

who by this time had been filled in on Icahn by Hammermill's investment bankers at Morgan Stanley (a WASPy firm that would back corporate management in the emerging M&A wars), was testy and contentious, asking repeatedly why Carl wanted the seats. Irritated by this interrogation, Icahn made it clear that he wanted to act as a catalyst in arranging for an acquisition of Hammermill.

To support his right to do so, Icahn reminded Duval that corporate management has a duty to maximize shareholder return. Naturally, the CEO agreed, but he took the opportunity to remind Icahn that management's duties extend beyond the shareholders to the employees and to the company itself.

But Icahn, who viewed this response as predictable management PR talk, reiterated that he wanted seats on the board and that he would use this position to encourage prospective suitors to step forward and acquire Hammermill.

In typical fashion, he began to turn the screws, intimating that he already had prospective buyers lined up as allies in the coming invasion.

From Duval's perspective, Icahn's request for representation amounted to an ultimatum.

"I did say to him, 'If I understand you correctly, Mr. Icahn, you've said that you want two seats on our board, and if you don't get them, there's going to be a proxy fight.' And he said, 'Oh, no, I don't like to put it that way. That sounds like I came here to threaten you.' Well, I said, 'How would you put it, Mr. Icahn?' 'Well,' he said, 'I guess that's just about it.' "

But Duval was determined to resist the pressure Icahn was applying. Saxon's failure to do so provided the inspiration.

"The board had determined that unlike the Saxon Company, Hammermill would not be blackmailed," Duval declared. "Therefore we felt . . . that a person who operated that way and who had declared to me personally and publicly, and the press, that he was a short-term investor only, and the quicker the better, would not be doing something constructive for those of us who depend on Hammermill, whether they buy from us, sell to us, work for us, own our stock."

"Duval was a tough guy," Olshan recalled. "He was a

fighter and he was up for a fight with Carl. Other CEOs trembled when Icahn came walking in. They feared losing their jobs. But not Duval."

Emboldened by the CEO's bulldog approach, Hammermill set out to block Icahn's admission to the board. With great urgency, Duval began calling the Hammermill directors to schedule a special board meeting for March 31. At this emergency session, held in a hotel at the Pittsburgh Airport, a "stop-Icahn strategy" was put in place. A key component of the plan called for reducing the number of directors by two, thus thwarting Carl's plot to win the seats of four directors up for election at the May 13, 1980, annual meeting. With two of the seats eliminated through a change in Hammermill's bylaws, Duval and prominent director Henry Curtis would be the only names up for re-election, greatly diminishing Icahn's chances. Still, Carl proceeded with the proxy contest, taking his case directly to the shareholders. Once again he drew a sharp contrast between the interests of management and investors.

Referring to his plan to find a third-party buyer for Hammermill, and management's assertion that it was in the best position to determine when and if an acquisition should be arranged, Icahn made this telling point in a letter to the shareholders:

"My associates and I have over $20 million invested in Hammermill stock. The President of Hammermill, on the other hand, owns stock valued at less than $170,000 and earned nearly $320,000 from Hammermill last year. *When he tells you that the time is not right to sell Hammermill, I question whose interests he represents.*"

Turning to the critical matter of shareholder value, Icahn castigated management for the company's anemic stock price and for an ambitious capital-spending spree that would likely sustain downward pressure on the shares.

"*Hammermill is entering, not completing, a period of heavy capital expenditures.* Management is planning expenditures of $240,000,000 over the next 2½–3 years. *I believe a capital-rich acquirer should be sought before these expenditures begin.* Should the deep economic recession that is widely predicted have an adverse effect on stock market prices, Hammermill stock may not rise to its book value per share unless the company is sold to a capital-rich acquirer. Might I remind you that *Hammermill stock has not traded even as high as $30 per share during the last decade!*"

As Icahn was well aware, even if he won a seat on Hammermill's board, his ultimate goal of arranging a buy-out would be hampered by a 1977 amendment to Hammermill's bylaws giving directors enormous power to veto such deals. To remove this obstacle, Icahn's proxy contest included a motion to repeal this amendment. A letter to the shareholders (titled "By-Law Changes Are Needed Now") noted that:

"In 1977—the Board of Directors proposed an amendment (which passed) to the Articles of Incorporation known as an '85 percent super-majority rule.' This amendment requires an 85 percent vote of all outstanding shares to approve any merger with another company which already holds 20 percent of Hammermill, unless approved by a majority of the directors who were directors prior to the other company becoming a 20 percent shareholder. *This rule has the effect of reducing the possibility of any tender offer which is not approved in advance by Hammermill's Board of Directors.*"

For its part, management tried to impugn Icahn's character by dredging up the details of his early run-ins with Wall Street regulatory agencies. A letter to the shareholders warned:

"You should be aware of the fact that Mr. Icahn and the companies with which he is associated have been the subject of several proceedings resulting in the imposition of censure and fines as a consequence of claimed infractions of statutes and regulations governing the securities industry."

The fact that Icahn's "censure and fines" had resulted in little more than slaps on the wrist was conveniently omitted. In fighting for survival, the "high-minded" captains of industry were willing to be as ruthless as the man whose ruthlessness they openly despised.

In another letter to the shareholders, management sounded this alarm: "Icahn Co. has in effect borrowed more than $4 million from banks for its working capital, and a substantial part of this has been used to purchase Hammermill stock. Other members of the Icahn group borrowed from Icahn & Co. to buy their Hammermill shares.

"The high costs of borrowed money give the Icahn group a strong incentive, in our judgment, to make a quick sale of their Hammermill shares. Under these circumstances, *your board believes Icahn would attempt to sell Hammermill at any price, even if it was significantly less than the fair value of Hammermill, so long as he and his group would profit.*"

In a cleverly designed counterattack, Icahn took this "quick profit" charge and turned it against management, revealing that a number of senior officers and directors, including Duval, had been quick to exercise their own stock options in the three-year period preceding the proxy battle. According to Icahn, the shares were sold for prices ranging from $14.56 to $17.81.

A "Memo from Carl C. Icahn to Hammermill Shareholders" (dated May 2, 1980) presented a full chart of officer/director transactions in Hammermill stock and concluded with this counter blow: "Management has stated that I am 'strongly motivated to promote a quick sale of Hammermill without regard to whether a fair price could be obtained.' I believe Hammermill is worth a great deal more than the prices at which management has sold. I am not advocating a sale of our Company at any price but only at a price in excess of book value (which was $36.84 at December 30, 1979)."

In the thick of the increasingly bitter proxy battle, lawsuits were filed by both sides. Hammermill's charges stemmed from the allegation that Icahn's 13-d filing failed to disclose his true plans and purposes as a Hammermill stockholder. In litigation filed in the U.S. District Court for the Western District of Pennsylvania, Hammermill charged that rather than buying the stock as an investment, Icahn was engaged in a "sophisticated scheme of corporate piracy . . . using borrowed money and funds which he has solicited for his get-rich-quick scheme. . . . Parroting a strategy he has employed on at least four other occasions, Icahn has given Hammermill the choice to pay the ransom he demands and buy back his shares at a substantial premium or to endure a divisive proxy fight which would materially jeopardize the long-term interests of Hammermill and the community of shareholders, employees, and customers which it serves. . . . Icahn and his cohorts have ignored and flouted the requirements of the federal securities laws which tolerate nothing less than full, fair and complete disclosure of all the material facts concerning those who acquire a five percent interest in public companies."

Icahn, in turn, countersued, seeking to remove the obstacles, such as reducing the number of directors, put in place to limit his influence on the company.

Taken together, the litigation launched by both sides represented in microcosm the greater battle between the pillars of the corporate establishment and the takeover bullies who would come to prominence in the 1980s. In the process, Icahn and his lot were forcing the American capitalist system to grapple with a critical question: Were management and boards of directors running America's giant corporations for their own self-interests or for the interests of the shareholders?

Whether or not Hammermill was correct when it charged that Icahn was out for greenmail, once this became an issue, the raider pledged to the shareholders that if he were elected as a director, he would not "accept any offer for the Hammermill stock owned by my firm, C.C.I. & Associates and Liba Partners unless all Hammermill shareholders are afforded the same opportunity to sell their Hammermill stock."

What's more, although Hammermill's management correctly labeled Icahn's strategy a "get-rich-quick scheme," Carl's pledge to the shareholders assured that if he arranged for an acquisition above the company's book value, they would all get richer along with him.

In responding to his efforts, management was proving to be the insulated, imperious lot Icahn pictured them to be. Every request Icahn made to shift decision-making power from the small clique of senior managers and directors to the shareholders was stonewalled. A call to appoint an independent committee of directors to review potential acquisitions was fought tooth and nail—as was the call to hire an investment-banking firm to seek merger candidates.

Management also tried to discredit Icahn by pointing to his previous moves on the likes of the Tappan Company. But what dire consequences could Hammermill's shareholders project from the Tappan episode? Icahn had successfully engineered an acquisition that substantially increased the company's stock price over the period he owned Tappan's shares. Would that be punishment for Hammermill's shareholders? Obviously, Dick Tappan, who had joined Icahn in the Hammermill investment, didn't think so.

Surely, the real threat from the Icahn bid was to a management that wanted desperately to stay in power.

As the date for the annual meeting approached, both sides knew the proxy voting would be close. At the first count, Icahn, who had spent more than $1 million on the contest, appeared to have eked out a narrow victory in securing one of the two board seats being contested (which required support of one-third of the voting shares) but had lost his bid (requiring 51 percent of the vote) to remove the obstacles to an acquisition.

However, Icahn's victory celebration was cut short when a final tabulation of the voting revealed a major impropriety in the Icahn proxies. It seemed that the Icahn faction had submitted proxies for a block of 70,000 Hammermill shares that were borrowed at the eleventh hour from Citibank and were not eligible to be voted. With this discovery, management's victory was complete, having turned back the Icahn assault on all fronts.

Icahn appeared to be the big loser. But in his inimitable way, King Carl managed to transform a defeat into a modest victory for his investment group. At the time the vote turned against him, Icahn countered a gloating management by declaring in his trademark don't-count-me-out-attitude: "We may have lost the battle, but I don't feel we lost the war, as yet."

Icahn continued applying pressure by using the most effective weapon still at his disposal: the ability to buy additional shares of Hammermill and thus to fortify his position for a proxy fight down the road. All the while, Duval knew that Icahn was free to build his equity stake, to create further dissension among the shareholders and to keep the pistol of an unwanted takeover at management's head. At this stage in his career, Icahn's capital base was inadequate to attempt a takeover in its own right— much of his tough talk was pure poker-faced bluff—but he could search for a deep-pocketed acquirer with the resources to buy Hammermill.

To get the Icahn episode behind it, Hammermill arrived at an agreement with its nemesis, whereby both sides dropped the litigation against each other, Icahn agreed to give Hammermill the right of first refusal on the purchase of his shares for a two-year period, and Hammermill agreed to pay Carl $750,000, thus enabling him to recover a substantial chunk of his proxy expenses. Ultimately, Hammermill stepped up to the plate, purchasing Icahn's 782,100 shares for $36 a share.

C.C.I. investors earned a net profit of $1.8 million on an original investment of $7.38 million. After the 20 percent general partner's fee to Icahn and a reserve for legal fees, the limited partners received $134,816.63 on each $100,000 investment unit. This was a modest return but one that proved Icahn truly could snatch victory from the jaws of defeat. It also protected an asset Icahn valued above all else: his credibility.

At this stage in his odyssey to control corporate destinies, Icahn was launching his attacks knowing that he would have to rely on his ability to frighten corporate management into a rapid settlement. Were they to call his bluff, forcing him to consummate a takeover, he would likely fall short. A big risk to take, but Icahn was betting that his targets—unaware of his true financial power—would never take the even greater risk of testing him to the limit.

Had Icahn folded his tent after the initial Hammermill loss, the manual on how to counter the lone wolf of Wall Street would have circulated through the nation's boardrooms in a matter of days. Take Carl to the mat, it would have read, resist his attacks on all fronts, and he will collapse. With that, his credibility as a heartless, calculating, unstoppable terror would have vanished. Determined to prevent that, Icahn had hung in with Hammermill, keeping his position throughout the standstill period, knowing that a victory in the end would be the only part of the Hammermill transaction the corporate community would remember.

But for Icahn and Kingsley personally, Hammermill had taught a lesson they would never forget.

"Hammermill was a tough one because we couldn't finish it," Kingsley said. "We couldn't raise the money to finish it off. During the course of the standstill, we were trying to raise the money but it wasn't there. We lost our clout because we didn't have the money to go all the way."

In the chess game they were playing, Icahn and Kingsley knew that the ability to go "all the way" was critical.

GETTING

RICH IN THE

EIGHTIES

Like "Taking Candy from a Baby"

"When it comes to making money, he doesn't care how his goals are achieved. . . . He wanted to make our relationship friendlier, but I wouldn't have it. I considered him a mortal enemy."
—DAVE JOHNSTON,
former chairman of Dan River, Inc., on Carl Icahn

Icahn intensified his pursuit of wealth in the early 1980s, a hurly-burly period in American finance. With the emerging pack of takeover titans proving that fast fortunes could be earned by acquiring, dismantling, dismembering, restructuring, or simply threatening the biggest (and in most cases the most defensive and lethargic) corporations, the sharpest minds in the nation's premier banks, brokerage houses and law firms tilted toward this twentieth-century gold rush.

In the past, the best and brightest in America had built their wealth and their reputations by creating powerful, innovative companies that became world leaders in commerce and industry.

But because intense foreign competition and corporate ineffici-
encies were taking a heavy toll on the traditional means of creating wealth, financial engineering emerged as an appealing
alternative. Rather than financing companies forced to compete
with the increasingly potent Japanese, Germans, and Koreans,
growing ranks of U.S. bankers switched allegiance to the financial alchemists who were promising and delivering bigger, faster
gains with minimum risk.

As Steven Brill, publisher of *The American Lawyer*, noted
in a trenchant and bitterly sarcastic editorial: "In the Roaring
Eighties everyone gets rich quick. In the Roaring Eighties credit
is there for the asking because the era's magic word—leverage—
is always a good thing. In the Roaring Eighties there are no
nervous Nellies at the SEC worrying about fraudulent or incom-
plete filings or insider tipping, because, again, everyone is getting rich. In the Roaring Eighties forty-year-old money managers
who think in time horizons of two hours to two weeks control
industrial America.

The eighties were first and foremost a decade of financial
wizardry in which the highest calling was to trade, transform, and
restructure business assets. In the process, fortunes were created
with smoke and mirrors. Market values of long-established companies would soar in a matter of days simply by dint of a raider's
interest in them or on the rumor that they would be acquired and
dismantled. In this environment, many of the pillars of the
corporate community were appraised for their "break-up" value
(meaning the price their assets would fetch on the auction block)
rather than for their ongoing financial performance. For this
reason, the venerable Walt Disney Company would come under
repeated attacks from a pack of raiders including New York-
based Saul Steinberg, who could sell off Disney's prized film
library and auction the rights to Mickey Mouse, Donald Duck,
and Jiminy Crickett. To fend off the raiders, a beleaguered Disney would reach into its treasury repeatedly, paying millions of
dollars in greenmail (the eighties' euphemism for "protection
money") to assure its independence.

Fueling the frenzy to manipulate corporations for quick
profits, investment bankers reinvented themselves, moving

beyond their traditional role as advisers on corporate finance to a more aggressive stance as catalysts in the mergers and acquisitions spree, concocting deals on their own. By alerting raiders to companies whose anemic stock prices and high "break-up" values made them vulnerable to takeovers, and by encouraging the raiders to take significant positions in the companies' stock, the investment bankers would effectively put the targets "in play." As other raiders circled the prey, they would ignite a heated competition for the companies' shares, prompting management to succumb to a hostile takeover, to seek an acquisition by a friendly suitor (best known as a "white knight") or to engage in a leveraged buy-out (LBO), whereby management (and/or other parties) acquired the business, using the corporation's assets to secure the financing and using its cash flow to pay off the debt. In this classic eighties brand of financial alchemy, the buy-out firm of Kohlberg, Kravis, Roberts and Company would reign supreme.

By churning the waters for all manner of deals, investment bankers collected enormous fees, running into the tens of millions of dollars for a single M&A transaction. With the money flowing in, managing directors at Merrill Lynch, First Boston, Drexel Burnham, Salomon Brothers, Goldman Sachs, and Morgan Stanley—many fresh out of business school—were earning annual bonuses of $1 to $5 million.

As the investment bankers speed-dialed raiders and CEOs in a frantic effort to identify opportunities, putting more and more companies into play, a new wave of arbitrageurs emerged as a force in the financial markets, buying huge quantities of stock in anticipation of imminent takeovers, and then aligning themselves with the raiders in order to bid up the price of the shares. When deals went bust (because the raiders took greenmail or because tender offers could not be financed), the arbs were just as quick to unload their positions, causing precipitous declines in share prices. In this frenetic world, where fortunes were made and lost on the basis of breaking news and on the ability to decipher fact from fiction, Ivan Boesky emerged as the king of the arbs.

The son of a middle-class Russian immigrant, young Ivan

dreamed of escaping his pedestrian roots. While still in college, including the University of Michigan (where he failed to graduate) and the Detroit College of Law, Boesky became fascinated with arbitrage. After marrying Seema Silberstein, daughter of wealthy real estate magnate Ben Silberstein (whose portfolio of properties included the Beverly Hills Hotel), Boesky moved to New York, taking a series of Wall Street jobs with brokerage firms before launching his own arbitrage partnership in 1975. The initial funding of $700,000 came primarily from Seema and her family. But as Boesky demonstrated an uncanny ability to pick stocks that would ride high in the takeover boom, private investors poured money into his fund, whose capital soared to more than $100 million by 1979. After a number of bad calls took a toll on his performance, Boesky severed his ties with the partnership and formed an arbitrage corporation. Although he would absorb heavy losses on busted deals, huge gains on a series of transactions reinforced Boesky's image as the street's premier arb. An image, the world would ultimately discover, that was based in part on a flow of inside information relayed to Boesky by Drexel Burnham managing director Dennis Levine and by Martin Siegel, who started out at Kidder Peabody and moved to Drexel, arriving there as one of the premier stars of investment banking.

Of all the forces reshaping the business community in the eighties, none had a greater impact than Drexel. The product of a 1971 merger that linked two small, struggling securities firms—Burnham & Company and Drexel Firestone—the combined entity would rise to power on the strength of a young Wharton School graduate, Michael Milken, who had launched his business career with Drexel Firestone.

Fascinated by a now-classic study of corporate bonds (conducted by W. Braddock Hickman), Milken came to the conclusion that bonds carrying low ratings from Moody's or Standard & Poor's were not the high risk instruments many thought them to be. In fact, by investing in a broad mix of long-term low-rated bonds (which paid higher interest than top-grade bonds) investors could secure more attractive returns without assuming additional risks. Based on this finding—which he supported with prodigious research of his own—Milken set out to change the investment community's perception of "junk bonds" from virtual untouchables to instruments of choice.

Blessed with an idea whose time had come, a brilliant financial mind and an instinctive gift for salesmanship, Milken built a powerful network of supporters (wealthy individuals and corporations) who were eager to avail themselves of the junk bonds' higher yields. Similar to Icahn's early work in options, Milken created a market in which junk bonds were bought and sold through his increasingly successful Drexel Burnham trading operation (which he relocated from New York to Century City, California, in 1978 and ultimately moved to Beverly Hills). Throughout the eighties, Milken's unparalleled ability to raise capital through his network of junk bond investors would give Drexel awesome clout, bankrolling clients, and, in turn, fueling the M&A boom. At the time, it seemed like a capitalist's dream. Whether companies could afford the debt they were assuming was hardly as important as staying in the Roaring Eighties game of buying, selling, or protecting corporate assets.

Only when the music stopped, and the cash cow stopped milking, would the impact of this financial myopia take its toll on debt laden companies from the Campeau Corporation's retail empire to TWA.

As prominent investment banker Felix Rohatyn warned at the time, "All of this frenzy may be good for investment bankers now but it's not good for the country or investment bankers in the long run. We seem to be living in a 1920s jazz age atmosphere."

Even Boone Pickens, a major catalyst in the M&A wars of the eighties, now concedes that it was a decade run amok.

"The eighties represented a necessary correction whereby shareholders got back some of the rights they deserved. But there was so much value out there to be tapped that it brought in crooks and incompetents. People with rinky-dink deals could come in and make all kinds of money because management would just roll over and pony up.

As the nation that had spawned the likes of Henry Ford, Alfred Sloan, Walt Disney, Bill Paley, and Ray Kroc witnessed the rise of a new kind of business force—one that sought to dismantle and restructure great corporations rather than building them from the ground up—Carl Icahn was at the head of the pack.

At this stage in his career, Icahn raised the volume of his monologue on corporate democracy and shareholder rights, but it was mostly background music, intellectual camouflage for the goal of getting rich quick. Although Icahn was truly outraged by the arrogance of corporate management his anger stemmed not from a populist concern for the masses, but because these entrenched CEOs controlled his money, his investments, his companies. Now he had found a way to turn the tables, bringing leverage and the power that went with it to his side. The idea Icahn and Kingsley had cooked up in their Manhattan offices was working. By God it was working. Millions were flowing into the coffers.

If there was a sweetener that came with the money, it wasn't so much that shareholders were benefitting along with him (in some cases they were paying for his greenmail), but more that Icahn the loner was sticking it to the corporate establishment and that all the Brahmin CEOs with their establishment lawyers and their memberships in country clubs were proving they weren't nearly as smart or as tough as King Icahn.

Accelerating his campaign to "control the destiny" of companies, he took aim at a shooting gallery of corporate targets. Forays similar to his assaults against Tappan, Baird & Warner, Saxon, and Hammermill were launched against Simplicity Pattern in 1981, and Owens-Illinois, Marshall Field, American Can, and Anchor Hocking in 1982. Throughout this period Icahn's power and confidence were growing.

Typically, the assaults began with Kingsley's analysis of hundreds of corporate balance sheets. At times—as in the Owens-Illinois, American Can, and Anchor Hocking raids—he would identify hidden value that ran through an entire industry.

"In the early 1980s, I looked at the container industry and saw that it was undervalued as hell," Kingsley recalled. "The business was in a down cycle, but where else could you get these

companies—some of the greatest names in American industry—
selling for garbage? Just buying them was like stealing.

"If we took them over, we knew they would be easy to break
up. Each of them had a lot of different businesses that if you
separated them out, you would reap tremendous value."

But as the Lone Ranger and Tonto were discovering,
Icahn's infamy had reached the point that they didn't have to
buy a company to reap the benefits. All they had to do was buy
a position and demand a seat on the board. In deal after deal, the
paydirt followed right behind.

"We hit on a hot streak," Kingsley said. "For a while there,
all we had to do was call up and they would pay. Some [including
Anchor Hocking] even called us first. They'd say 'We know you
have our stock and we want to buy it.'

"I mean, it was like taking candy from a baby."

In total, Icahn had acquired 6.2 percent of Anchor Hocking's shares for a blended price of $13.94. The price he named
for the buyback, $18.75 a share, represented a $3.75 per share
premium over the market, producing a tidy profit of slightly less
than $3 million.

A month later, Owens-Illinois cried "uncle" in the face of
an Icahn assault by agreeing to pay $29.50 (a premium of $4 over
the market price) for the 1.3 million shares of its stock Icahn
controlled. In return for signing a standstill agreement, in September 1982, whereby he agreed to forgo the purchase of the
glass company's shares for ten years, Owens-Illinois ponied up
what amounted to $5.2 million in greenmail.

Just how rewarding it was to let Carl "do the driving" was
becoming increasingly clear to the fortunate few who were funneling money into his deals. Questioned about his participation,
Icahn's friend Stanley Nortman revealed that he was on the
financial joyride of a lifetime:

Q. How much money did you make personally in
Owens-Illinois . . . ?
A. I think it was above $100,000.
Q. What about American Can?

A. I think I made over $100,000.
Q. Over a period of how much time?
A. A couple of weeks.
Q. Do you make money like that in your business, Mr. Nortman?
A. No.

In February 1982, the Icahn group filed a 13-d revealing its threatening position in the Chicago-based retailer Marshall Field. Soon after, Icahn met with Field's CEO, Angelo Arena, at the O'Hare Airport Hilton. Attempting to intimidate his adversary in typical fashion, Carl boasted that he had enjoyed considerable success pursuing other companies through big stock purchases. Then he locked in on the current target, warning Arena that he had substantial financial resources, that he intended to use those resources to continue buying Field stock until he captured 35 percent of the company's outstanding shares. As Icahn weaved his tale of fear, he raised the specter of a proxy contest giving him control of the board and ultimately of the company.

Always the tactician, Icahn anticipated Arena's thought processes and raced ahead to close off his escape routes. If the CEO was thinking that his lawyers at Skadden Arps could bail him out, Icahn himself raised the issue of litigation, declaring that all the lawyers in the world might slow him down but that they would not be able to stop him.

Icahn's appetite for Field grew from an observation by Al Kingsley that the retailer was sitting on valuable real estate—including its grand flagship store on Chicago's State Street—carried on the books for a fraction of its market value. By selling the company's retail sites and leasing them back, Icahn believed he could unleash tremendous value that was currently locked up in brick and mortar.

Although Field had been the target of a takeover attempt by the retail conglomerate Carter Hawley Hale in 1979, that would-be combination had fallen apart when Field won a court order blocking the takeover on antitrust grounds. Arena, who had moved from Carter Hawley Hale to take over Field only days before the would-be takeover took shape, had led the fight against his former employer. At the time, Icahn & Company, which had an arbitrage position in Field on the assumption that the Carter Hawley Hale takeover would succeed, lost heavily the day the deal imploded and Field shares tumbled.

Always persistent, though, Icahn had not given up on Field, and he saw fresh opportunity as Field's stock was pummeled from a high of $36 to a low of $12. By the time Icahn launched his asset-oriented bid, he was able to buy the stock for bargain basement prices.

"After the Carter Hawley Hale bid fell apart, we retained the stock in our portfolio and I kept an eye on the shares," Kingsley says. "Well, I'm watching and watching and I see it's dropping down to $13 or $14 a share. And I say to myself, 'This is just unreal. It's a beautiful situation. Here's an old line company with old line stores, not just Field's but they own Frederick and Nelson stores in Seattle and a bunch of shopping centers.'

"Well, I thought this was the greatest thing and so I brought it to Carl's attention. He doesn't bite at everything I bring him and a lot of times it can take me three pitches to get his interest. But with Field he jumped right away. He saw the value in that real estate."

So thrilled was Icahn over his attack on the retailer—an adventure he code-named "Foxfield"—that he bragged about it at a New Year's Eve party attended by investors and a clutch of young women.

Icahn had a decidedly negative view of incumbent management when he arranged for the February meeting at the O'Hare Hilton. Specifically, he held Arena in low regard, considering him responsible for failing to accept the snubbed bid from Carter Hawley Hale. Icahn also complained that Field had undercharged for the corporate assets it sold and had overpaid for the businesses it purchased in a buying campaign conducted under Arena's watch.

As the CEO squirmed in his seat at the hotel meeting, he saw his company slipping through his hands. But just as the picture appeared unequivocally bleak, Icahn tossed out a life preserver. Providing Field allowed him to purchase sufficient treasury stock to boost his holdings to 35 percent of the outstanding shares, and that he be granted two seats on the board, Icahn would sign a standstill barring him from increasing his stake in the company for two years.

To Arena, the prospect of Icahn taking a place on the board with 35 percent of the shares was hardly a cause for celebration, standstill or not. Recognizing that Icahn's proposal would make him the new CEO in clout if not in title, he asked Carl to accept a compromise, tying the standstill agreement to a ceiling of 15 percent of the shares—an idea Icahn shrugged off as preposterous. No way was he going to settle for a minor equity position frozen at that level by a two-year standstill. As he knew full well, that would shift all the leverage from his side of the table to Field's. This violated Icahn's cardinal rule: If you can't act from a position of power, don't act at all.

With this in mind, Icahn presented an alternative of his own. If the 35 percent cap was too threatening for management, he offered Field the opportunity to rid the company of its newly emerged nemesis by—surprise, surprise—agreeing to buy back his stock for $26 a share, a premium over the market price. In arriving at this figure, Icahn engaged in convoluted mathematics that had more to do with chutzpah than with fundamental share values.

"He discussed the fact that he might be interested in selling back to the company his stock," Arena recalled. "When I asked him how much he would want for the stock, he linked back to the prior conversation, at which time he said to me that if he was able to buy Treasury stock, he would be willing to pay $26 a share for that Treasury stock and that since he would be willing to pay $26 for Treasury stock, we should be willing to pay him $26 for the stock he had. . . ."

After this came the now familiar Hobson's choice:

"If we didn't agree to either of these other two courses," Arena said, "namely, his coming on to the board . . . or our buying back his stock . . . that he would pursue his activities in the market to acquire that level of stock ownership, and he thought once he got to that level of stock ownership, he would have control of the company anyway."

Here again, the self-proclaimed champion of shareholders' rights felt no compunction about proposing a sweet deal for himself—one that would come at the expense of the other owners of Field stock. At this point, however, Field management was unwilling to submit to pressure, and so Icahn—always the aggressor—moved to put teeth into his threats, building his stock position from 5 percent to nearly 30 percent in the space of six weeks.

This preemptive strike was funded by the biggest war chest Icahn had assembled to date. In addition to the usual investor entourage, a number of big hitters joined in the Field attack—including Alan Clore, the Geneva-based son of Sir Charles Clore, one of Britain's wealthiest financiers; Marvin Warner, chairman of Miami's Great American Banks; Picara Valley, an investment outfit based in the Netherlands Antilles; and Banque Commerciale Privée, a small Paris-based lender. Clearly, Icahn's impressive performance as a raider was attracting capital into the fold, enabling him to expand the magnitude of his deals.

"Carl had a moving group joining him in Marshall Field," recalled Ted Altman, Icahn's lawyer on the transaction. "As the deal progressed, and as we were fighting in the courts, new and different people kept joining the group. In this way, Carl's resources, and his position in the company, kept growing."

At times the group was unwieldy and contentious. "We had rooms full of investors, each with their babbling lawyers," Kingsley recalled. "All of the investors had to sign the 13-d's and each time that happened, the lawyers had to show how smart they were."

Still, Icahn was delighted to have the band of investors joining his raid. As always, he recognized that the financial system, for all of its apparent complexity, boils down to a simple yet irrefutable rule: He who has the stock has the power. The more money at his disposal, the more he and his supporters could gobble up equity, the more power he could wield.

"At that point in history, before the advent of the poison

pill, there were limited defenses companies could rely on to protect themselves from those who bought their stock in the market," Altman said. "They could fight in court, and they could search for a more favorable buyer, but as Marshall Field discovered, there was little they could do to stop an acquirer intent on acquiring shares through a tender offer or open-market purchases."

Ironically, as the Icahn juggernaut was succeeding, Carl's loose-knit investor group became even more of a headache to control. "As the stock was going up, the investors were getting antsy," Kingsley said. "These guys were saying, 'Let's sell out— take a profit.' But we had to keep them in line so that we could accomplish what we'd set out to do."

In his drive to acquire Field shares, Icahn may have employed the same scare tactics with major shareholders that he used to intimidate corporate management. In a March 15, 1982, letter to the SEC's enforcement division, Field's attorneys at Skadden, Arps charged: "In order to amass a control block at the lowest possible cost, it was essential that the market be kept in a state of uncertainty about Icahn's plans. . . . Icahn reinforced this uncertainty by personally contacting large shareholders and telling them that they had better sell to him, because he intended to sell out soon, at which time the stock price would drop precipitously."

Although Carl had warned Field that litigation would not stop the Icahn juggernaut, management turned to Skadden anyway. The firm claimed that the Icahn group had violated the securities laws by failing to disclose its true intentions in the 13-d filing—specifically that it intended to "acquire a 'large amount,' approximating 30 to 35 percent of Marshall Field common stock—for the purpose of 'influencing' the destiny of the company."

Continuing along this line, Skadden, Arps also alleged that Icahn's 13-d was written to camouflage his group's motives while still covering its bases for any action it chose to take.

"The Icahn group told the public that it intended to pursue 'one of two' evenly balanced and equally favored 'alternative courses of action' with respect to Marshall Field: either to seek control of the company by open market and privately negotiated purchases, a proxy contest and/or a tender offer for some, but not all, of the company's shares, or to sell its shares in the open market or in privately negotiated transactions to one or more purchasers, including possibly Marshall Field. This statement of purpose, which includes within it virtually the entire universe of conceivable alternatives, is so broad as to be virtually meaningless."

Pointing to a trend that could only be seen as a sign of the times in the Roaring Eighties, Skadden noted that in a growing number of 13-d filings, "the filing person makes a 'boilerplate' disclosure, which includes within its terms every possible course of action, thereby protecting the filer (which, like the Icahn group here, simply takes the convenient position that it has not made up its mind what to do) against a later claim of nondisclosure while leaving it free to pursue its plans in a market that is really no better informed about its intentions than it was before the filing. This totally subverts the purposes of Section 13-d."

In addition to the run-of-the-mill securities lawsuits that Icahn and his lawyers had learned how to pulverize, Field tried a new tactic, slapping Icahn with a charge under the Racketeer Influenced and Corrupt Organization Act (RICO) claiming that the money used to acquire his position in the embattled retailer was gained through a pattern of racketeering, allegedly evidenced by his previous raids. With the suit, Skadden was seeking to lump Icahn together with the Mafia figures that were the original RICO targets. This was a calculated attempt to step up the power of takeover-defense litigation, threatening a raider not only with legal roadblocks but also with the prospect of seeing his name associated with notorious criminals.

Field's lawsuits particularly enraged Icahn because of the RICO provisions and because he felt he had been misled by Arena.

"When Carl first met Arena at the airport, they walked arm in arm back to the plane and Arena said, 'You'll hear from us in a day,' " Kingsley claimed. "That sounded promising. The next day we did hear from them but in the form of a lawsuit. They must have said, 'Okay, we met Icahn, now let's sue the shit out of him.' "

Charging that Field's executives had "publicly blackened" his name, Icahn countersued, demanding $25 million from Arena and Field's directors. Icahn's complaint also charged that Field's management had violated its fiduciary responsibility to the shareholders by seeking to block the Icahn group without shareholder approval.

From Icahn's perspective, the filing of RICO charges was another clear-cut case of corporate management abusing the system to protect its own interests. Although he was stung by the tactic, he told a friend that he was an "economic animal" and that he could not let emotions get in his way.

Behind the scenes, Field hired investment bankers Goldman Sachs to search for a white knight alternative to the Icahn group. In a frantic rush to save the company from Icahn's clutches, Goldman held talks with more than a dozen major retailers including May Department Stores, Batus, Inc. (parent of Gimbels and Saks Fifth Avenue) and once-spurned Carter Hawley Hale, which compared to Icahn, looked like the lesser of two evils. For weeks the talks zigzagged all over the lot, with Field holding out for terms that appeared unattractive to all of the would-be buyers.

In the end, however, Field boiled down to a case of money, clout, and stock—just the way Icahn and Kingsley had projected. Soon after Icahn struck a deal with Banque Commerciale Privée to lend $20 million, which opened the way for a huge increase in margin purchases of Field stock, the retailer recognized that it had to act or risk falling into Icahn's hands. With that sense of urgency, Field struck a deal with Batus, the American unit of London–based B.A.T. Industries.

Kingsley first learned that the battle had been won while in the enemy camp, giving a deposition at Skadden, Arps New York offices. Ironically, just as a Skadden attorney was threatening, as Kingsley recalled, "to sue us," another of the firm's lawyers walked in with a press release saying that the board of directors had agreed to put the company up for sale.

On March 16, 1982, Batus U.S. announced a tender offer for 65 percent of Field's stock, agreeing to pay $25.50 for the common shares and $45.90 for the preferred. But to Icahn—and almost everyone else in the financial community—this was too little too late. Calling it "unconscionable" that management would recommend in favor of a $25.50 common stock bid when it had spurned a $42 offer from Carter Hawley Hale, Icahn balked at the terms and threatened to continue amassing his Field position. After considerable jockeying on both sides, Batus raised its offer to $30 for the common and $54 for the preferred.

Still, in an eleventh-hour display of brinksmanship, Icahn balked, insisting that Batus sweeten its offer again. Seeking to keep Icahn at bay, Field made a public request for Batus to up the ante one more time. Capitulating, Batus agreed to extend its $30 per share offer to all of Field's outstanding common stock. Soon after, Icahn would sign a standstill, agreeing not to oppose the new terms or to buy additional Field shares. Both sides dropped their litigation against each other, and the Icahn group tendered its shares for a $30 million profit.

No one could accuse the merry Icahn band of making money the old-fashioned way. With the new 1980s style of wealth accumulation, working for a living appeared to be a fool's game. In this case, Icahn's personal interests dovetailed with those of the broad base of Field shareholders. In pursuing his own gain, he had forced an insulated management to respond to the goals of the company's owners, providing a rapid increase in shareholder values. Reflecting his pride as an outsider tilting against the corporate establishment, the reception room of Icahn's Manhattan offices featured the annual reports of the companies he had conquered in the financial markets, in the back rooms, and in the courts of law that made up the three venues of the takeover arena. Like a great white hunter proudly hanging the horns of his slaughtered prey over the mantel, Icahn was displaying the trophies as evidence of his intellect and machismo.

Continuing his terrorist strikes against the corporate community, Icahn moved next against Dan River, Inc., a century-old textile manufacturer set in the sleepy company town of Danville, Virginia. A sprawling sign erected atop the roof of the company's main building declared this to be the HOME OF DAN RIVER FABRICS.

A major producer of denim and dyed yarns, Dan River was in the throes of a deep sales slump affecting much of the textile industry when Icahn started buying the company's stock in the summer of 1982, building a position of 398,900 shares—6.9 percent of the company—by the time a filing was made with the SEC in September.

Once again Icahn was buying at a time of uncertainty that kept most other investors at bay. Dan River was struggling to reverse a slide in earnings that saw the bottom line drop from $22 million in 1979 to $19 million in 1980 and $14.5 million in 1982. Although management had spent $250 million to modernize the company and on this basis was predicting an imminent turnaround, Wall Street remained mostly skeptical. This was a company on its knees.

Still, Icahn's interest in Dan River was clear and, to those observers now familiar with his modus operandi, quite predictable. Given the wide spread between his average purchase price of $12.80 per share (prices ranged between 10⅝ to 15) and Dan River's book value of $38 per share, Icahn inhaled the aroma of opportunity.

"Carl obviously saw that Dan River was a company worth more than the value the stock market had assigned to it," said Frank Nickell, president of Kelso & Company, a New York investment banking firm that would play a major role in deciding the fate of Dan River. "Traditionally, textile and apparel companies had been undervalued by Wall Street. Carl knew this. He also believed, I'm sure, that with new management brought in to stir the pot, the company's performance would improve."

As with most of the deals of the decade, there was also the specter of a takeover. As Icahn was mulling over investment opportunities, a June 1982 L.F. Rothchild research report came across his desk. Referring to Dan River, the report noted that "less than 2 percent of the outstanding shares are closely held, rendering the company particularly vulnerable to a takeover."

A follow-up Rothchild report issued in August was even more optimistic: "There has been recurrent takeover speculation about textile companies and, in our opinion, Dan River is a likely candidate because of the big discount and the fact that holdings of the stock are not concentrated. Either in a takeover, or on prospects of a major recovery in earnings, we believe the stock has considerable appreciation potential."

But in setting his sights on Dan River, Icahn was navigating unchartered waters. For the first time in his career he was taking on more than a company—he was taking on a town. The vast majority of Dan River's 12,500 employees lived in and around Danville. As far as the locals were concerned, the company and the city were just about one and the same.

"I grew up in nearby Greensboro, North Carolina; and my family would frequently drive through Danville on our way to summer vacations in other parts of the state of Virginia," Nickell remembered. "I was always struck by the omnipresence of the Dan River company. All of those red brick buildings with the Dan River name on them. It was the archetypical company town."

A threat to Dan River, especially one by a "sinister force" from Wall Street, was a threat to jobs, homes, a way of life. As Icahn moved on the company, threatening to control it, Dan River executives capitalized on these fears by whipping the locals into a frenzy, filling their heads with nightmarish visions of Icahn taking control, liquidating the company's assets and, leaving the employees—many of whom had known no other job, no other life—on the dole.

"To the Dan River employees, Icahn was the devil incarnate," Nickell recalled. "The way they saw it, Carl was going to go through town in a pickup truck and sell off the buildings brick by brick."

Dan River's management used the fear of Icahn to rally employee support, blaming the company's woes on the threatening bully. "People are concerned, and frequently it's difficult for them to concentrate on the business," said Dave Johnston, former chairman of Dan River, "because of the fear of the consequences of this company being looted by Icahn."

A widely circulated memo designed to support this impression fueled the local fires and rallied the hometowners' opposition to the "devil" from New York. Entitled "Icahn and Dan River, Inc.," the memo declared:

"Dan River employs some 8,000 people here and therefore represents the backbone of the community. The danger to Danville is not so much that Icahn would take it over and run it. . . . The danger is that he might break it up and sell it as separate corporations. Some of the buyers might be interested purely in the equipment. Some might be interested only in warehouse space. Some might not find it profitable to keep open everything they bought. . . . Carl Icahn is in the business to make money— not to see how much community good he can do. . . . In fact, what's good for him could be extremely bad news for Danville."

To say nothing of "bad news" for Dan River's senior management, whose concern for their own plight was never mentioned in the "Icahn and Dan River" memo. Although Icahn was hardly in business for the good of backwater communities, management's posturing about a deep-seated concern for the town and the shareholders appeared, at least in part, a convenient means of camouflaging its own self-interest.

The clash between Icahn and Dan River's management began on September 14, 1982, with a telephone call from Carl to Johnston's office in Danville. Traveling to New York on business that day, Johnston—a gruff, assertive man—was informed by his secretary that Icahn had requested a return call as soon as possible. When Johnston complied, he learned directly from the source that the Icahn group had acquired more than 5 percent of Dan River's common stock and was filing a 13-d with the SEC.

Ironically, Johnston was in New York to meet with his lawyers at the prominent New York firm of Paul, Weiss, Rifkind, Wharton & Garrison and with investment bankers from Kidder Peabody to discuss a possible leveraged buy-out of Dan River by the investment firm of Wesray Capital. For this reason, news of the Icahn purchase could not have come at a worse time. Just as management was exploring potential deals with friendly sources, a man with a reputation for controlling corporate destinies according to his own agenda entered the scene.

Quickly, Johnston's focus shifted to the Icahn threat. During his visit to New York he presided over an evening skull session with Kidder Peabody at Dan River's Manhattan apartment and followed up the next morning with a session at the Paul Weiss offices. At both meetings, "what to do about Icahn" dominated the conversation. Although Icahn tried to arrange a face-to-face meeting with Johnston at this time, the CEO stalled, saying he would have to review the 13-d. With this, Icahn fired off a copy of the document to Johnston's attention.

When Johnston failed to respond, Icahn placed a follow-up call on September 20, declaring that it would be in the best interests of Johnston and the company to meet with him immediately. By this point Johnston, who had been briefed by Kidder Peabody and Paul Weiss, had come up to speed on this fellow Icahn and had formed the opinion that he would be "a person very difficult to deal with, and that his history of activities with other companies was dreadful to contemplate."

Recognizing that the "devil" could not be ignored, Johnston agreed to meet with Icahn on Friday, September 24. But in his inimitable fashion Carl began making a series of demands, counteroffers, and adjustments that are part and parcel of his negotiating style and that tend to wear down, confuse, and frustrate his adversaries.

When Johnston suggested a meeting on the 24th, Carl responded that he preferred to meet on Thursday, September 23, ostensibly so that Al Kingsley, who was not available on the 24th, could be present. Accommodating Icahn, Johnston agreed to meet on Thursday, but within a matter of hours Icahn called again, saying this time that he refused to come to Danville, based on his lawyers' objections, and demanded a change of venue to New York.

Johnston, who says Icahn wanted the change because "he thought we would have him arrested," told Carl it's "strange indeed that a man who had just made a significant investment in a company wouldn't come to its headquarters' location."

When Carl remained adamant about steering clear of Danville, Johnston reiterated his willingness to meet on Dan River's home turf. That this was the only acceptable option was communicated to Carl by phone and in a subsequent letter from Johnston. But if Dan River's chairman had determined to hang tough against the Icahn onslaught, he had no way of anticipating the relentless force that would be unleashed against him. On September 23, Johnston learned, much to his consternation, that Carl had scored a major coup by purchasing the Dan River shares previously owned by Unitex, Ltd., a Hong Kong company that had been Dan River's largest single shareholder with 8.6 percent of the stock.

Calling Johnston on September 24, Icahn referred to the Unitex purchase, which significantly increased his leverage and put more teeth into his still unannounced takeover threat, using this new equity as a club to pressure the chairman into a meeting on Carl's terms. When Johnston volunteered that he would be returning to New York for company business on October 4, and would be willing to meet on that date, Carl turned up the heat. October 4 was too late, he complained. His investors were growing impatient and—repeating his warning—it would be in Johnston and Dan River's best interest to meet with him promptly. This implied threat infuriated Johnston, but he saw no other choice than to accelerate the timetable in spite of his pride.

The first face-to-face encounter between the opposing factions took place September 30 at Dan River's New York sales office on 111 West 40th Street. In attendance were Icahn, Kingsley, Johnston, Dan River president Lester Hudson and the company's financial vice president Fred Zahrn. The Dan River people—southern textile men who had thought themselves to be continents away from the takeover fever that had gripped Wall Street, and thus free to conduct the company's business as they saw fit—were incredulous at what they saw and heard.

At first they may have been lured into a sense of complacency by Carl's persona.

"I was shocked by his appearance," Hudson recalled. "He seemed sloppy, poorly dressed, ill-prepared, inarticulate. Could this be the guy I'd heard about?"

But if Icahn appeared at first blush as a harmless, absent-minded bumbler, that impression vanished as he got down to business.

"He shocked me with his bluntness," Hudson remembered. "He said he wanted to take over Dan River."

Icahn's plan was simple and direct. He expressed the strong likelihood that he would issue a tender offer to purchase between 40 to 50 percent of Dan River's shares for $16 to $17 a share. Combined with the roughly 15 percent of the stock already in his group's possession, he would gain control of the company.

"Then he made me an offer that shocked me even more," Hudson said. "He asked for my help in taking over Dan River. If I helped him, he offered me a ten-year contract for full salary and a compensation package that I could cash out for 100 percent of the money at any time. In other words, he would pay for me to do nothing if I helped him. I thought that was obscene and I told him so."

Johnston, who also rejected what he characterized as a bribe out of hand, said, "I thought Carl Icahn was an evil person trying to take advantage of the shareholders. Foreign competition in the garment business had flooded our market here and caused great problems for the company. He was seeking to take advantage of that."

For his part, Icahn denies trying to bribe anyone. "There were several people at that meeting," he recalled. "Would I do that with all of those people there? I might have given them employment contracts for a couple of years, but not a ten-year deal."

By offering management one type of deal or another, Icahn was hoping to arrange for high-level blessing of the tender offer at the bargain price of $16 to $17 and to gain swift control of the company, putting him in position to sell off the assets for a handsome profit. But as always, there were alternate plans. At the September 30 meeting, Icahn raised the specter of another scenario that would be even more suitable to his style: the purchase of his interests by a white knight.

Icahn's 13-d had also announced that his investment group might seek control of Dan River or "seek to sell the shares in the open market or in privately negotiated transactions to one or more persons, which may include the issuer." As far as Icahn was concerned, he had a bunch of country bumpkins ripe for the plucking.

But as events would prove, Icahn misjudged the "hicks" from Danville, assuming they could be steamrollered into submission or bought out with a generous parachute. Neither approach would prove effective.

"Icahn threatened, persisted, cajoled, but Johnston, also a very persistent man, fought Icahn at every turn," Hudson recalled a decade later. "He was determined not to hand the company over to him."

The reason behind Johnston's obstinance may have had less to do with his alleged concern for the townspeople and the shareholders, and more to do with the chairman's determination to remain in power. Icahn's march on Dan River had come soon after Johnston's election as chairman and thus threatened to undo the crowning achievement of his career.

"Dave Johnston had his flaws, but undue subtlety wasn't one of them," Nickell said. "You knew where he stood all the time, and he stood square against Carl. Icahn had the gall to come along and ruin his kingdom.

"For his entire life, he had been in the textile business and he'd worked his way up to achieve the pinnacle for a man like that—to become the chief executive officer of a company. Now to have someone come along and buy that company, well what was Johnston going to do at this stage of his life, look for a job? Johnston reacted the way other CEOs react when they find themselves in that situation."

On every front, Icahn vs. Dan River was a clash of cultures, of geography, of insiders and outsiders, of company men and a corporate raider. But most of all, it was a clash between two individuals: one who wanted to keep control over a public corporation and one who wanted to earn a fast profit on the value of its assets. Both were determined to have their way.

.   .   .

To block Icahn, management put in place a series of measures that might well thwart the raider, but that brought into question their alleged concern for the shareholders. Dan River's first move was a sprint to the courthouse, seeking legal protection from a man whose presence had already propelled the stock price several dollars a share—an act of wizardry management had proven itself unable to do.

Claiming that the Icahn group had violated federal securities laws from previous takeover attempts, the company insisted that Icahn had built his Dan River position with "proceeds derived through prior acts of extortion, mail fraud, and securities fraud." The company also complained that it was "the latest (and at least the eleventh intended) victim of Icahn's tactics."

By picturing Icahn as the embodiment of evil, Dan River management was trying to further its cause with the shareholders.

Counterpunching with charges of his own, Icahn fired off a statement declaring, "I consider it an abomination that a company's management should resort to these gutter and smear tactics."

Dan River lost their first fight in the courthouse. The U.S. District Court refused to support the company's case. Pursuing a backup strategy, the board approved the issuance of a new series of cumulative preferred stock for the purpose of funding an employee stock-bonus plan. In the cozy way Dan River structured it, the new preferred would be locked up for five years in a trust fund controlled by management. Making the arrangement even sweeter for the men at the helm, merger proposals would have to be blessed by the holders of two-thirds of the preferred. Cutting through the legalese, this meant that management, which controlled the trust fund, would have virtual veto power on offers to buy the company.

In filing a lawsuit of his own, Icahn charged that Dan River's management had "secured, at no cost to itself, voting control of Dan River and has done so without obtaining common shareholder approval and at the expense of common shareholders."

Since the preferred shares represented about 22 percent of Dan River's voting stock and was now effectively controlled by management, Icahn's point was well taken. What was held out to be a move designed to protect shareholders' rights was actually a poorly camouflaged plan to protect management's power.

Icahn would have none of it. Charging ahead, he launched a tender offer at $15 per share for 700,000 shares, or 12 percent of the outstanding stock, and then raised the ante to $16.50 for up to two million shares. Combined with the 15 percent of the stock the Icahn group already owned, a successful tender of this magnitude would give the raider and his band voting control of the company.

Later, Icahn said he would increase his offer to $18 a share for 54 percent of the company if Dan River would drop its litigation and would otherwise refrain from blocking his tender.

Fearing Icahn's advances, Dan River returned to court, seeking a preliminary injunction preventing Icahn from voting his shares, launching a proxy solicitation or in any way seeking to change the company's management. Because the federal district judge who heard the case rode a circuit in western Virginia, the venue would shift from one remote town to another. At one point in the proceedings, the judge announced that the next session would be held in "Big Stone Gap." Hearing that and then getting travel directions from Dan River's counsel, Icahn's New York lawyer Ted Altman imagined himself taking a small plane to a car, a car to a mule, and then having to hike for miles to the courthouse.

Naturally, Dan River's board and management were hostile to Icahn. "At one point, when Johnston was asked what would happen if Icahn was successful in taking over Dan River," Altman recalled, "he said, 'It would be too terrible to behold.' "

Ultimately, the judge granted the preliminary injunction preventing Icahn from voting more shares. In typical fashion, Dan River was required to post a bond that serves as compensation to the injured party should the temporary injunction prove to be wrongful. As Icahn recalls it, the episode reinforced the impression of Dan River, and the town of Danville, as one and the same.

"At the end of the proceedings, the judge stands up and says, in this thick southern drawl, 'I'm gonna rule. You can have all the stock you want, but you can't vote it.'

"With that, Altman shouted, 'I want a bond!' And the Dan River lawyer said, 'Judge, I have no problem with that. We have a bond. It's all the buildings Dan River owns.'

"And the judge said okay to Dan River's case."

But Icahn was in no mood to concede the battle to the good old boys from Danville. Instead he fought lawyers with lawyers, lawsuits with lawsuits, this time moving the battle to the Court of Appeals, which ruled in his favor. This enabled Icahn to continue building leverage as he tendered for a controlling block of Dan River shares. But in a disturbing outgrowth of the Dan River litigation, the Securities and Exchange Commission pursued a charge that Bayswater was an unregistered investment company. The implications were clear: By allegedly using Bayswater as a vehicle for investing in other companies, but failing to register it as such, Icahn was freeing the company from the legal provisions spelled out in the Investment Company Act. The SEC launched an investigation into the matter, resulting (in typical SEC fashion) in a consent decree skirting the issue of whether Bayswater was an investment company but obtaining an agreement that Bayswater would not conduct business as an unregistered investment company. Ultimately Icahn registered Bayswater as an investment company, distributed most of the cash to the shareholders, and then de-registered it.

Concurrent with Dan River's defensive move to block Icahn in court, management was aggressively pursuing a white knight. From October to December of 1982, investment bankers at Kidder Peabody met with thirty-four potential acquirers or merger partners in an all-out effort to sell the company. Against this backdrop, one must ask, why management was beating the bushes for a buyer when it already had a buyer, cash in hand, in the name of Carl Icahn.

The answer is found in an agreement prospective white knights were required to sign as a prerequisite for the privilege of taking a close-up look at Dan River. The document specified that for a period of from three to five years, potential acquirers would not "purchase or offer to agree to purchase any securities or assets of Dan River or enter into any acquisition or other business combination transaction with Dan River or any subsidiary of Dan River, or propose any such offer, unless such purchase, offer or proposal have been previously presented to and approved by the Board of Directors of Dan River."

Few serious candidates emerged from Kidder Peabody's frantic search, though, and only Hanson Industries, a U.S. subsidiary of UK-based Hanson Trust PLC, entered into formal negotiations. Determined to pursue a backup strategy, the company engaged in a costly effort to outbid Icahn, committing $15 million to open-market purchases of Dan River shares. The idea was to stymie Icahn's tender by driving the market price of the company's shares over the price Icahn had offered to pay for them. This would neutralize Icahn's strategy by eliminating the spread that was critical to the appeal of his tender offer.

It was a shrewd strategy, but one that relied on a questionable use of corporate funds. If an investor is willing to pay the shareholders a premium for their stock, on what grounds— besides its own self-preservation—should management be spending corporate funds to match or exceed that premium? Icahn labeled the management buy-back a "scheme" and an "illegal tender offer," and a *Barron's* editorial called management's actions "another heavy blow to sound corporate governance."

At the same time that Icahn and Dan River were trading blows, executives with the investment banking firm of Kelso & Company were meeting in Atlanta with a local associate. Founded by San Francisco lawyer Louis O. Kelso, the firm had emerged as a major force in promoting and structuring leveraged buy-outs through so-called Employee Stock-Ownership Plans. Under this arrangement, employees purchase equity in their corporations from the principals or public shareholders, thus becoming owner/employees rather than simply salaried workers. The concept would theoretically both boost productivity by giving employees a stake in the business, and create opportunities for investment bankers, who would collect fees and, in some cases, equity interests in the businesses they guided through the process.

Throughout the 1960s and much of the 70s, ESOPs were touted as a boon for employees. But in the turbulent 1980s, frightened corporate managers began to view ESOPs as a means for warding off takeover bullies. Under this arrangement, ESOPs would be used as vehicles for taking corporate shares out of reach of the raiders by funneling them into management-controlled trusts.

As the Kelso group discussed developments in the market-place, the Dan River name—which had been under the media spotlight ever since Icahn filed his 13-d—came up for discussion. The firm's associate, who had done financial planning for Dan River's president Lester Hudson and had developed a working relationship with him, believed Kelso might help the beleagured textile company. With this in mind, a Kelso team visited Hudson. What was scheduled for a brief session so excited Dan River's president that the Kelso people stayed through the weekend, working out a proposal for creating an ESOP that would purchase Dan River's shares, thus keeping the company out of Icahn's grasp.

The ESOP proved attractive to Dan River's management from a debt management standpoint. At the time, $96 million of Dan River's $130 million debt carried a relatively low interest rate of 8 percent. Before Kelso came along, a management-led buy-out was being considered as a means of blocking Icahn. But this option necessitated new borrowings in violation of the existing loan covenants, meaning management would have to refinance the 8 percent loan at about 14 percent. Because this would have had a burdensome impact on Dan River's debt load, there was strong motivation to keep the current financing in place.

The Kelso plan allowed management to accomplish its goals through a complex transaction whereby an Employee Stock-Ownership Plan bought the shares without upsetting the loan covenants. That's because technically the ESOP, rather than the company, arranged for new financing to buy the stock.

The ESOP approach gave management a financially attractive means of buying back the company's shares using more of the employees' money than their own. The way the deal was structured, Kelso created two classes of equity. Class A common

stock, valued at $22.50 per share, went to the ESOP for a total
of $110 million. This accounted for about 70 percent of the Dan
River equity. The balance, mostly in the form of Class B common, was purchased for $4.3 million by twenty-six senior Dan
River managers and a Kelso investment fund.

The ESOP plan satisfied a wish list of management goals.
According to the terms of the deal, Dan River's employees—who
made the transaction possible by trading in their established
pension plans for the ESOP—were able to offer $22.50 a share
for the outstanding stock, a price that was sweet enough to make
Icahn a seller. With Carl's block acquired by the ESOP, the
threat of a takeover was eliminated.

Second, the stock gave management an equity stake for a
bargain price while allowing the executives to retain much of the
control of the company. As *Business Week* explained the deal:

> The Class A common stock will always be worth
> about $22 more than management's Class B. But if the
> company grows, management's stock will get a dispro-
> portionate share of the upside. The value of the stock
> is reviewed once a year by an independent appraiser. If
> Class A climbs to $26, for example, Class B will have
> a value of $4—a 100 percent gain, compared with a 16
> percent rise for the ESOP. . . .
>
> Employees are able to vote on a merger or sale of
> the company, but they cannot vote on any other mat-
> ters, including election of directors. Control still rests
> with the "dirty 30," the workers' term for Dan River's
> officers and directors. Employees' stock will be voted
> by United Virginia Bank, the ESOP trustee, as di-
> rected by a management-controlled committee.

Whether intentionally or not, Dan River whipped its employees
into a frenzied state of fear over Icahn, and then played on that
fear to promote a deal that was clearly in management's self-
interest. For a modest cash outlay, management neutralized a
persistent nemesis and gained a chunk of equity in the company.
By comparison, the employees agreed to have the value of their

pensions frozen while the ESOP was in place—this for a long-shot stab at capital appreciation based on a hoped-for rise in the value of the company's shares.

It was a rise that never came. Suffering from continued foreign competition and burdened by the debt load that was part and parcel of the ESOP transaction, Dan River's numbers continued to deteriorate.*

From the beginning, many Dan River employees felt that they had been hoodwinked by, as one salaried worker put it, "a shuck and jive act." A twenty-eight-year-old weaver would go further, saying, "Frankly, I wish Icahn would have taken over Dan River."

But not Carl. Without having to accept the financial risk of a takeover, or to wrestle with Dan River's unions, he had once again used the threat of a takeover to achieve his goals. In selling out for $26.50 a share, Icahn's group earned a profit of $8 million. Once again Icahn had used the system to profit from it.

Although Dan River's management claimed that they had stood up to Icahn and limited his gain, Icahn knew that he had won again. In commemoration of the deal, the raider named his newly purchased German shepherd "Shiloh," a reference to the Civil War battle at Pittsburg Landing where the Union forces defeated the Confederates.

The Dan River battle was an acid test of Icahn's determination. Unbeknownst to the company's management, Icahn was in danger of going over his head. Put to the test, he would have been hard pressed to come up with the financing to take over Dan River. At this point in his career, Icahn was using brains and moxie to whip corporate America. With financial resources far from unlimited, he had to stage such an extraordinary show of strength that his adversaries would fear calling his bluff.

"In the beginning, I was playing poker," Icahn admits. "I didn't have the money to fight for the long haul—to pay the

---

*Ultimately, the company was sold to an investment group, leaving the employees with no appreciation on the original value of their shares.

interest on the shares I held. If push came to shove, I would have had to find a way to protect my credibility but it never came to that because those companies didn't have the guts to really fight me."

Flush with the profits from his corporate raids, and flattered by his sudden status as a Wall Street celebrity, Icahn decided to reinvent himself by adopting the persona of a country squire. In 1982, King Carl moved his family from Manhattan to the equestrian enclave of Bedford, New York, taking up residence in an imposing twenty-two-room Norman stone mansion Icahn purchased from actress Jennifer O'Neal. At first Icahn used the estate as a retreat, living in his Manhattan apartment at 900 Park Avenue Monday through Friday, and joining his family in Bedford on the weekends. Although he thought he would maintain the split residence, the country home became ever more appealing: the city, which he had enjoyed so much in his bachelor days, less so.

Naming the estate "Foxfield," a reference to the code name for his successful attack on Marshall Field, Icahn has created an old-money environment to add a veneer of respectability to his newly minted 1980s fortune.

The setting is tasteful and elegant, furnished in a nineteenth-century English motif replete with regal tapestries, needlepoint hunt scenes and floral chintz. Everywhere there are oriental rugs and leather-bound books. A maid attired in a linen apron solicits wine orders and a chauffeur inquires if "Mr. Icahn" will be in need of a limousine. Somehow, the staid, majestic environment is meant to compensate for the fact that this man of nouveau wealth has nothing in the way of ancestral tradition.

But to observe Icahn close up is to see that he is a bundle of contradictions—a man with one foot firmly planted in his humble background on the streets of New York City and another set gingerly on the terra firma of American nobility.

A set of tennis at "Club Icahn," the lavish indoor complex he has erected on the Bedford estate, is testimony to this. Built at a cost of $1 million, this is a grand facility, complete with a soft surface court designed to absorb the shock to the king's legs, an English living room viewing area, wood burning fireplace, men's and women's locker rooms and an attendant, wearing a uniform bearing the Foxfield logo, who plays umpire and chases balls. At first blush, club Icahn is a shrine to the sport the owner loves, a Taj Mahal of tennis, no expense spared. A reflection of the grand vision and the brute power that brought Icahn to the zenith of the financial world.

But there is another side of King Carl, the miserly, count-every-penny grown-up-kid who never got the taste of being middle-class out of his system.

Stories of Icahn's pecuniary peccadillos are legion.

"I remember running into Carl's wife Liba on this godawful snowy day and having her tell me how safe she felt driving on the snowbound roads because she'd just bought a Jeep Cherokee," said a Bedford neighbor and prominent member of the local business community. "I said, 'If you like the Jeep, you'll really love a Range Rover. The Jeep is fine and all but it's so spartan. Take it from me, I just bought a Range Rover and I'm mad about it.'

"She seemed interested, so I took her over to see my Rover. At first, Liba appeared to like what she saw, but then she started shaking her head as if to say 'No, no, no.'

"When I asked what was wrong, she pointed to the price sticker still on the window and said, 'Carl would never let me spend that. He's too cheap. My Jeep has roll-up windows because Carl wouldn't spend the extra $300 for electric.'"

Carl Icahn's nature is to be both an insider and an outsider simultaneously. In the business world, he is on one level a shareholder and a CEO, and on another, a pariah to the corporate establishment. The same captains of industry who respect his intellect and his negotiating skills despise him for his ruthless tactics and bellicosity.

A similar dichotomy marks his place in the Bedford community, where he is admired for his wealth and his business

acumen but is dismissed by the Brahmins for his lack of style and
social grace. To some in the Bedford upper echelon, Icahn is a
real-life Jed Clampett.

One of the stories the locals love to tell is about the time
Icahn attended a posh party at a nearby polo club. It seemed that
cliques of members had arranged to have catered buffets delivered to their private tables. The unwritten rule was that you
confined your eating to your group's buffet.

But from Icahn's perspective, this was one big smorgasbord
and when you are hungry, you eat. As he was making chit-chat
with a grand dame of the horsey set, he eyeballed the lavish
spread on the table beside them. Reaching for a tray of hors
d'oeuvres, Icahn started noshing the goodies as if he were alone
in his kitchen. That's until one of the members who had catered
the table spotted Icahn's transgression and slapped his hand,
saying loud enough for all to hear, "That's not your food."

To be fair, Icahn's outsider status stems in part from a refreshing
lack of pretension and an aversion to the effete airs of those
born-in-the-manor-house neighbors who have never even been
inside a public school or had lunch in a cafeteria. Although he
surrounds himself with the trappings of royalty, in many ways he
remains surprisingly accessible and down-to-earth.

"Carl is a straight shooter," said a local real estate broker.
"He refuses to ride on a high horse. When he sees me in town,
social events, whatever, he always makes a point of saying 'hello.'

"One time I drove Carl home after viewing a property. The
security guard at the gate didn't recognize my car, so we were
flagged down. After the guy saw that it was Carl, and we were
waved through, Carl did something no one else in his position
would do: He apologized for having a guard. He said something
about the insurance company making him have it. I could tell by
the sheepish look on his face that he was embarrassed by it.

"Carl doesn't play the rules of the superrich. He snubs his
nose at their conventions, their pomposity. I remember attending a dinner party at the home of a wealthy Bedford industrialist.

When I reached to pour myself a glass of champagne, the host admonished me.

" 'Don't do that,' he said. 'That's why we have a butler.' So we had to wait for the butler to come from the next room to serve us.

"Carl would never do that. He wouldn't think twice about pouring the champagne."

PHILLIPS PETROLEUM MEETS THE "BARBARIANS FROM HELL"

"In every deal, in every negotiation, in every raid, the question 'What does Carl want?' can be answered the same way: 'Carl wants more!' "

—BRIAN FREEMAN, investment banker

In the first C.C.I. partnership, investors could ride the Icahn bandwagon for as little as $100,000; by 1982, Carl put a $5 million floor on investment shares in his Crane limited partnership. Based on his early success, the raider was lifting the cover charge on what was proving to be one of the decade's most exclusive and profitable clubs.

As Icahn wrote to the Crane prospects: "I have invited a select group of friends and associates to join me in a partnership which I have every belief will be both extremely interesting and profitable. . . ."

Once again, Carl was spelling out his manifesto, this time as a proven strategy (worth the higher ticket price). As the Icahn letter continued:

"It is intended that the partnership shall invest in one or several companies selling well below book and/or 'real' value. It is also contemplated that the partnership will be an 'activist' concerning the destiny of its own investment and possibly the destiny of the company or companies whose shares it has purchased."

Deal by deal, year by year, Icahn's ambitions continued to grow. In 1983, he scored $19 million on a stake in Gulf & Western. The payoff came when G&W's investment bankers at Kidder Peabody found an institutional buyer for Icahn's stock.*

Then in 1984, Icahn snared $41 million in greenmail from B.F. Goodrich Co. In this transaction Icahn followed his familiar pattern, acquiring 1.7 million Goodrich shares—4.9 percent of the stock—then calling for a meeting with the company's CEO John Ong. At this session, held on October 25, 1984, Icahn laid out a series of possible moves including a threat to raise his holdings to 30 percent and to seek a seat on the board. But just in case management preferred to live without a dreaded raider in its camp, Icahn offered to sell his stock back to the company for a substantial premium. Six days later, on October 31, Goodrich capitulated, paying an Icahn investment entity $35 a share at the same time the stock was trading on the Big Board for $28.

The unusual twist in the Goodrich case is that the company tried to disguise the fact that it had sold out the shareholders to pacify Icahn. Although Goodrich announced in a press release and in its 1984 annual report that it had repurchased a block of its own shares, management failed to mention Icahn or that greenmail had been paid. Subsequently, the SEC charged the company with making "materially misleading statements." In what was the first greenmail case against a public company, Goodrich settled with the SEC without, in typical SEC speak, "admitting or denying guilt." The company did,

---

*In 1985, Icahn would acquire an even larger block of G&W stock. Although there was talk of Ivan Boesky, who also amassed a major G&W position, working as a partner with Icahn, this never came about. Instead, Icahn sold his shares in the open market.

however, pledge to abide by the SEC's disclosure rules in future transactions.

Also in 1984, Icahn made a major move to legitimize himself, changing from an attacker/greenmailer who made his money by threatening acquisitions to a financier who would actually take possession of his corporate prey. The shift had begun the year before with Icahn acquiring a 13.5 percent stake in ACF Industries, a New York–based manufacturer of rail cars, automotive, and energy-related equipment. As usual, Icahn's timing was perfect. Suffering in the midst of an economic recession, ACF profits had declined from $27 million ($3.01 a share) in the first half of 1982 to $433,000 (five cents a share) by mid-1983. In light of this steep earnings slide, the dividend was cut, causing consternation among shareholders. As Icahn knew full well, growing dissatisfaction with the company's performance could serve to his advantage in a proxy battle.

Icahn also recognized that ACF, in spite of its cyclical woes, was a strong company carrying an estimated liquidation value of at least $60 a share. Considering that Icahn's 13.5 percent block was purchased at prices ranging from $32 to $41 a share, he saw the favored combination of substantial upside potential with minimum downside risk.

ACF's management, led by CEO Ivan Burns, saw the same value and was determined to keep the diamond in the rough from falling into Icahn's hands. As Icahn increased his stake to 18.3 percent, ACF announced a series of defensive measures it was considering to halt the Icahn juggernaut. These potential roadblocks included a sale of all or part of the company, a recapitalization, a tender offer for its own shares or a management-led leveraged buy-out.

The announcement that management was pursuing these options came as part of a ploy to raise the price of ACF's stock, making it more difficult for Icahn to acquire a controlling interest in the company. After a halt in the trading of ACF shares preceding the announcement, the stock price soared $6.25 to

$48.50. Although Icahn and Kingsley pushed ahead as if they could acquire the company, secretly they worried that they lacked the capital to finish off the deal.

As ACF's management was searching for the financing to consummate a leveraged buy-out, Icahn's group increased its stake to 27 percent and offered to acquire the company in a two-step transaction that would reduce their capital needs. Under the terms of the Icahn proposal, ACF's WKM division, a manufacturer of oil-field equipment valued at more than $200 million, would be spun off to ACF's shareholders. Icahn would then pay $31 per share for the remainder of ACF.

In an effort to buy time, ACF proposed a standstill agreement that would keep Icahn at bay while management searched for a more appealing suitor. Considering that the standstill would require Icahn to freeze his offensive in midstream, a concession that left him unnerved, he deliberated over every line of the agreement. Although he was ill, and confined to bed at the time, Icahn quarterbacked every move attorney Ted Altman made in negotiating with ACF in his behalf. Ultimately, an agreement was signed in September 1983, giving the company seven months to find another buyer. Icahn retained the right, however, to compete against any higher bid secured by ACF. In effect, Icahn had the best of both worlds: He would sit by as ACF scoured the market for a richer deal, thus boosting the value of his holdings, and he could work to strengthen his own financing should he decide to outbid all comers and seize the company for himself.

In January 1984, ACF's management launched round two by announcing it had worked out a leveraged buy-out with a new entity created by the investment banking firm of E.M. Warburg, Pincus & Company. The Pincus group would pay $50 a share in cash.

Clearly, ACF's management believed it had found the magic formula for keeping the company free of Icahn. At the time Burns announced, "We look forward to working with E.M. Warburg, Pincus in consummating this transaction as soon as possible and to a long and fruitful relationship once the transaction is completed."

Even after Icahn, exercising his right to make a competing

bid, offered $53 for ACF, management insisted that it preferred the Warbug, Pincus bid, which it would put to a shareholder vote in April. Shortly thereafter, Icahn raised his offer to $54.50 a share, a sum that would make him the winner in the bidding for ACF. Surprising many on Wall Street who had viewed Icahn's months of maneuvering as simply another attempt to raise his profits before bailing out, Icahn agreed to purchase the company for $405 million. As part of the financing package, ACF would sell the WKM division for $230 million. After approval by the shareholders, the deal was consummated in June 1984. With the company taken private, Icahn was named chairman, Kingsley vice chairman and Joseph Corr, an ACF executive who had caught Icahn's attention, was named president and a member of the board.

But Icahn didn't stop there. In a twist unusual even for the "creative financing" of the 1980s, he played two takeover attempts simultaneously, using the leverage of both to maximize his total return. At the same time that he was jousting with ACF, Icahn acquired about 5 percent of the stock of Greenwich, Connecticut-based Chesebrough Pond's, Inc., the diversified consumer products company that counted Q-Tips and Vaseline among its premier brands.

The move on Chesebrough took a most unorthodox turn. In the course of the negotiations, Icahn made it clear that whatever else he got, he wanted Chesebrough's choice box at the U.S. Open tennis matches. For the high rollers in New York's financial community, a premier box at the Open is a requisite status symbol, ranking up there with an entry in the Forbes 400. Because Open boxes rarely came on the market, even the rich and powerful have to resort to creative methods to get one.

Sitting by Foxfield's English gardens and outdoor tennis court, Icahn, deep in discussions with Chesebrough's CEO Ralph Ward, complained that the corporate elite were up to their ears in perks, so much so that they monopolized the seating at the Open. Responding that tennis is a "wimp sport," as Icahn recalls it, Ward offered to give the raider the seats.

Throughout July, Icahn and Chesebrough engaged in negotiations. Then in August, Chesebrough agreed to purchase

Icahn's block of stock at $38.1 a share, the NYSE closing price on the day of the transaction, August 7. No premiums for Icahn? Well, not exactly. As part of the deal, Chesebrough agreed to buy ACF's Polymer Corp. unit, a Reading, Pennsylvania-based plastics manufacturer, for $95 million. After consummating the purchase, Chesebrough admitted it had been pressured into acquiring Polymer. Said a Chesebrough spokesperson: "It is fair to say we were not looking for a company like this."

When Icahn showed up to sign the papers cinching the stock sale and Polymer deal, he was told that the ownership of the U.S. Open box could not be assigned to him for legal reasons. At first Icahn threatened to walk out of the closing, but when his own lawyers backed up Chesebrough's claim, he agreed to complete the transaction and to move away from Chesebrough with the promise that they would always give the seats to him. (Ultimately, Icahn pulled strings with Open officials, getting the box assigned to his company.)

ACF laid the groundwork for Icahn's relationship with Drexel, Burnham, Lambert, which refinanced ACF at year-end 1984, taking out the bank loans in exchange for junk bonds and filling Icahn's coffers with an additional $150 million of takeover capital, known in Drexel parlance as a "blind war chest," meaning the raider could commit the capital as he saw fit without clearing his plans with Drexel.

Actually, Icahn's first contacts with Drexel dated back to 1980, when he was introduced by an intermediary to the firm's corporate finance executives. First impressions were hardly favorable. At the time the Drexel men viewed Icahn as a backwater figure fiddling around with "nickel dime deals." There were also concerns about Icahn's methods, specifically how close he came to crossing the line on securities laws. Although there was no evidence of wrongdoing, the feeling at the top was that this was someone Drexel could live without.

But by 1984 Icahn's star had risen significantly, and his acquisition of ACF did wonders for his respectability. This time when he was reintroduced to Drexel, they were interested. At first Drexel CEO Fred Josephs dispatched investment banker Leon Black, then a rising star, to build bridges to Icahn. When the financing proposal was on the table, Josephs got personally involved, working with Black to ice the deal.

From the outset, Drexel learned that Icahn would be a fee chiseler, pushing for discounted fees, for special terms, for concessions on every price that was quoted to him. Internally, Icahn was regarded as a difficult client; at the same time he was respected as the smartest of the corporate raiders, virtually all of whom had links to Drexel.

"I knew all the raiders of the era," said a former senior Drexel executive. "Boone Pickens, Jimmy Goldsmith, Saul Steinberg, and on and on. They all had their talents and they were all exceptionally smart. But Carl was the smartest of all.

"He was so smart I would find myself getting lost in conversation with him. We'd be talking about a transaction, and Carl, who is always studying every possible angle, no matter how remote, would say, 'Think of what would happen if A does X. If he does, then I'll do Y. But if I do Y and A does X, what happens if B does XY? In that case, I might have to do Z.'

"I could engage in this kind of chain thinking for maybe eight moves, but Carl was only getting warmed up at eight. He'd go on to think out fifteen, twenty, twenty-five scenarios. With Carl it was always classic chess. He was so bright, so determined, so tenacious, you just knew he was going to beat out A, B, C, or whoever he was up against. He was orders of magnitude above most everyone else."

This fit perfectly with Drexel's master plan to forge relationships with mavericks like Icahn who had the moxie to take on the corporate establishment and to propel the takeover boom that Mike Milken and his team were in business to finance. They knew the truly colossal deals were still waiting to be done.

Icahn crossed the threshold into the mega deal arena in February 1985 with a two-page letter to William C. Douce, chairman of the giant Phillips Petroleum Company. In the letter Icahn offered to buy Phillips through an $8.1 billion leveraged buy-out valued at

$55 a share. But in typical Icahn style, the letter included more than a friendly offer to buy a company. Were Phillips to reject the bid—which everyone on Wall Street believed Douce would do—Icahn threatened to launch a takeover.

As the terms of the confrontation took shape, Phillips's only means of avoiding a battle with the notorious Icahn was to buy all the outstanding stock for the same $55 a share Icahn was offering. Only then, Icahn promised, would he step aside, assuring himself of a handsome profit on his 7.5 million shares and leaving the company free of his clutches. It was a shrewd and calculating attack on a takeover target that had already been bloodied by another dreaded predator of the 1980s, Texas oilman Boone Pickens.

The story had begun the year before the Icahn move when Pickens, head of Amarillo-based Mesa Petroleum, little more than a gnat of a company in the oil patch, made the audacious announcement in December 1984 that it had acquired about 6 percent of Phillips shares and that the upstart company was on the verge of tendering for another 14.9 percent block of Phillips stock at $60 a share.

Since Phillips stock then hovered around $40, the bid promised to appeal to shareholders and to put the fear of God in management, which had heard more than it cared to of Pickens's pronouncements (eerily similar to Icahn's) touting himself as a great ally of the shareholders in a noble battle against entrenched management.

In this case, the essence of Pickens's message was that Phillips management had failed to realize the company's inherent value. To rectify this untenable situation, Mesa's canny and media-savvy chairman held out the specter of a three-stage seige: First he would acquire the 14.9 percent block of Phillips stock, then he would seek control of the company, and in the pièce de résistance, he would work to engineer a merger with another company whereby all Phillips stockholders would collect $60 a share.

Although Pickens's plan was predicted on a parcel of ifs, ands, and maybes, as well as on a flimsy package of securities to pay off shareholders, Phillips management knew that in the wild and woolly eighties the financial system was intoxicated with big deals and that with Wall Street's support, takeover artists could accomplish miracles. With this in mind, the Mesa threat was taken very seriously.

Acting immediately to ward off the raider, Douce hired an all-star cast of takeover specialists who had become the glamour boys of the decade. The defense team included investment banker Joe Fogg of Morgan Stanley and M&A legal whiz Martin Lipton, generally regarded as the father of the poison pill. Although Phillips appeared determined to repel the backwater arbitrageur from Amarillo by bombarding him with lawsuits and launching a media assault designed to paint him as a greedy opportunist, the advisers from Wall Street knew they could not win this one in the courts.

And so a complicated "recapitalization" plan was hatched, whereby Phillips shareholders could sell part of their stock back to the company for cash and securities. In a move reminiscent of the Dan River scheme to evade a predator, Phillips would issue new shares totalling about 32 percent of the stock, distributing this equity to an ESOP. Based on the notion that the employees would always side with management, the ESOP shares plus other blocks of stock loyal to management would give Phillips's reigning executives an iron-handed grip on the company.

To pacify Pickens, Phillips agreed to pay him $53 a share for his stake, which would yield a profit of nearly $90 million. Although Phillips insisted that the package of cash and securities it was offering to the other shareholders was also worth $53, Wall Street sources pegged the real value in the mid- to low-$40s. Once again the management of a major American corporation had acted to protect itself from a corporate raider. As the price of his deal, Pickens signed a standstill agreeing to keep his distance from Phillips for fifteen years.

But if the CEO and the board believed that the siege was over, the sigh of relief they let out at the sight of Pickens backing away (presumably smiling all the way to the bank) was premature. Once news of the peace treaty with the raider hit the Dow

Jones wire, Phillips stock—previously inflated by the prospect of a takeover—plummeted from the mid-$50s to the mid-$40s as uncertainty swirled around the recapitalization.

While the arbs and long-term shareholders were fuming over the stock's dizzying fall, Icahn recognized that once again the system had created an opportunity for profit. Believing that Phillips was still selling at about half its book value, and that it remained appealing prey for other takeover artists or acquisition-minded oil companies, Icahn saw that the time was right for a move on the company.

This took Pickens by surprise. Considering the psychological warfare that Phillips had waged against him—including the staging of anti-Pickens prayer meetings in and around Bartelsville—Pickens could hardly believe that Icahn was wading into this kind of hornet's nest. One informed source claims that Pickens, who had announced that he would move to Bartelsville were he able to take over Phillips, was warned that he'd be shot within the first month of his arrival.

But whether Icahn was aware of this or not, from his perspective such threats would be viewed as a sideshow. To Carl, Phillips was pure economics.

"Boone Pickens comes and he bids $60 for the stock," Icahn recalled. "He has the nerve to bid $60 for a stock when the stock is $37. It's a terrible thing. They say, 'Get out of here. We don't want you.' Just get lost and we will give you $90 or $100 million and you go away. He goes away. And then the real arrogance of this thing emerges. Management said we are turning down $60 because we want to give you $43. Well, that was contemptuous. Unthinkable.

"I was watching the situation and I said to myself, 'Look, something has to happen here.' I have been an investor for many years. I have done a lot of work in this area. I have read a lot of balance sheets. I took a look at Phillips's balance sheet and the cash flow, and I said this is worth more than $60. Boone Pickens is not stupid. He is not paying $60 for charity. He is not doing it because he wants to help us out. He is paying $60 because he thinks it is worth more.

"So I said, the stock is now $46, $47. Pickens is willing to pay $60 and they are willing to pay $43. Well, they have got to pay more. It's an insult to my intelligence."

With this, Icahn and his investors jumped into the stock in the waning days of 1984. A little more than a month later, in early February 1985, Icahn had acquired about 5 percent of Phillips and was set to launch his own attack. In a letter to Douce, relayed through Joe Fogg at Morgan Stanley, Icahn complained that the package being offered to the shareholders was "grossly inadequate." As an alternative, Icahn offered to purchase the company for $55 a share. However, if the company was willing to offer all of the shareholders a package worth $55, he would step aside.

As usual, however, a thunderbolt followed the offer: Should management reject his bid, Icahn was prepared to launch a proxy fight to quash the recap plan, along with its cozy ESOP provision, and to tender for all of the company's shares, 51 percent to be paid for in stock and the balance in debt instruments. The takeover offer would total $8.1 billion, dwarfing Icahn's previous attacks.

At first the Phillips team attempted to belittle Icahn. On one occasion Icahn called to speak to Douce, only to be told that he could not come to the phone. No offer was made to return the call. This left Icahn steaming. Bad blood between Icahn and Douce would drive both sides throughout the confrontation.

In addition, because Drexel was emerging as the new power on Wall Street, making its mark picking off the kind of blue-chip companies that had been served by Morgan for generations, a searing animosity between Morgan and Drexel also poisoned the air over the Phillips talks.

"Joe Fogg thought of Carl and us as the barbarians from hell," said a former Drexel managing director. "He made no attempt to deal with Carl on his own terms. Instead, Fogg always acted as if he was dealing with the chairman of a Fortune 50 company who always did everything prim and proper."

Assuming that a face-to-face confrontation with mighty Morgan Stanley would send Icahn away with his tail between his legs, Phillips arranged for Icahn to meet Fogg at Morgan's offices. The session was scheduled for 6 P.M. But Icahn, still assem-

bling financial reports being churned out by Kingsley, kept calling on the half hour with word that he would be delayed. By the
time he arrived, it was after 8 P.M.

The scene was surreal. Icahn, savvy, street smart, still very
much a kid from Queens, entered Morgan Stanley, the WASP
citadel of investment banking. Spit and polished in his dark suit,
Fogg looked the part of a Dickensian overseer granting an audience to a wayward clerk. Icahn, his suit slightly wrinkled, his tie
off center, was the picture of a man about to be excoriated. For
a moment Fogg must have believed he held the upper hand.
Surely, this Icahn could be intimidated.

As Icahn recalls, Fogg leaned across his desk, looked him
square in the eyes and said, "You say you want to buy one of the
largest oil companies in the world. That's preposterous. What
the hell do you know about the oil business?"

Whatever Fogg was attempting to accomplish, he could
never have anticipated Icahn's response.

"You don't understand, Joe, I'm not here for an interview."

Kingsley was equally irreverent.

"Morgan Stanley had sent us this questionnaire," he recalled. "Oh, it must have been two or three pages of questions.
'Will you be going to move the company out of Bartlesville?
What's your background in the oil business?' When we met with
them, they said they wanted to know if we were 'good applicants.'

"That's when I said, 'Cash! We have cash. That's all we
need to be good applicants. We'll hire people who know about
the oil business.' "

On the legal front, Icahn matched Phillips with high-priced
talent, and then some.

"By the time Icahn surfaced, Phillips had already cut a deal
with Pickens, so they thought Icahn was a scavenger working on
the pickings," said Denzil Garrison, a local Bartlesville lawyer
who represented Phillips in the early rounds. "But I'll tell you,
Carl had a ton of lawyers down here. Maybe twenty. New York
lawyers and Oklahoma lawyers. They were all dressed in their

dark suits, and hell, I was wearing a sport coat and I felt like I was walking into the lion's den.

"We filed suit here to try to enjoin Icahn's takeover attempt. The grounds were that such a takeover was not in the public interest. The fact is we were trying to create some new law, and we weren't very successful at it. A federal judge threw out the case when it got to Tulsa."

Although Phillips was learning that it had to contend with Icahn, management didn't know that behind the scenes Ivan Boesky was secretly jockeying to form an alliance with the raider in the hope of driving up the price of the stock. Boesky's motive was clear: As a major buyer of Phillips during the Pickens raid, he was sitting with a big position that had dropped nearly $10 per share in the aftermath.

On the last Friday of December 1984, Boesky—whose Mt. Kisco, New York, estate was only minutes away from Icahn's Bedford Ponderosa—invited Carl to visit him at his home the following Sunday. The proposed topic of conversation: Phillips Petroleum.

"He said that I really should look at Phillips because the company had really done a very bad thing in turning down the Mesa deal and coming up with this recapitalization that was very inadequate," Icahn recalled. "He felt that the stock was cheap . . . and he was very upset about it. . . ."

Meeting in a breakfast room of the Boesky estate, Icahn, Kingsley, Boesky, and a Shearson Lehman energy analyst talked over the current state of Phillips. The consensus: Phillips remained an attractive stock, primarily because the recap plan was too cheap and would have to be sweetened. From Boesky's perspective, the best way to draw out the sweetening was to unleash Icahn the intimidator on Douce and his board, pressuring them to raise the ante. This would spike up the stock, wiping out Boesky's loss and putting him in the black.

But apparently, Boesky wanted even more. According to Icahn, about an hour into the meeting, "Ivan the terrible" proposed a partnership.

"He discussed that maybe we should do something together . . . being partners to make something happen," Icahn recalled. "To buy stock and sort of get the company to sweeten the deal. . . ."

The response was not what Boesky had been hoping for.

Icahn said, "I remember telling him that, generally, I don't like having partners in these deals, and that for him to be a partner of significance in such a situation, he'd have to come up with at least $150 million. And he said that was a lot because he already had stock in it. And then I said, 'Well, if you don't do that, I really don't like having partners because it's difficult doing these deals.' I'd never done it before except where I controlled the whole situation."

At this point Icahn was uncertain if Boesky had the money to form an alliance with him. But Carl was willing to hold out the possibility of a "partnership" with the hope of using Boesky's money to buy more Phillips stock.

The meeting adjourned without an agreement and, more important, without Icahn letting on he had already purchased a block of Phillips shares and was considering an assault on the company. Because Icahn had no agreement with Boesky of any kind, he saw no reason to tell him anything of substance. But Ivan, who was wired into the Wall Street rumor mill like no one else, soon learned of Icahn's position in Phillips. Furious, he called Icahn, charging that he had been double-crossed.

"I first asked whether or not he indeed was buying any Phillips, and he said he was," Boesky recalled. "That's why I was taken aback because I said, 'Well, I would have thought that you would have extended the courtesy of letting me know that you were going to do that, having discussed the matter together.' . . . I was a little peeved at the time."

Icahn viewed the call as an attempt by an anxious arb to get a fix on where the stock was headed.

Clearly, Boesky was fishing for information about Icahn's intentions, knowing what Carl did or did not do would have a major impact on the price of Phillips stock.

"Ivan was always mirroring deals other guys did," said a former Drexel investment banker. "If Carl was buying, Ivan would want to buy. If Carl was selling, Ivan would want to sell. He was a magnet for information. That's how he operated."

For days Boesky called Icahn—sometimes several times a day—cajoling, badgering, asking the same questions over and over again. But Icahn remained tight-lipped. "Look, Ivan," he said, "I don't know what I'm going to do. You're not my partner. You didn't put up $150 million. . . ."

On January 28, about a week before announcing his Phillips tender offer, Icahn did agree to purchase 2.7 million Phillips shares from Boesky. But even then Boesky discovered the futility of trying to manipulate Icahn.

Referring to Carl's agreement to purchase his stock, Boesky asked, "Well, what if you buy it and then sell out at a higher price? What if you buy the stock here, the two million, and you sell it at 50 or something, back to the company. . . . Would you give me any?"

Boesky, one of the shrewdest operators on Wall Street, was trying to cut himself a slice of Icahn's profits. If he seriously expected to get anywhere with Carl, he grossly underestimated the guy on the other end of the line, who responded to his request with a terse "No, not at all. Why the hell should I? You didn't marry my daughter."

"In his heyday, Boesky had feelers out to everyone on every deal," said the former Drexel managing director who worked on the Phillips deal. "He was all over the place—a buyer, a seller, a trader, a conduit of information. He was so pervasive, it was spooky. We used to think of him as the Wizard of Oz.

"And he was very clever, but surely he miscalculated Icahn when he thought Carl would do anything for him. Drexel would come to his aid because Ivan was one of Milken's best customers. He'd buy junk, he'd sell junk, if we needed a job to be done, Ivan would do it. So we wanted to take care of Boesky. But Carl never felt any such need. Carl is always so into himself, he doesn't think about helping someone else. He won't give you ice in the winter."

The Boesky block gave Carl greater leverage in his takeover bid and, as a backup, provided a greater profit opportunity should another raider or corporate suitor make a run at Phillips. At this point, Minneapolis-based takeover artist Irwin Jacobs (aka "Irv the Liquidator") had a stake in Phillips, and Penzoil was also known to be sniffing around. If either one, or others waiting in the wings, made a move on the company, the stock price would soar, giving Icahn a profitable exit.

He knew, though, that he was maneuvering in treacherous waters and that circumstances could change rapidly. His bet was that Jacobs was going to remain a passive player, angling to earn a profit from the sidelines. And although Penzoil was talking to Phillips, a bid did not appear to be forthcoming. So Icahn decided to act.

On a Sunday morning in early February, Carl plotted strategy with investment bankers from Donaldson, Lufkin, Jenrette (DLJ) and Drexel, Burnham, Lambert. Drexel, which had already backed hostile raids on Gulf Oil and Disney, was champing at the bit to pick up with Phillips where Pickens had left off. Mounting an all-out attack on Phillips promised huge fees and the opportunity to bail out Boesky.

"At this time, we already viewed ourselves as invincible," said the Drexel managing director. "We were confident that anything we would take on would work. With the Gulf deal behind us, Phillips, another oil company, loomed as the ideal target.

"The only thing we had to decide was who to unleash on Phillips. But after talking among ourselves and to a number of candidates, we realized that a deal of this proportion, going against a card-carrying member of the corporate establishment, would take a tough motherfucker who would be oblivious to the heat. An unstoppable force. When we thought of it that way, only one name seemed right: Carl Icahn."

Contact with Icahn actually began with a call from Icahn to Leon Black, with Carl musing on the Phillips situation. At this point, the arbs—who held much of the Phillips stock—were bashing the recap plan, waiting for someone to pick up the ball. Initially, Black took little stock in Icahn's call, knowing from experience that Icahn was always looking at dozens of opportunities. But in a flurry of follow-up calls, and a subsequent meeting at Icahn's offices with Black, Drexel's M&A chief David Kaye, and managing director John Sorte, the Drexel men started to believe that this was more than Carl thinking out loud. He was prepared to make a move.

As Icahn was contemplating his options, though, he was talking to DLJ as well as Drexel. This connection had come about only weeks before through a chance meeting with Jocelyn Javits, whose great uncle, Jacob Javits, served as U.S. Senator from New York. Mingling with Icahn at a cocktail party, Jocelyn used the opportunity to drum up business for her firm, DLJ, by offering to set up a meeting between Carl and Donaldson's people, including respected oil analyst Kurt Wolff. Soon after, the Sunday session was arranged.

Immediately the participants—which, at Icahn's request, included Drexel Burnham—started airing their Phillips strategies. Donaldson's approach was purely tactical: Icahn should proceed full-steam ahead with a proxy fight, convincing the shareholders to reject the recap plan on the grounds that it was too cheap and therefore contrary to their best interests.

But Drexel proposed a proxy coupled with a tender offer. Once the investment bankers put their proposals on the table, the squabbling started. Donaldson, which viewed Drexel as invading their turf, belittled the tender idea, insisting that a proxy against the recap was sufficient to kill it. For its part, Drexel countered that Donaldson's plan was half-baked and would collapse in the marketplace. From Drexel's hard-nosed viewpoint, the Donaldson plan was toothless.

"DLJ's approach was the stupidest idea I'd ever heard," said the Drexel managing director. "A proxy without an offer would have amounted to bullshit, totally lacking in credibility.

"You have to understand that at the time, Icahn was still a bit player. All of his previous deals were on a relatively small scale. Here he is going to take on one of the bulwarks of the corporate club—the goddamn Phillips Petroleum Company—and if he's going to get anywhere he'd better go with a hell of an attack. A proxy without a tender offer just wasn't going to cut it."

Kingsley agreed, saying at one point, "Look, just a proxy fight. People will laugh at you if you say that. . . ."

Drexel's plan would be a momentous step, launching, in a decade already known for the megadeal, the daddy of all hostile tenders, requiring a staggering $8 billion. Could it be done? DLJ was skeptical. But Drexel had Mike Milken and Milken had his junk bond network and although he had never raised anything close to $8 billion, Milken was confident.

Behind the scenes, an interesting component of the Icahn/Drexel strategy unfolded. Rather than seeking commitments from its junk bond buyers in anticipation of the deal—thus requiring him to pay substantial fees up front—Icahn suggested that Drexel simply provide him with a commitment letter of its own. From Icahn's perspective, there was little risk to Drexel, which was certain it could raise the money.

But even fast-and-loose Drexel was unwilling to go out on that kind of limb. Making a point-blank declaration that it would raise the money would force Drexel to take a charge on the firm's capital. Were the firm unable to raise the sum from outside sources, it could be forced to draw down its own cash, thus putting it in jeopardy.

As negotiations with Icahn continued, Leon Black huddled with Carl at his offices, placing dozens of phone calls to Fred Josephs, then head of Drexel's corporate finance department. The goal was to come up with a letter that would "make a commitment without making a commitment." To this end, all sorts of possibilities were raised. "We feel confident we can raise the money" looked like a strong possibility. As did "We believe we can raise the money." But as close as this language came to making the point, it somehow missed the mark. Only when Leon Black came up with the idea that Drexel would say it was "highly confident" that it could raise the financing did lightning strike. Instantly everyone knew they had hit upon the magic words.

But so new was the concept that Josephs, still three months away from being appointed Drexel's CEO, felt the need to seek approval from the firm's chief operating officer. Josephs also pressed Black to make certain the letter would not fail. If Drexel was going to put its credibility on the line, it would have to deliver. With that ultimatum, Black had his marching orders to confirm with the junk-bond salesmen, up to and including Milken, that the financing could be raised. As enthusiastic as Black was over the idea he had concocted, he wouldn't be selling the paper. Josephs wanted to be sure that the Drexel team charged with that responsibility would deliver. Quickly, Black checked with the troops and reported that the money was as good as gold. With that, the "highly confident" letter was signed, putting the deal in motion.

Or so it seemed. But the next day, the always unpredictable Icahn decided that, on second thought, the wording was not strong enough and he wasn't proceeding with the deal. At this point, Icahn was striking in two directions. He was making a last-ditch effort to press Drexel into biting the bullet and making an even stronger commitment. At the same time, he was still uncertain whether he wanted to pay for the "highly confident" letter—for which Drexel would charge him $1 million—or to go with DLJ's proxy-only plan.

In deliberating over the issue, Icahn consulted with his lawyer, Ted Altman, who advised him that the "highly confident" language had little strength as a legal document. Were Drexel unable to deliver the financing, Icahn would have no recourse, and in fact, would look like a fool. But Altman also reminded Icahn that Drexel had a reputation as a firm that could deliver on its pledges. With the ACF financing a fait accompli, Icahn had every reason to believe in Drexel's commitment. A day after holding up the works, and after seeing that Drexel was determined to draw the line at "highly confident," Icahn gave the green light.

At this juncture in American business history, Drexel Burnham was a financial powerhouse of extraordinary proportions. Although the firm was detested by the business establishment, which considered it the command post for a Wall Street mafia that was rewriting the rules of finance and in the process intimidating corporate management, Drexel was universally respected for its awesome ability to raise capital. In time, when

Drexel, via Milken, said that it was "highly confident" of the ability to finance a deal, the world would view the assurance as an iron-clad guarantee.

At the time of the Phillips deal, however, the concept was new and untested. Capitalizing on this, Phillips ridiculed the Drexel letter as a worthless piece of paper that proved Icahn lacked the financing to consummate a tender offer. That was the word Phillips received from its investment bankers at Morgan Stanley, who, with their white-shoe mentality, had little respect for Drexel Burnham, which it viewed as Wall Street's version of a house of ill repute. With Morgan still locked in the time warp of a more genteel era, Drexel's fast-and-loose style, inventing as it went along, was repugnant to everything Morgan stood for.

"In the tradition of investment banking I grew up in, you had a commitment or you didn't have a commitment," says a Morgan investment banker. "Where you had a commitment, a financial institution would issue a letter stating so. In effect, you had a guarantee. In contrast, the 'highly confident' letter was simply an opinion that a firm could get the financing, but there was no guarantee. So we didn't take the letter very seriously."

With Drexel sending up a trial balloon on a revolutionary form of financing, one would think that Josephs and his team would be holding their breath, praying that tactic didn't blow up in their faces. But Drexel's self-image as an invincible power was growing day by day, deal by deal, and there wasn't a moment of second-guessing.

"We felt just as the letter said, 'highly confident' that we could raise the money," says the former Drexel executive. "When Mike Milken said we could do it, we believed it. We figured, 'What does Morgan Stanley know about junk bonds?' We were the only guys on Wall Street who knew how to use them."

After Phillips took out newspaper ads portraying Icahn as a paper tiger, Carl agreed to pay Drexel $7.5 million in fees to go beyond the "highly confident" letter and to secure commitments from Milken's junk bond buyers. The way the deal was structured, Icahn would have to pay the investors ⅜ of 1 percent of the money they pledged if the deal went through, ⅛ of 1 percent if the deal fell apart after the funds were pledged. On top of this, Drexel would be entitled to 20 percent of the profits (known as the "ups" in Drexel parlance) when Icahn sold his Phillips shares.

Based on this rock-solid financing, Icahn counter-attacked with newspaper ads of his own, declaring in the *Wall Street Journal*'s February 20, 1985, edition:

> MY TENDER OFFER IS FOR REAL.
>
> I announced on February 15 that the investment banking firm of Drexel Burnham Lambert had already obtained $1.5 billion in commitments for my tender offer financing—all in 48 hours. . . . In addition, ACF Industries and other of my affiliates are putting up $400 million of Phillips shares as a portion of the equity needed to support the financing. I also announced yesterday that I have given Drexel instructions to obtain the balance of the financing for the tender offer upon defeat of the board's recapitalization plan, and that I will deposit in escrow $102 million, $15.5 million to be paid to Drexel and the institutions committing to the tender offer as commitment fees when the conditions of the tender offer are met, and $86.5 million to be paid to Drexel as financing fees when the tendered shares are purchased. The question now remaining is whether Drexel Burnham can perform. Drexel has stated they are highly confident they can—so am I!

At a secret meeting with Drexel, Phillips advisers tried to halt the Icahn juggernaut by sweetening its offer just a bit. At that point Drexel stated that the offer was still inadequate and that Phillips would have to tack at least $2 per share to its price. When the Phillips negotiators complained that they had gone an extra mile to make a deal and that they couldn't see any way that the price could be spiked up any higher, a Drexel man jumped in, saying, "We know how to do it. We'll do the junk bond offering for Phillips." An icy silence made it clear that the message had sunk in.

By the time of Icahn's announcement, Drexel had lined up an impressive clique of investors that included First City Financial, controlled by the Canadian-based Belzberg family ($187.5 million commitment); Reliance Insurance Co., controlled by Saul Steinberg ($60 million); Pacific Investment Management Co. ($145.3 million); and Kemper Investors Life Insurance Co. ($50 million). Among the forty-seven investors listed in a February SEC filing, many were in the deal for two reasons: to collect the commitment fees due them even if Icahn failed to take over Phillips and, in a secret agenda, to give credence to his takeover threat. Because many of the backers assembled by Drexel had Phillips blocks of their own, they were eager to see Icahn force Phillips to sweeten its recap offer. By standing behind Icahn with a treasury of cash, most believed that Phillips would indeed blink and that the battle would be won without cashing in a dollar of commitments.

As part of this plot, and to give further credence to its "highly confident" claim, Drexel intentionally omitted some of its biggest investors from the original list of junk bond buyers.

"The investors' names would have to be filed with the SEC and we knew everyone would be checking the list to see who was on it," said the former Drexel executive. "So we left out some of our biggest names, like First Executive and financier Carl Lindner. The idea being that Phillips and others wouldn't think we were tapped out in arranging for the initial commitments. Seeing that the likes of Lindner and First Executive were not included in the initial wave would be a sure sign that we had even bigger guns ready to join the battle."

As Icahn and Drexel proceeded on this basis, they were setting a critical precedent for the takeover binge that terrorized American business in the 1980s. The Phillips deal represented the first time that the banking community was excluded from a major M&A transaction. Considering Drexel's awesome clout, represented by Milken's junk bond investors, the mighty money center banks were dispensable. This gave raiders more power than ever. Whereas once they had to pick their way through a patchwork of sensitive banking relationships, complicated by the fact that no bank would finance a hostile takeover of a major client, they could now detour around all of that.

"The banks used to put raiders through a gauntlet," said the former Drexel man. "They would worry about conflicts. They would worry about the caliber of the guy they were bankrolling. They would worry about the guy's image in the business community.

"But there was none of that with Milken. He'd finance the entire capital structure so there'd be no need for any other source in the deal. With Mike it was one-stop shopping.

"And Mike never worried about conflicts or image or any of that etiquette crap. If a guy could pay the fees and get the job done, Mike would back him. That was a godsend for guys like Icahn. They weren't big deals when they got started with Drexel, but we kept feeding them and feeding them, and as in *Little Shop of Horrors*, they kept getting bigger and bigger.

"Carl was never part of the Drexel inner circle. He was never one of the boys, as was Boesky. Carl was always his own man. But he had a wonderful banker in Drexel. When he needed to finance a deal, he would call Leon Black, who served as gatekeeper for Milken. Carl would call Black and Black would call Mike and Mike would make the decision."

On Saturday evening, February 9, Icahn held a cocktail party at his house. The guests included Ivan Boesky. After a few moments of idle chatter, the two men slipped away into Icahn's library to talk about the Phillips deal. Once again Boesky raised the issue of tackling Phillips as partners. They agreed to meet the next night at the offices of Carl's lawyer, Gordon Horwitz, to discuss the matter further. But as before, the talks about some kind of partnership arrangement went nowhere.

At this point Icahn wrote off Boesky as all talk, no action, when it came to Phillips. Either he lacked the money to play on the level Icahn was demanding, or he lacked the guts to take a high-profile role in a hostile tender. The more Icahn watched Boesky dance around the sidelines, the more he pegged him as a scavenger for information and nothing more.

Still, Boesky put himself back into the Phillips action by acquiring another block of stock, based, apparently, on his conviction that Icahn was on to something.

"The man [Icahn] bought two million shares, that's pretty good," Boesky said, reflecting on his decision. "He's a pretty smart investor. Maybe I made a mistake. Maybe I sold too much. Maybe I should keep a little bit more. You know, maybe he sees more value in it than I do. I respect his judgment."

Now back in the Phillips arena, Boesky tried to quarterback the deal by telling Carl how to gain credibility for his tender offer. Once again his meddling met with an icy response. The idea that he should take lessons from Boesky hardly sat well with Icahn.

At the same time, Icahn claims he was hearing from another armchair quarterback, a mysterious deep throat who seemed to have radar on Carl, allegedly calling him on a private number in Bedford and tracking him, on vacation, to a hotel line in Palm Beach.

"This guy . . ." Icahn recalled, "said his group . . . is going to make an offer for my stock. So I said, 'Who the hell are you?' He said, 'When the time comes, you will know.' He didn't give me inside information about the company, but he knows the facts backwards and forwards about the company. . . . Normally, I wouldn't talk to people like this, but there is something about it that makes me stay with it. . . . He really knows the company. . . . I pride myself in being an analyst. . . . I think I know Phillips probably better than anybody outside of Phillips and probably a lot better than many of those inside. This guy knows it better than I do. . . . He knows a lot more than any arbitrageur would. . . ."

The moment Icahn announced his intention to launch a hostile tender offer, Phillips countered with lawsuits charging the raider with violating the securities laws. But at the same time it was mounting a barrage of litigation, the company was also taking practical steps to protect itself. First, it sugar-coated the initial recap plan with goodies that it claimed sweetened the offer by $2 a share—a claim Wall Street discounted, viewing the sweetener as worth about $1. On a second front, Phillips authorized use of a poison pill. The way it was structured, if a buyer acquired at least 30 percent of Phillips stock, the shareholders would be entitled to exchange their stock for debt instruments valued at $62 a share. The pill's toxin stemmed from the fact that the 30-percent buyer would be the only shareholder ineligible for the $62 in notes. Even worse, he would face huge debt as he was forced to make good on the commitment to the other stockholders.

This seemed to be a good time for Icahn to cash in the modest profit he had made on the rise in Phillips shares to date. But instead he plowed ahead, motivated by the profit motive and by rage that the system, this time reflected in the poison pill, would further entrench management at the expense of the shareholders.

"The poison pill is what I consider to be legal trickery," Icahn said. "What it amounts to is a law firm trying to rewrite the law. One law firm said at the time that the law should be changed to bar any shareholder from buying more than 20 percent of a public company. Well, the law wasn't changed, so they put the poison pill in effect. The pill said that if anybody bought more than 30 percent of Phillips, the company would turn into a debt instrument. Anybody who owns shares gets $62 of debt, which is ridiculous."

Determined to keep moving the chess pieces, Icahn launched his proxy battle, exhorting the shareholders—most of whom, by this point, were arbs and institutions eager to keep the company in play—to vote against the recapitalization plan. Although Douce and his colleagues discounted Icahn's chances for victory, when the results of the voting were announced in early March, the recap was defeated. At that point Phillips—which kept saying that its previous offers represented full value for the shareholders—sweetened its offer again, this time to a package worth between $53 to $56 a share, and Icahn called off his tender offer. But in typical fashion, he "wanted more."

Quickly the action shifted to a Morgan Stanley conference room, where the Icahn and Phillips forces engaged in a marathon bargaining session that began shortly after seven o'clock in the evening. The key issue was Icahn's demand for $30 million in fees to cover his out-of-pocket expenses incurred in the Phillips attack. Although Phillips was prepared to pay a substantial sum, management drew the line at $25 million and demanded that it be linked to a ten-year standstill agreement, during which time neither Icahn nor Drexel could move against the company.

At first Icahn, acting unilaterally, agreed to a five-year standstill that would be binding both on himself and Drexel. But when Black and Sorte got wind of this, they objected vehemently. Meeting in a huge conference room that served as the evening's command post for Fogg and Marty Lipton, the Drexel team insisted that they would go no further than three years. They viewed Phillips as a fluid situation that would present new opportunities in the near future.

Phillips agreed to the Drexel time frame, but would not budge on the issue of fees. They would pay $25 million and not a penny more. But Icahn, who was betting that he could wear his adversaries down, had decided from the start to negotiate through the night, insisting on the $30 million figure and refusing to leave until he got his way. In what would become a trademark tactic, he had slept especially late the morning before and had napped in the afternoon, all with the idea of gaining an advantage over his opponents.

Just as Icahn had planned, the meeting dragged on and on, to midnight and then into the morning hours. Teams of lawyers and investment bankers, plates of cold and coagulated Chinese food all around them, shuttled back and forth between opposing sides, making offers and counteroffers. On two occasions—again true to his practiced shtick—Icahn stormed out shouting that he had had enough and was calling off the negotiations. The second time he was gone for over an hour, leading the Phillips team to believe that he might in fact make good on his threat. But then he returned, warning his adversaries that his patience had worn thin and that an acceptable offer had better be placed on the table. But even so, Phillips held the line at $25 million.

"Icahn knew that the chances of getting the $30 million were slim," said the former Drexel man. "But you can't blame a guy for trying.

"You have to understand the way Carl thinks. He probably said to himself, 'Maybe I won't get $30 million. Maybe I'll only get $26 million. But is it worth staying up an extra few hours to make a million bucks? You bet it is.' "

Unknown to Icahn, he might well have succeeded in his efforts had he prolonged the negotiations into the following day. That's because the Phillips board had held a secret session right before the negotiations began. The purpose: to set limits for Fogg, Lipton, and others representing the company at the Icahn meeting. The number settled on, $25 million, could not be exceeded without approval by the board, whose members were asleep in their respective houses and hotel rooms during the all-night marathon. No matter how great a show Icahn put on, the Phillips team was unable to go beyond the $25-million limit. But had Icahn really abandoned the talks, leaving with the threat of a resumed tender offer, chances are Douce would have rewired the board and found another few million.

Still, Icahn fared superbly, walking away with the $25 million expense check plus profits on his Phillips stock of more than $50 million—all earned over a period of less than three months.

Although the public and the press viewed the Phillips battle as another chapter in the eighties saga of rich takeover barons getting richer and public companies getting raped, the story is more complicated. In many of the confrontations between raiders and corporate management, the shareholders benefited from a sharp and rapid rise in the value of their stock. This could not have happened unless a wealthy and persistent individual, driven by the lure of profit, was willing to take on the corporate establishment whether he cared about his fellow shareholders or not. And in what would make Phillips a watershed event, the shareholders soundly defeated the kind of management-supported plan that in the past rarely succumbed to a challenge. With Icahn as their cheerleader, the Phillips shareholders were effectively saying to management: "Our opinion of what is best for us is much more valid than yours."

For its part, Phillips management debunked the idea that the Icahns of the world brought anything of enduring value to the company or the shareholders. As each side made their points, they reflected, in microcosm, a great national debate flaring over the issue of corporate takeovers that were changing the landscape of American industry. To a growing number of observers, the binge of corporate raids was a threat to jobs, to capitalism, to the American way of life. As the great names of U.S. industry, from Gulf Oil to Walt Disney, fell prey to a new breed of capitalist who earned Carnegie-sized fortunes by intimidating and dismantling free enterprise, a grass-roots wave of concern swept across the nation and into the halls of Congress. Motivated by fear of mass unemployment as raiders broke up venerable corporations, by concern for the great American company and by outright envy over the raiders' nouveau wealth, constituents urged their representatives to do something to restore "order" to the system.

It was against this backdrop that a congressional subcommittee convened to look into the question of whether legislation was appropriate to curb or limit corporate takeovers. The ongoing battle for Phillips Petroleum was at the heart of the issue.

As subcommittee chairman Timothy Wirth asked, "Is fear of takeovers simply paranoia on the part of corporate managers? Does it reflect the desire of corporate managers to insulate themselves and protect their jobs, or are corporate managers justified in taking steps to protect corporate assets from raiders such as Mr. Pickens and Mr. Icahn, whose desire, they argue, is simply to turn a quick profit in the market at the expense of companies, employees, other shareholders, and the long-term economy?"

For the most part, the infamous financial engineers of the eighties viewed these public forums as witch-hunts to be avoided at all costs. "Why," the thinking went, "subject yourself to the pious rumblings of liberal politicians seeking to win points by taking on the laissez-faire capitalists." But Icahn—whose knowledge of history and keen intellect distinguished him from his peers, relished the opportunity to justify takeovers by turning the tables on his critics.

In his testimony, Icahn used a historical example to illustrate his point that poorly managed companies die not when they are challenged but when they are shielded from challenge.

"Did any raider take over Chrysler?* Did any raider take over the railroads? And yet these companies had to be closed down. . . . Thousands and thousands of people, indeed a whole section of this country, has been closed down . . . *not because raiders came in but because raiders did not come in.*" (italics added)

Not surprisingly, Phillips viewed the issue from the other end of the spectrum. In a speech, "The Pirates of Profitability," Phillips Executive Vice President C. M. Kittrell attacked Icahn and his fellow corporate raiders for raping the shareholders.

"Mr. Pickens and Mr. Icahn claim they reaped a windfall for Phillips shareholders. And to some degree that's true. In the short term they did help drive up the price of Phillips stock, which benefited all shareholders.

"These benefits can be quantified. But what about the costs of a hostile raid? They're not so easy to determine.

"When money is diverted from research, exploration, construction, jobs, and charitable contributions in order to pay an immediate shareholder premium . . . to what degree will shareholders, and consumers, bear these costs in the long run?

"And to what extent is the long-term strength of a company—and its ability to serve shareholders, employees, and communities—undermined?

"In Phillips's case, we will not know the answer to these questions for many years, if ever.

"But there's one thing we know today; corporate raiders who say they represent shareholders . . . represent them, not by proxy, but by piracy, and they do so at great risk to everyone but themselves.

---

*Chrysler never closed down but went into bankruptcy before being bailed out by the government.

"As such, they are nothing more than pirates of profitability."

The argument between Icahn and Phillips had as much to do with power as with economics. For generations, America's corporate establishment had ruled virtually without challenge. But suddenly, CEOs across the nation found themselves being held accountable by a new breed of capitalists who in case after case had seized power with proxy battles and tender offers. The charge that these raiders (who were clearly threats to the CEOs' privileged status) were wholly evil forces was simplistic and self-serving. Although the Icahns of the world were, in a sense, pirates in search of instant profits, the threat they posed to corporate management came as a wake-up call that, slowly but inevitably, would force the corporate community to be more responsive to shareholders. This evolution, still underway today, is evident in the pressure being brought to bear on corporate boards to reduce the princely salaries of chief executives, or at least to tie compensation to the companies' financial performance. Although excesses of the financial engineers would bring hardship to once grand companies forced to assume excessive debt, the shake-up of insulated and imperious management was long overdue.

In the end, there was one issue no one would argue about. Icahn's extraordinary tenacity and resourcefulness had produced an enormous profit. He had tested his manifesto on one of the largest corporations in the world, and he had emerged victorious.

In retrospect, Phillips was a watershed deal, for both the evolution of Carl Icahn and the M&A craze that defined the decade.

"Before Phillips, Carl Icahn was just Carl Icahn—a successful takeover guy with brass balls and a pretty good record for getting things done," said the former Drexel managing director. "But after Phillips, Carl became *the* Carl Icahn. The deal firmly established his image as the best intimidator, the best takeover practitioner around.

"Think about it this way. For Pickens, a creature of the oil patch, to launch an assault on Phillips was audacious. But for Carl Icahn, this Wall Street operative who'd never even seen an oil well and who had no ties to the business establishment, to attack Phillips, that was unholy, incredible, awesome. And it was proof positive that in the eighties, there were no rules, no boundaries, no limits on what a guy with the right weapons could do."

With ACF and now Phillips, Icahn also recognized the enormous firepower of having Drexel, this virtually unlimited bank, lined up behind him. In the early eighties, before junk bond financing became widely available, Icahn had established himself as a force to be reckoned with, using the modest resources that were available to him. After junk bonds, the man didn't change, but the scale of what he could and did accomplish changed dramatically.

But every action has an equal and opposite reaction. On the one hand, the Phillips deal was a coming-out party for the increasingly powerful financial engineers of the Roaring Eighties. But equally important, the spotlight that the deal cast on Drexel would come to haunt the firm and the takeover bullies it backed with such ruthless abandon. When the names of Drexel's institutional investors reached the Capitol, Congress was shocked to find that savings and loans were investing in junk-bond financed takeovers. Considering that Phillips was a high profile company with high-powered lobbying, the Icahn attack would stir up a hornet's nest in the House, subjecting Drexel to intense regulatory scrutiny and producing antitakeover roadblocks all over the place. Ironically, Drexel was so intoxicated by its success at Phillips that it was blinded to the price it would have to pay for it.

Although Icahn would go on to attack even greater names than Phillips, there is evidence that he recognized all along that there were limits to how far a raider could go in threatening the bedrock of the corporate establishment.

In the mid-80s, Kingsley brought Icahn two deals he thought were guaranteed winners. The only problem was that they required attacks on the best-known companies in America—AT&T and General Motors.

When Kingsley touted AT&T to Icahn, he based his pitch on the premise that they could buy the behemoth for $22 billion, and then quickly extract $12 billion from an overfunded pension fund, replacing much of the excess cash with annuities. But Icahn wasn't biting—not for a takeover attempt. Although he did acquire more than 30 million shares, he stopped there, feeling that a tender for one of the corporate elite, considered to be part of the American fabric, would be crossing a line that raiders, for all their moxie, were advised not to trespass.

Similar thinking prevailed over the GM plan. Although Kingsley saw the company as a bargain, and was gung-ho about buying an enormous position, Icahn's answer was blunt and to the point. As Kingsley recalls it, Icahn sized up the idea in three words: "They'll hang us."

ICAHN VS.
LORENZO

The Taking of TWA

"There's no such thing as a 'gimme' with Carl. You know in golf, when your ball lands within a few inches of the hole, your opponent concedes the putt—it's a gimme. Not with Carl. Everything has to be negotiated. Everything has a price. I never heard Carl say, 'Hey, let's split the difference.' "
—SKADDEN, ARPS PARTNER JAMES FREUND

In the spring of 1985, Icahn attended the power event of the eighties, the annual Los Angeles junk-bond conference hosted by Drexel Burnham. At this ostentatious assemblage of financial Schwarzeneggers, mostly investors in Mike Milken's junk bonds and the raiders who used them to intimidate corporate America, Carl happened to hear a presentation by Robert Peiser, chief financial officer of Trans World Airlines, a relatively weak carrier that had been spun off from its parent company, Trans World Corporation, in February 1984. In the course of the presentation, Icahn found himself intrigued by the enormous cash-flow potential of a major carrier. Although he had fancied the idea of investing in an airline for years, this set the wheels in motion.

"The TWA guy's main point was that airlines are terrific cash generators," said Brian Freeman, an investment banker who would wind up playing a key role in the unfolding saga of Carl Icahn and TWA. "This was nothing Carl didn't already know. It was no secret. But it had the effect of focusing him on airlines."

Through the remainder of the conference, Icahn made the rounds, schmoozing with Drexel's high muckety-mucks, but all the while the TWA idea dominated his thoughts. At the time, he may have forgotten a conversation he'd had previously with Marty Whitman, a financial bottom fisherman who had made millions buying and selling the bonds of distressed companies. Knowing Whitman to be a shrewd, street-smart investor, Icahn took the opportunity to pick his brain about the airline business. As Whitman remembers the conversation, which occurred while the men were playing tennis at a club in Banksville, New York, Icahn said, "Hey, Marty, the airlines look pretty good, don't they?" To which Whitman responded, "They look pretty good to people who don't distinguish between gross cash flow and net cash flow."

Although Whitman's response was insightful, and would prove to be prophetic, Icahn dismissed it as an irrelevant wise-crack. He would attend the Drexel conference with the sense that there was something attractive about airlines in general, TWA in particular.

"I think TWA's former CEO Ed Meyer inadvertently gave Carl the idea of buying TWA," said Kent Scott, former head of the TWA pilots union. "In 1984, when Meyer was negotiating with the flight attendants, he boasted in a magazine piece that he had built up a $400 million cash horde to use if they went out on strike. This was what he needed to keep TWA afloat if the flight attendants shut things down. The cash gave him a strong bargaining chip, so he was bragging about it.

"I picture Carl sitting around his pool saying, 'Holy shit, Kingsley, get me the 10 K on TWA. We can probably buy that company with their own money.' "

Kingsley's research, produced soon after the Drexel bond conference, indicated that TWA was undervalued. In addition, a report prepared by an airline analyst concluded that a restructuring—principally the elimination of unprofitable routes and excess aircraft—could have a major impact on TWA's bottom line. But even more compelling to Icahn was the discovery that TWA, then on the verge of renegotiating its union contracts, stood a reasonable chance of winning substantial concessions.

Spurred by this confluence of positive fundamentals and promising omens, Icahn began buying TWA stock, purchasing his initial shares for $9.50 each, less than the company's book value. Convinced that he could capitalize on this critical spread as he had done so often before, Icahn accelerated his purchases, acquiring more than 5 percent of the outstanding shares by the end of April and roughly 20 percent by the first week of May.

By this time Icahn was being driven by dual forces. First and foremost was the opportunity for profit. "It's the old Graham Dodd philosophy," Icahn said. "He wrote the book in the thirties where you really buy these things when nobody wants them, and you have to sort of see that there is value there. . . .

"The value is there. I think it can be appreciated. It has a very good cash flow and the cash flow is very important in this situation. When you really analyze these companies, to get into it more deeply, depreciation isn't always true depreciation, and so when you look at earnings, it isn't always a true picture. . . . Cash flow is a much better picture . . . and TWA has good cash flow. . . . If you look ahead, I think they have to get concessions eventually with labor, and that is going to add a lot more to the cash flow and to the earnings."

But Icahn was enamored with more than the numbers. As he read about the company's glamorous history, including the tenure of its one-time owner Howard Hughes, he found himself succumbing to the romance of aviation. For a former bookworm from Bayswater, the prospect of commanding a global airline replete with an arsenal of jets and a small army of war-trained pilots was the stuff of Walter Mitty fantasies. So much so that a man who to this point had consciously eliminated emotion from his business decisions was about to violate his own principles.

On a practical level, TWA was a particularly vulnerable prey. Precisely because the beleaguered carrier, whose cumulative profits over the years had been virtually wiped out by an equal volume of losses, never expected to hear a raider knocking at the door, it had failed to install the legal defenses most of corporate America had already put in place.

Skadden, Arps partner Jim Freund, who represented TWA, said, "It had none of the shark repellents. . . . In particular, TWA did not have a staggered board; the directors could be removed without cause, and there was no provision outlawing shareholder action by written consent. Thus a raider had the ability to throw out the entire board in one fell swoop, without ever calling a shareholders' meeting. This is exactly the threat that Carl Icahn was to use throughout the whole affair, and it affected our strategy at all points along the way."

Icahn launched his assault on TWA with the usual bravado.

"Icahn meets with Ed Meyer, and he says to Carl, 'You can't take over this venerable company,' said Kent Scott. "Carl says, in effect, 'Just watch me.' Ed had no idea of corporate finance as it is practiced in the Manhattan jungles. Icahn had a bird he could pluck the feathers from."

In typical fashion Icahn presented a dizzying range of possible actions designed to befuddle and therefore thoroughly frighten TWA's management. As paraphrased by his lawyer, Weil Gotshal partner Steve Jacobs, Carl's 13-d filing declared that the raider is "currently evaluating his position; he may determine to seek control in the future, and he may explore the feasibility of making a proposal to TWA for a merger or business combination. . . . Icahn will also explore acquiring additional shares from time to time."

For Meyer, who had spent the bulk of his career managing an airline's internal dynamics, coming face to face with an external force like Carl Icahn was a new and disconcerting experience. "When you sat across the table from him, you got a picture of a guy who never answered a question straight," Meyer said. "He answered a question with a question. If there was an answer, it was buried in a long discourse."

Interestingly, Drexel Burnham was TWA's investment banker. Although the firm had few rules limiting its freewheeling activities, it did have a self-imposed ban on financing hostile raids on client companies. That didn't stop Wall Streeters from speculating that Drexel had set up TWA, filling Icahn's war chest and then leading him to the carrier at the West Coast bond conference. Although Drexel was not above that kind of double-dealing, the evidence suggests that Icahn was acting independently. In fact, when Fred Josephs heard that Icahn had acquired a major block in the airline, he tried to step between his clients, appealing to Icahn to back off. In doing so, Josephs presented himself as a friend with a word to the wise. Airlines are capital intensive and highly cyclical, he told Icahn, and this will give you more headaches than even you can take. "If God invented a business you cannot run," Josephs warned, "it's an airline."

Meyer too claims that he tried to dissuade Icahn from entering the airline business on the grounds that it was more difficult than it appeared from a distance. "I met with Icahn several times and each time I said, 'You don't want to get into this business,'" Meyer recalled. "He was mesmerized by the $400-500 million cash flow he saw in TWA. But I said, 'Carl, that won't even cover the airplanes you'll have to buy.'"

The last thing Drexel wanted was a war between two of its clients. But Drexel's conflicts were of no concern to Icahn. Nor did he give much thought to Josephs' advice to avoid the airline industry. He had already amassed a fortune pursuing his own instincts. The thought of taking his cue from paid advisers just rubbed him the wrong way.

In May, Icahn decided to seek control of TWA. Toward this end he arranged two meetings with Meyer to discuss his intentions and to assess management's response. At the meetings, Carl stressed the need to cut costs by selling up to $500 million of domestic assets. The idea was related to a consultant's report that called for eliminating most domestic flights that did not feed into TWA's main U.S. hubs in St. Louis and New York's Kennedy

Airport. The strategy was designed to concentrate on those routes that generated traffic for the carrier's more profitable overseas business.

Because this conflicted with a recently completed study conducted for TWA's management by Cresap, McCormick & Paget, Meyer and his senior aides attacked the Icahn plan. The Cresap strategy envisioned strengthening the domestic system in order to feed more traffic to the international routes. To achieve this, TWA had set aside the cash to buy new planes for domestic service. Since Icahn was thinking in terms of shrinking domestic assets and management favored a buildup, the discussions left both sides at polar extremes. Compromise seemed remote.

In an attempt to find common ground, Icahn and Meyer met first at a bar in the Waldorf Astoria. The men detested each other from the start. As a career corporate manager who had earned his stripes on the accounting side of the business, Meyer, a rather sober executive given to horn-rim glasses, struck Icahn as a man over his head. His mild manner and bookish appearance reinforced this impression. One can imagine Icahn thinking to himself, "What's a bean counter like this doing at the head of a global airline?"

According to Icahn, Meyer accused the raider of wanting a "fast buck." Icahn countered that Meyer's only interest was to protect his job. The two men left more disgusted with each other than before. As the carrier's major shareholder, Icahn was convinced that he would have to take control of the carrier in order to achieve substantive change in TWA's performance.

On May 21, Icahn submitted a letter to TWA, proposing to pay $18 a share for all of the carrier's outstanding stock. In deference to the rising backlash against greenmailers and takeover artists—one he feared could quash his effort to acquire TWA—Icahn made an uncharacteristically diplomatic offer.

"He committed himself not to vote his shares in favor of this cash merger unless a majority of the other shareholders voted in favor of it," Steve Jacobs recalled. "In other words, he would not jam it down the throats of the other shareholders. . . . He disclaimed any intention to be interested in greenmail; he stated that he would operate TWA in the best interest of the employees; he pointed out that $18 was a substantial premium."

Icahn implored the board to present his offer to the share-holders, backing up his request with a threat to put in motion a consent procedure seeking to replace TWA's board with a slate of directors that would agree to place the $18 offer before the shareholders. However, he would refrain if the current board permitted the shareholders to vote on his bid.

For a company that had considered itself virtually immune from hostile raiders, the idea that an outsider had acquired nearly a quarter of the company and was now seeking majority control came as a shock. Confused, angered and determined to ward off this unwelcome intruder, management mounted an of-fensive designed to stop Icahn in his tracks. In short order, the company launched a slick campaign to discredit Icahn in the press and in the halls of Congress. The idea was to whip up a groundswell of anti-Icahn sentiment, using this to pressure Con-gress and the Department of Transportation to throw roadblocks in the raider's path.

As Icahn's attorney Steve Jacobs remembered it, TWA was "conducting a brilliantly orchestrated campaign of attack. TWA's chairman is making speeches, seeking protectionist legis-lation, and accusing Carl of being the greediest man on earth. The stories are rampant that Carl is going to take over TWA, which has been miraculously transformed from being the third-least-respected company in the United States into a national treasure. TWA is claiming that Carl is going to shut down routes, close the Kansas City and St. Louis facilities and lay off employ-ees, all to his own personal advantage. Moreover, he is going to issue—these dirty words—'junk bonds,' to TWA shareholders. TWA employees are standing behind the airline's ticket counters and walking down the streets of New York exhibiting big buttons saying STOP CARL ICAHN.

"When we tried to hire lobbyists in Washington to convey the Icahn message to Congress, we found that none were avail-able. TWA had retained them all."

On the legislative front, the principal action centered around the House Subcommittee on Aviation. TWA, playing to a growing public sentiment against takeovers, sought to influence the committee to curb hostile raids on airlines and to endorse a bill, already introduced in Congress, that would require the Department of Transportation to investigate TWA's fitness to continue as a commercial carrier under Icahn's control. During the investigation Icahn would be barred from restructuring the carrier by selling routes and aircraft. Although Icahn promised at the outset that he would not dismantle TWA, but instead would run it as an ongoing enterprise, he had to counter the concern that his motives were sinister.

Representative John Paul Hammerschmidt of Arkansas, noted that he was "somewhat sympathetic" to the proposition that takeovers were a positive force for rooting out inefficient management, but he worried about the impact this kind of activity could have on "the traveling public and the U.S. international aviation interests. This concern is based at least in part on the reputation of the so-called corporate raiders such as Mr. Icahn. They have the reputation for buying up the shares of an undervalued company and then milking or selling off the assets solely for the purpose of personal financial gain. It has been alleged that this is done without regard for the company's employees or for the customers that the company serves."

Ed Meyer used the forum to attack Icahn and to try to discredit his pledge not to dismantle the carrier.

"Following an extensive review of Mr. Icahn's track record, and the results of numerous face-to-face meetings in recent weeks, we are convinced that one strategy he is not willing to pursue is to manage TWA in a competent, responsible manner, seeking to maximize the long-term interests of our constituencies . . . ," Meyer told the committee. "What we seek is that a hearing be held and a determination begun . . . that hearing should be instituted expeditiously and his stock holding should be held in trust pending the outcome.

"Given the range of our responsibilities, we are unwilling to turn over TWA to Mr. Icahn and his unnamed cohorts without pursuing available alternatives and without seeking appropriate regulatory review."

That TWA shareholders would want the opportunity to decide for themselves whether or not Icahn's offer was in their best interests was never mentioned. Instead, Meyer shifted attention from management's intransigence by citing the popular notions about the evils of corporate raiders.

". . . last month's *American Lawyer* published an Icahn memo on his tactics, none of which concerned management of a target, and quoted 'his enemies and even his friends' saying that Mr. Icahn is one of the greediest men on the planet . . ." Meyer continued, "No one has said that Mr. Icahn has anyone's interests at heart other than his own. With that in mind, our board feels strongly that one of the greediest men on earth should stay right where he is, and out of our skies. . . .

"Mr. Icahn has written to several committee chairmen assuring that he has changed his stripes, that he will not dismantle TWA, that he has the long-term interests of the public at heart. I hope so, but the assurances bring to mind the joke that my kids used to tell me about the world's biggest lies. . . . On Wall Street, this year's version of the old joke is that the three biggest lies are, first, 'I am buying your stock only for investment purposes'; second, 'We have no interest in liquidating the business'; and third, 'We have the long-term interests of the employees, customers, and communities in mind.' "

Responding to Carl's demand that his $18 offer be presented for a shareholder vote, management and the board decided to delay this for a two-month period, allowing time for Salomon Brothers, TWA's investment bankers, to search for a white knight. Appeals for legislative and regulatory relief were designed to give credence to management's action and to stall for time.

If Ed Meyer had expected a warm embrace from the congressmen, though, he was disappointed. Instead of joining in a lynch-Icahn movement, a number of the committee members turned the heat on TWA's management, noting that the company's performance was abysmal. In this context, they asked, why shield the carrier from a high bidder, and quite possibly from a force for positive change?

Representative Hammerschmidt stated, "Mr. Meyer, during the first quarter of this year your operating and net loss was the second worst in the industry. Your yield was one of the lowest in the industry and your expenses were among the highest. In addition, over the last few years, you have shrunk the size of the airline considerably. In light of that, I wonder what your thinking is on why Congress should block the new ownership who might be able to improve that situation?"

Representative Tim Valentine also forced Meyer to confront the critical question of why Congress should meddle with the free market in the name of protecting TWA's management. "What is the broad national interest that is violated by this takeover? I know you love your corporation and I know you talk about these overseas routes, but what is it that Congress should be concerned about?"

Meyer responded, "Well, the broad national interest is that the wealth of the country is increased by manufacturing, service industries coming into business, remaining in business, growing. I think the broad national interest is hurt if we get massive liquidation or forced liquidation of companies. I will say I am concerned about—"

"Well, how do we pass a law avoiding that type of liquidation if the stockholders want to dissolve it?"

What TWA had predicted would be a platform for the villification of raiders was evolving instead into an inquisition into the self-interest of corporate management.

Representative Glen Anderson asked, ". . . why do you believe you will get an offer higher than $18?"

Meyer answered, "Because our investment advisers have deemed it inadequate, and I feel very strongly that it is inadequate."

"Well, it is my understanding that TWA is now considering a leveraged buy-out as an alternative to presenting Mr. Icahn's bid to the shareholders. Is that still confidential?"

"Yes, Mr. Anderson."

When Representative Anderson asked if a management-prompted leveraged buy-out would result in a greater debt burden for TWA than Icahn's bid, Meyer answered, "It's possible. I don't know."

Given his turn at the microphone, Icahn counterattacked, first challenging the notion that his pledge to keep the carrier intact was a calculated deception. Suddenly he was Carl Icahn, Eagle Scout.

". . . I haven't appreciated the efforts by TWA's management to impugn my personal integrity and misstate the terms of my offer. As you have heard this morning, TWA's management continues to claim that I would seriously damage or even destroy the airline. This would make me both a liar and a fool, and I am neither. I am in a business where my word is my bond. I buy and sell increments of hundreds of thousands of shares, solely by oral agreement. My reputation as a man of my word is something that I would not risk for any transaction."

As to TWA's primary goal of prompting the committee to enforce a freeze on Icahn's activities while the DOT investigated his fitness to run an airline, Icahn argued that this would be playing into the hands of an insulated management.

"If you gentlemen give TWA what they want, and make me wait ninety days, what you will be doing is entrenching this management, because in this type of a transaction, where we make an offer of $600 million, ninety days is an eternity. Even thirty days is an eternity, because what TWA will do under these circumstances will be to dilute stock—*Business Week* mentioned that they already talked to Boeing concerning this—dilute the stock and give the stock to a 'favorite son' or to a friend. Perhaps that friend or favorite son . . . will be put on the board.

"During this period I will be held helpless. My hands will be tied. . . . This is what they call 'greenmail,' but usually in the 'greenmail' we are the guys that are threatened. What they will do is come to me and say, 'Look, Mr. Icahn, we are issuing all the stock to this or this or this person. Your hands are tied. We suggest very strongly that you now sell your stock, or we are going to do poison pills. We are going to do more dilution and a number of other things. . . .'

"This is exactly why TWA is doing this. They want to entrench themselves. . . . My offer would be the model of shareholder democracy, if only TWA's board would submit it to TWA's shareholders for prompt consideration. Compare the terms of my offer with the recent response by TWA's managers: thirty-two golden parachutes, contracts to insulate themselves from the possible effects of my proposed acquisition and a vote to withhold my offer from the shareholders for sixty days.

"It is interesting to note Mr. Meyer's response concerning these thirty-two golden parachutes, mentioning the fact that they are afraid headhunters will rob them of this valuable management. I just wonder how many headhunters and how many other companies in the airline industry are going to be so anxious to rob a management that has lost money for the last five years. . . .

"The Congress has consistently rejected requests to intervene in isolated transactions. Given the terms of my offer, the Congress should reject TWA's request to enact a law here.

"The ultimate irony is that they are forcing me to go to Congress, suing me in every state of the Union, calling me every kind of name in the book, writing up things about me that I never even heard of myself. . . . Then the irony is they come and say, 'Look at Icahn, all he wants to do is sell out,' and they are forcing me to do it. In other words, if this law is passed, what is going to happen, I predict to you gentlemen . . . I will have an offer in about twenty days on the table to sell my stock and then they'll say, 'Look at Icahn, what a bad, bad guy he is. He never wanted to buy the company.' "

In the end, the committee decided against interfering with the free market, rejecting TWA's pleas to freeze Icahn or to restrict airline takeovers. But comments from Representative E. Clay Shaw, Jr., should have served as a warning to Icahn of the challenges he would face in a business he knew little about.

Questioning Icahn, Shaw asked: "I don't mean to be disrespectful, but how in the world do you feel you are going to come into a company that the chief executive officer sat in front of us today and he couldn't even remember when it last paid a dividend; you have got labor problems right now, you have two or three contracts that are on the table. You are going to start talking about scaling them down at the same time United is out in the marketplace looking for cheap pilots. . . . With all these things, how are you going to turn that around even soon enough to pay the interest on what you are going to borrow?"

Although defeated in Congress, TWA played another card, dispatching Salomon Brothers to search for white knights to top Carl's offer. If a better offer failed to materialize within sixty days, only then would management take Icahn's bid to the shareholders.

The first prospective buyer, Resorts International, put forward a weak bid of $22 a share for a merger, 60 percent of which would be in cash, the balance in debentures. In addition, Resorts simultaneously proposed an alternative plan, known as a front-loaded tender offer. A popular strategy of the day, front-loaded tenders were designed to prompt shareholders, in some cases stampede them, into the raider's camp for fear of winding up in the back end of the deal. Under this scenario, Resorts would pay $24 for 60 percent of the stock and a $19 debenture for the balance of the shares. The idea amounted to a poorly camouflaged strategy to box Icahn into a corner.

In this case, Resorts would attempt to use the two-tiered takeover strategy to coerce Icahn into accepting its $22 bid. Central to this, Resorts knew that as an owner of more than 10 percent of TWA's stock, Icahn had a "section 16 (b)" problem, which meant that if he sold his shares of TWA within six months of buying them, any profit would revert to the company. This would leave Icahn unable to benefit from Resorts's front-loaded price.

In this context, Resorts was prepared to warn Icahn that if he fought their bid to acquire TWA, they would proceed with the front-loaded tender, forcing Icahn to take the back-end debentures. But if he did not oppose them, Resorts would switch to the one-step merger with an equal price for all the shareholders. As part of its strategy Resorts planned to create an artificial deadline, giving Icahn an hour to decide which way he would go.

As a seasoned M&A negotiator, Freund knew the Resorts attempt to stymie Icahn would fail. Presented with an ultimatum in which he is told to choose between evil A or lesser evil B, Icahn moves into intellectual overdrive, expanding the range of options. In this way, he turns the tables on his adversaries, who find themselves facing a more ominous threat than they hurled at the raider.

"We felt that Carl would have said no on principle," Freund said, referring to the Resorts ultimatum. "He would challenge it in the courts and buy in the market underneath the tender, presumably sweeping the street to get 51 percent. Then he would provide the TWA shareholders with a lower-than-$18 back end."

In other words, Icahn was likely to retaliate by acquiring enough additional shares to gain control of TWA. From that position of strength he could offer the shareholders a lower debenture price than Resorts was contemplating. With the prospect of a Resorts offer backfiring on the company, TWA's advisers counseled against it.

As weak as it was, Resorts's bid turned out to be the highest white-knight offer. Texas Air, run by airline maverick Frank Lorenzo, had expressed interest but at a maximum of $20 a share. This left TWA's board with only the Resorts bid to ward off Icahn. And even that deteriorated. As the negotiations proceeded from the conceptual to the practical, Resorts weakened its position, complaining, among other things, that it might have trouble coming up with the money to do the deal. Insiders saw this as a ruse by Resorts to cut its offer at the eleventh hour.

Just as the prospects of countering Icahn were fading, Texas Air suddenly indicated that it was willing to go beyond its original offer. With that the picture brightened considerably. A white knight was willing to contend for the company, and to make the news even sweeter, Icahn indicated through back channels— from his lawyer Steve Jacobs to TWA's counsel Jim Freund— that he would not stand in the way of a friendly deal, providing Texas Air paid an adequate price. Being the financial chameleon that he is, Icahn has always been willing to turn from buyer to seller and vice versa, depending on where the dollars are. If Texas Air was going to make a healthy bid, Carl would cash in his chips for a quick killing, banking his proceeds until the next opportunity emerged. That prospect delighted TWA, which launched into intensive negotiations with Texas Air.

Lorenzo, who coveted TWA for his growing business empire, had emerged as a force in the aviation industry by launching Jet Capital Corp., a vehicle for acquisitions, and then raising the money to purchase Texas International Airlines in the early 1970s and then Continental. In his quest for TWA, only Icahn stood in the way, and Lorenzo was convinced he could outmaneuver him.

Because Icahn held a big position in the carrier, and was free to continue buying stock, Lorenzo knew that a tender offer—ordinarily a white knight's favored option—would not suffice in this case. Once Texas Air began to buy, Icahn could do the same, quickly increasing his stake to 51 percent, thwarting the would-be white knight or extracting a huge price for his shares.

A possible solution called for Texas Air to preempt Icahn through the back door by purchasing one of TWA's most valuable assets, such as a critical piece of the airline's route system. This radical surgery, the thinking went, would diminish the carrier's appeal as a takeover target, thus forcing Icahn to halt his attack. But the air leaked out of this trial balloon when TWA's lawyers argued that Icahn would challenge this kind of "asset lock-up" in court and that he would likely prevail.

The only safe way to structure the deal was to come up with a transaction Carl would not oppose. In this context, a merger—whereby Texas Air would pay $23 a share—appeared to be the best approach. Texas Air and TWA focused on this approach, structuring a merger proposal, filing a proxy statement and seeking to obtain approval from the DOT. But as lawyers for both sides hammered away at the issues, Lorenzo worried that he would somehow fall victim to an Icahn trap. To reduce the likelihood of an eleventh-hour ambush, Texas Air looked for a gun it could hold to Icahn's head.

"As Texas Air became more and more nervous about Carl, Frank's people pressed TWA for lock-ups, such as a supervoting preferred stock," Freund recalled.* "TWA's position was that in

---

*Supervoting preferred gives the holders of this class of security lopsided power in voting on corporate issues.

order to grant lock-ups, we needed 1. the Texas Air financing commitments to be in place; 2. a substantial bump in the merger price; and 3. a hell-or-high-water merger agreement."

Because these conditions could not be met—most important, Texas Air refused to budge on its bid—TWA confirmed its decision not to issue lock-ups. Behind the scenes, the company worried that Icahn would view the lock-ups as an act of war, prompting him to seize control of the carrier. At this point TWA hoped to neutralize Icahn with the carrot rather than the stick. The consensus was that for all of Icahn's threats, he was hoping to bail out in the wake of a rich deal.

In refusing to raise his bid, Lorenzo was indicating that he too believed Icahn was looking for an exit, and though he might rant and rave at a $23 take-it-or-leave-it price, when it came down to the wire, he would grab it. This would be the first of two critical blunders on Lorenzo's part. Had he raised his offer to $25, he would have armed TWA with the grounds to grant the asset lock-ups, placing an imposing roadblock in Icahn's path. In all likelihood he would have defeated Carl, emerging from the negotiations with another airline grafted on to his empire. But by remaining steadfast at $23, he failed to preempt Icahn, and, in turn, to take him out of the contest at a critical juncture.

Even at the lower price, Lorenzo had a golden opportunity to rid himself of the Icahn nemesis. This came just after TWA agreed in principle to accept Lorenzo's $23 bid. For the deal to proceed, Icahn would have to back out, taking his profit of roughly $80 million and leaving Lorenzo free to capture his prize.

Determined to use his power as a bargaining chip, Icahn signaled his willingness to accept the Lorenzo offer. But as the price for supporting the merger, Icahn worked out a tentative agreement with Leon Black, then Lorenzo's investment banker, calling for Texas Air to pay Carl $9 million in fees—in addition to $7 million already coming to him—as the price for peace. Although Black believed this was a fair price to pay to neutralize Icahn, Lorenzo stunned everyone involved by refusing to cover the penny-ante expenses.

"After Drexel worked out the financing for Frank, I advised him to get a standstill from Icahn because Carl owned one-third of the stock," Black recalled. "I said, 'I worked it out and we will be covering incremental fees of $9 million.' That's when Frank said, 'Fuck him—he's a pig' and hung up.

"I called Frank back. I said, 'This is crazy. I understand you don't want to pay fees, but you have a gorilla on your doorstep who can disrupt this.' But Frank said, 'Carl will never take over the airline.' "

In rejecting Black's informal agreement with Icahn after the fact, Lorenzo appeared to be playing games. But from his perspective, this was clever negotiating. Convinced that Icahn was in the stock as an arb, he was certain Carl would sell out for his $80 million profit on the speculative run-up in the shares. His belief stemmed in part from a concern that Drexel's greater loyalties lay with Icahn, who, after the Phillips and ACF deals, had emerged as a Milken favorite. Fully aware that Drexel was playing both sides of the street, Lorenzo was skeptical of the advice he got from Black.

In his assessment of Icahn's position, Lorenzo made a second major mistake: He overlooked TWA's labor unions, principally the pilots and the machinists. To them Frank Lorenzo was the devil incarnate. Ever since he had angered the unions by taking Continental Airlines into voluntary bankruptcy in 1983, he had been despised by organized labor. As he prepared to take over TWA, the unions were determined to play the role of spoiler. They would do so by enticing Icahn to re-emerge as a serious bidder, arming him with a potent weapon to battle Lorenzo. That weapon was wage concessions.

Knowing that they would be under pressure to reduce labor costs in order to make TWA competitive with such carriers as American and United, which were already restructuring their wage scales, TWA's unions accepted the fact that they had to make concessions. Rather than having these cuts extracted by a Lorenzo-headed management, which might go further than the unions could stomach, they would preempt the process, putting the concessions in Icahn's lap.

Ironically, these same unions had joined with management

in a "Stop Icahn" movement when he had first emerged as a
takeover threat. But that was when they had to choose between
Icahn and Ed Meyer. Nonetheless, true to form, Icahn wanted
more than labor was willing to give.

These strangest of prospective bedfellows—a lone wolf capitalist and a clutch of trade unions—began round-the-clock bargaining sessions held at Weil, Gotshal's law offices, high in the
General Motors Building across the street from the Plaza Hotel.
At times the meetings turned to shouting matches, as positions
hardened and tempers rose. At its worst point, a nasty war of
words broke out between Icahn and the machinists' negotiator
Tim Connolly.

Although Icahn is said to have found these episodes amusing, when the heat was turned his way, he was unwilling or
unable to take it.

"It was very late at night—maybe 2 A.M.—and I was grab-
bing a nap on an office couch," recalls Brian Freeman. "Then
suddenly, I was awakened by this yelling and screaming, and as
I sat up I saw Icahn putting on his suit jacket and storming out
of the room. He was muttering something like 'I don't need this
crap. I don't have to take it.' When I told Carl to calm down, he
told me to 'bug off.'

"Just like that, Carl was gone—and he stayed away for at
least a half hour. We were worried that he'd gone off to Lorenzo.
Leon Black and Lorenzo had been putting pressure on him to
return to their side, and we thought, maybe he did.

"But then Carl finally returned. It seemed he'd gone for a
walk and that had taken the steam out of him. He said, 'We're
here to do a deal. Let's get on with it.' "

Throughout the union bargaining sessions, Icahn used the
specter of Lorenzo to force labor to make concession after concession. At any point, he reminded the leadership, he could sell out
to Lorenzo, bagging a guaranteed profit. Although the unions
had never seen anything like it, this "Do as I say or face the
consequences" strategy was classic Icahn.

Fearful that Icahn would make good on his threat, the pilots
kept sweetening their offer.

"[Pilots' representative] Harry Hoglander was actively

working with the three unions to get Icahn to jump in," said Kent Scott. "But Carl was playing reluctant. 'Why do I want to go in? I can have a profit on my shares if I sell to Lorenzo. I don't want to get bogged down running a company.'

"This was mostly an act. The more Carl objected, the more money the unions threw at him. They were throwing so much money at him I bet he had to leave the negotiating sessions every half hour just to laugh to himself."

"When you negotiate with Carl, you know that his strategy is to threaten, continuously threaten," Freund said. "I call it 'confrontational negotiating.' That's his modus operandi.

"One day in the midst of the TWA negotiations it got to me. I said, 'Carl, if you continue with these threats, we are going to get up, walk out of here, and never negotiate with you again.' That's when he said, 'Okay, no more threats.'

"But then thirty minutes later he began threatening again. I said, 'Carl, there you go with the threats again.' To which he responded, 'No, no, I was just showing you the consequences of your action.' At that point everyone broke up laughing."

As with the Phillips negotiations, Icahn scheduled late-night meetings so that he could attack his adversaries when they were bush-tired, mushy-brained, and eager to go home.

"I remember a meeting during the TWA negotiations that was scheduled to start at 9 P.M.," recalled TWA's investment banker, Mike Zimmerman, of Salomon Brothers. "As it turned out, Carl didn't show up until eleven. While everyone else was negotiating, he went home, napped and showered. By the time he made his entrance, the TWA people looked like trash and Carl walked in looking like a million bucks."

"Carl wears you down," said former pilots' representative Tom Ashwood. "He negotiates into the night. Five, six, seven hours. He'll ramble on about baseball and artificial insemination. Then when you lose your train of thought, he'll pick up right where he left off, hammering at a point he wants to make.

"He's impossible to deal with. When you think you have fully reached an agreement with Carl, you come back to the table after a break and there is no deal. Because he's changed a number or added a hitch that throws everything out of whack in his favor. If you say five, Carl says six. Say six, he says seven. Say seven, he says eight."

Another Icahn gambit is to prepare his opponents for an all-out fight.

"One time when we were negotiating, Carl told this story of his high school days when a bunch of tough Irish guys were bullying him, pushing him around, trying to intimidate him," recalled William Jolley, a partner with Jolley, Walsh & Hager, attorneys for TWA's flight attendants. "But one day Carl says he turned on one of the toughs in a stairwell and either through physical violence or threats, made them see that they could never do that to Carl Icahn again. This is Carl's way of telling you that no one messes with Icahn and wins. In the end, he's saying, 'I'll get you. I'll get you.' "

At one stage a plot was hatched to force Icahn to accept more modest wage concessions than he was demanding. The plan developed when Icahn, who had settled informally on a wage package with the International Association of Machinists, found that he could win deeper concessions from the pilots. With the commitment in hand, Icahn returned to the machinists to force them to dig deeper into their pockets. Although they were determined to hold the line, the machinists worried that a hard-line approach could prompt Icahn to walk out.

Rather than risking the worst-case scenario of a Lorenzo acquisition, the IAM kept the negotiations alive and apparently open to substantial compromise while Icahn struck his deal with the pilots. In effect, the IAM used the pilots as bait, hoping their deep concessions would keep Carl in the game as a TWA buyer. Only after Carl was hooked would the machinists return to serious negotiations, giving Icahn more than they originally intended but far less than the pilots had conceded.

In the course of these hard-fought wage negotiations, Brian Freeman, who advised the IAM, concocted his plan to manipulate Icahn. Whenever he was negotiating with Icahn, Freeman instructed IAM chief John Peterpaul to leave one of the phones in his office unanswered.

"Every time Carl demanded this or that, I would say that I have to check with my client," Freeman recalled. "With that, I would call the line Peterpaul knew not to answer. Carl would scream at me, 'You're incompetent. You don't even know where your client is.' I'd say, 'Fine, Carl, if it will make you feel better to take out a tombstone in the *Wall Street Journal* saying FREEMAN IS AN ASSHOLE, do it, but I can't seem to get in touch with Peterpaul at this time.' What Carl didn't know was that when I wanted Peterpaul, all I had to do was call the other line. Which is precisely what I would do when he raised a point I knew we could support."

At the same time the unions were arm wrestling with Icahn, they were secretly pitching the deal to other prospects capable of making a credible bid for TWA. The list of candidates included Jay Pritzker, the billionaire Chicago industrialist who had purchased Braniff Airlines.

They realized from the start that Pritzker's interest was genuine, but he would make the deal only if he could extract 25 percent wage concessions from the pilots and machinists. Although they could bargain further with Pritzker, Freeman and the unions concluded that there was no time for this. The imperative was to lock up Icahn and shut the door on Lorenzo.

The unions also sought out Eastern Airlines' CEO Frank Borman. This was the ideal match for several reasons. Borman relished the idea of combining the Eastern and TWA fleets and route maps, and the unions believed the former astronaut would be generous with them.

Serious talks commenced in mid-July when an Eastern executive team joined TWA's pilots and machinists for extensive negotiations at the Manhattan law offices of Sullivan & Cromwell. Although Borman's terms proved satisfactory to labor, Eastern's investment bankers at Merrill Lynch could not provide assurance of Borman's ability to finance the deal. With the clock still ticking, labor decided it was more important to tie down Icahn.

As much as the unions had come to detest Icahn's pettiness, in the back of their minds they recognized that he was right about one critical point: In the life and death battle to block Lorenzo, he was their only ace in the hole. For this reason, each time they reached what they thought was the limit of their largesse, they found themselves forced to dig deeper and deeper.

In the hard line he took with the unions, Icahn wanted both the pilots and machinists to take 20 percent cuts in wages and benefits. The pilots agreed to the concessions as the price of keeping out Lorenzo but the machinists, who were lower paid and less viscerally opposed to Lorenzo, drew the line at 15 percent. Claiming he would have to sell out to Lorenzo if this was all he could get, Carl returned to the pilots, demanding that they make up the difference. With consternation, the pilots caved in, agreeing to wage and benefit reductions of 26 percent. Taken together, these deep cuts in payroll and fringe benefits promised to put an Icahn-controlled TWA $200 million to $300 million in the black. The turnaround would be shouldered by organized labor.

"Carl is smart—in some ways too smart for the unions, management, bankers, everybody to deal with," said Brian Freeman. "You get mad at him—say he's greedy, insensitive.

"But people are always getting mad at Carl. Not because he's done something unethical but because he keeps outsmarting you. He's always maximizing his returns at your expense. Always pushing the deal as far as he can without blowing it up."

Interestingly, as Icahn was making inroads with the unions, Lorenzo was beginning to realize that his assessment of Carl's character—specifically that he didn't have the stomach to take over TWA—had been a dreadful miscalculation. With this in mind, Black worked feverishly throughout the summer to resolve Icahn's fee issue in a way that would save TWA for Lorenzo.

With this in mind, Black called Icahn, virtually pleading with him to resurrect the talks. After repeated rejections, Black was determined to make a connection no matter what Icahn said. Before allowing Carl to hang up, Black learned that he was headed for a dinner meeting at Christ Cella.

An hour later, Icahn, dining with a friend at the clubby Manhattan steakhouse, looked across the dining room to find

Black seated by himself, fussing with a menu. Icahn knew from experience that Black was persistent, but this was more than he expected.

When Carl's dinner guest left, Leon darted across the room to Icahn's table, picking up where the telephone conversation left off. Black insisted that they find some way for Carl to make a deal with Lorenzo, but Icahn countered that he would not negotiate with Lorenzo through intermediaries.

From Icahn's perspective, this demand had settled the issue for the night. But Black had other plans in mind. Asking Icahn to sit tight for a few minutes, Black whirled out of the restaurant and on to the Manhattan streets, returning, in a matter of minutes, with Frank Lorenzo in tow.

Although Black was delighted with his magic act, both Icahn and Lorenzo were tense, edgy, even annoyed at the sight of each other. Although they began to talk, it was clear from the start neither one was in a conciliatory mood. Quickly the conversation stalled, leaving Icahn cranky and upset. When Carl announced that he was going home, Black, with Lorenzo in tow, followed along.

As Icahn and Lorenzo walked in virtual silence through the darkened New York streets, Black struggled to build bridges between them. By the time they reached Icahn's building, Carl couldn't wait to escape. But Black pleaded for them to go up to Icahn's apartment.

Once they were upstairs, though, the scene grew even more bizarre. Quickly, Black hustled Lorenzo into a bedroom, trying to convince him to pay Carl's fees. A heated argument ensued, and Carl—sitting alone in the living room—could hear every word. At one point the squabble became so loud that Icahn told Black and Lorenzo to quiet down, warning nervously that he would be evicted from the building.

In the end, Lorenzo emerged with a counteroffer. No, he would not pay the total of $16 million to cover Icahn's fees. That, he believed, would be asinine. In return for the fees, Icahn would simply agree to vote his stock in favor of a Texas Air/TWA merger. But Lorenzo worried what would happen if another bidder, say Northwest, emerged from the woodwork to acquire

TWA before the Texas Air voting came to pass. Icahn could sell his stock into the higher offer. Net effect: Lorenzo would pay Icahn $16 million for nothing. Although the odds of a successful bidder surfacing at that point were remote, Lorenzo's competitive nature, and his determination not to be taken by Icahn, blocked him from rolling the dice.

Instead he offered to pay for an option on Icahn's stock, upping the ante to $22 million for a lock on Carl's shares. But since Icahn was determined to remain free to capitalize on opportunities, if and when they emerged, the options offer was killed on the spot.

Another factor played into Icahn's decision. Armed with union agreements assuring deep cuts in TWA's cost structure, Icahn began to believe for the first time that he could acquire the carrier and, based on his partnership with labor, turn it around. With the smell of a good deal in the air, and the romance of owning an airline softening his typical steely approach to business decisions, Icahn brushed aside Lorenzo's too-little-too-late offer, raised his bid to $24 and started aggressively acquiring stock again, this time boosting his holdings to 45 percent of the outstanding shares. Now Lorenzo was in a quandary.

"Texas Air was faced with a 45 percent shareholder who was now favored by all TWA employees," said Texas Air's attorney Dick Katcher. "We did not have many options. We raised our price from $23 to $26. Carl was at $24. Obviously, if Carl did not go along with the $26 deal, there would be no deal unless TWA did something for us.

"We had several reasons for raising our bid. We thought that perhaps at this price, Carl would be a seller. He had said back in June that he would not use his stock position to be a spoiler. We also thought that the new bid would induce him not to buy more stock."

Once again Lorenzo's negotiators sought lock-ups that would give Texas Air leverage over Carl, helping to cinch the deal at $26. Specifically, Texas Air wanted TWA to: 1. call all of its convertible securities for redemption, thus diluting Icahn's holdings; 2. give Texas Air an option on one of its crown jewel assets, such as its transatlantic routes; 3. sell Texas Air a super-voting preferred stock.

Clearly, Texas Air had little choice but to ask for the lock-ups. Because Icahn held 45 percent of TWA's shares, he could easily quash any move on the carrier's part to merge with Lorenzo. The only hope was that in granting Texas Air the lock-ups, and thus diluting Icahn, he would be discouraged from proceeding with an acquisition.

As TWA mulled over the options, however, it became increasingly clear that granting the lock-ups would put the company on shaky legal ground, making the move vulnerable to an Icahn court challenge. Even more ominous, Icahn was making noises that in retaliation for the lock-ups, he would lower his offering price to the shareholders. This was a shrewd tactic. From Carl's perspective, Lorenzo's $26 bid was simply a pressure tactic to force Icahn to raise his price, ultimately increasing the profit Texas Air would earn on its TWA stock. By refusing to take the bait and instead threatening to drop his offer, Icahn was putting the fear of God in TWA. Using Texas Air's wishy-washy offer, dependent as it was on questionable lock-ups, to challenge Icahn's solid bid could actually drive the price down, subjecting the board to the collective wrath of the shareholders. As Icahn had read all the cards on the table, he played his hand masterfully.

Freund tried to pressure Icahn to raise his bid by another $1 a share, holding that this could assure Carl's success. But in the process he ran square into the inner strength that makes Icahn so frustrating but is so critical to his success.

"We were negotiating in a Skadden, Arps conference room for hours on end," Freund recalled. "I told Carl if he came up with another dollar per share, the board would be much more disposed to go with him. If he didn't come up with the extra dollar, the board might well go with Lorenzo, and I warned him that the decision would definitely go down to the wire.

"I worked on Carl for three hours to try to get that dollar per share. I showed him why it was in his best interest to kick in that dollar. But he wouldn't budge. Other guys in a similar situation would probably say, 'Here's 50 cents or 75 cents,' but not Carl—not an extra cent for him. He had the courage of his convictions and obviously believed he would get TWA without increasing his bid."

One of the tactics that Freund used in this negotiation was to remind Carl of his previous assurances that if a better bid than his was put on the table he wouldn't be the spoiler.

At this point Freund asked Icahn to live up to his familiar declaration that he may be tough and he may be incredibly hard to pin down, but once he makes a deal, he is a man of his word.

"You gave me your word you wouldn't be the spoiler, and now you are being just that," Freund charged. "You said you are a man of your word, but you are not behaving like one. If you do this, you are only 50 percent a man of your word." Indignant, Icahn shot back with examples in the TWA deal where he had kept his word.

Freund nodded his head. "Okay, Carl, let's say you are 75 percent a man of your word."

"Come on," Icahn countered. "Give me 80 percent. I'm at least an 80 percent man of my word."

For a man who sees all of life as an auction, putting his own honor up for bids seemed entirely appropriate.

Clinging to the hope that it could somehow derail the Icahn juggernaut in the eleventh hour, TWA continued to court its white knight, offering limited lock-ups including a supervoting preferred that had as many votes as Icahn. Were the board to decide in favor of Texas Air, the lock-ups would increase the chances of neutralizing Icahn and ultimately of awarding the carrier to Lorenzo. With this in mind, Freund had a lawyer poised in Delaware with a charter ammendment for the supervoting preferred, and the documents were all drawn up, ready to be signed.

The contest between Lorenzo and Icahn came to a head at a board meeting on August 20. At this pivotal session, held at TWA's world headquarters at 605 Third Avenue in New York, Lorenzo,

Icahn, and the unions addressed the directors. On the same day the unions formally approved their deals with Carl, underlining the clout Icahn brought to the table.

Presenting a united front before the board, the raider and his labor bedfellows made for an impressive show of force. "There was a veiled threat running through that room that if the board selected Lorenzo, labor would shut the deal down, if not the entire airline," said a TWA adviser present at the meeting. "If you closed your eyes, you could see visions of guys pouring sugar into gas tanks and using switchblades to tear up the seats. There were no direct threats—just a sense that labor was not going to be denied without damaging recourse."

In spite of management's strong preference for Lorenzo, TWA's directors—including such "names" as former Defense Secretary Robert McNamara, one-time Lyndon Johnson aide Jack Valenti, Peter Ueberroth and former Pepsico president Andrall Pearson—had to face the fact that Texas Air's bid was riddled with holes.

"The additional $2 in the Texas Air proposal was gratifying, to be sure, but the board had previously approved $23 as being a fair price," Freund said. "Unfortunately, there was no instant gratification to the Texas Air deal; it would take six or seven months to accomplish. The legality of the lock-ups was far from certain."

As the board discussed the decision at hand, the directors found themselves uncomfortable with the Texas Air bid and, equally important, impressed with Icahn's ability to strike a deal with the unions. When the vote was taken, the decision was in favor of Icahn. Although TWA had an obligation, forged during the merger negotiations, to present Lorenzo's bid to the shareholders, Texas Air walked away, collecting $18 million in termination fees (also specified during the merger negotiations) and a black eye from its bruising battle with Icahn.

The board's decision stands as an extraordinary episode in the 1980s takeover wars. In dozens of similar battles in which a raider challenged management, the board sided with the "good guys." But in this case the board recognized that the "bad guy" had put the best offer on the table.

From Meyer's perspective, the Icahn victory was a matter of leverage and skill. "I was never a skilled negotiator on Icahn's level—that I admit—but the fact is I had no real cards to play," Meyer said. "But given Icahn's skills and abilities, even with cards to play, I probably would have had a tough time."

Icahn had triumphed in an arena filled with tough and determined adversaries including hostile lawyers, investment bankers, Frank Lorenzo, and the TWA board. That he had done so is testimony to his talent as a financial tactician and negotiator. Even on Wall Street—where self-proclaimed geniuses are as ubiquitous as MBAs—there is a consensus that Icahn is in a class by himself.

In part, his success is based on an intellectual skill that enables him to plot dozens of moves in advance. While his adversaries are thinking in linear fashion—"If I can get from A to B, then I'll proceed to C"—Icahn sees dozens of possibilities on a single screen. The mental agility that enables him to zigzag from C to F to Z and back to R, leaves his opponents so thoroughly confused and frustrated they are on the verge of shorting out.

"In trying to beat Carl, and failing to do so, people come away baffled," said Brian Freeman. "But I can tell them why they fail. Because they think they know what Carl's goal is when in fact he has no fixed goal.

"Carl is a buyer and a seller. He goes forwards, backwards, and sideways. He has 360 degree vision. Everything to Carl is an opportunity."

When the day was done, Icahn had emerged victorious. Hours after the board meeting, he strutted around his office in a TWA flight jacket, proclaiming in a rare burst of exuberance, "We just bought ourselves an airline."

At the time, he failed to heed unsolicited advice from Uncle Elliot.

"One evening, right before Carl purchased TWA, I was a guest at his house," Schnall recalled. "He was having this late-night meeting with Kingsley and some TWA people, and I remember saying to him, "What the hell do you need an airline for? Keep away. Let Lorenzo have it. Why don't you buy Bergdorf Goodman instead? That's the kind of business I like."

Assuming control of TWA was clearly the high point in Icahn's life. From every vantage point, the middle-class loner from Queens had arrived. Surrounded by wealth, power, status, position, and now a budding respectability, he appeared to be on the verge of the true greatness he aspired to. Reflecting the mood of the moment, Liba marked her husband's fiftieth birthday in February 1986 by throwing a lavish party at Foxfield. Among the guests were Ivan Boesky, who, wearing a cape, cane, and top hat, appeared to one of the guests like "Count Dracula."

Reflecting Carl's distaste for formal parties, Liba had a buffet served rather than a sit-down dinner. As musicians played in the background, the guests made speeches, alternately toasting and roasting Icahn. A huge cake, crafted as a replica of a TWA jet, marked the buoyant optimism of the latest Icahn conquest. The gifts ranged from the raunchy to the sentimental. Schnall's was the most poignant. Along with leather bound rare poetry books purchased at New York's Argosy book shop, he gave his nephew a Tiffany framed picture of nineteen-year-old Uncle Elliot holding the hand of a smiling three-year-old Carl Icahn, bundled up in a snow suit.

CHAIRMAN

ICAHN

Role Model or Reverse Robin Hood?

"Carl takes every possible position. He'll say black is black, black is white, black is red, black is blue, black is green, black is pink. He covers every base. That way he can say to you later 'I didn't lie to you. I told you black is really pink.' "
—BRIAN FREEMAN

Judged by any of the recognized financial yardsticks, TWA had never been a successful airline. Its most significant coup had come soon after World War II when it was granted the rights to compete with Pan Am as a U.S. flag carrier overseas. But Howard Hughes, who owned TWA in the postwar period, was more of an aviation buff than a airline manager. His biggest blunder was in moving slowly to embrace the jet age, leaving his propeller-driven fleet to compete against the sleek new 707's Pan Am was buying as fast as Boeing could make them.

After Hughes departed, the carrier brought its fleet up to date and, blessed with protected routes in a regulated era, managed to earn reasonable profits. Intoxicated by the 1960s romance with conglomeration, management then embarked on an asset shopping spree, making a series of acquisitions that brought Canteen Corp. and Hilton International Hotels under the corporate umbrella.

Preoccupied with this growing empire, management's focus shifted away from its airline component—which was always capital intensive and subject to harrowing dips and curves in travel, fuel costs, and profitability. Ultimately, the conglomerate's holding company, Trans World Corp., jettisoned Trans World Airlines. By the time Icahn made his move, the airline was an anemic beast, its profitable transatlantic routes drained by a weak and poorly managed domestic system.

Still, Icahn commenced his TWA tenure with a great burst of enthusiasm. Here was an opportunity for the fearsome raider—loathed by the corporate establishment as a parasite of the capitalist system—to reinvent himself, undergoing a dramatic metamorphosis from takeover arbitrageur to captain of industry. Increasingly sensitive to the public hue and cry over the payment of greenmail, Icahn had already begun to disavow this form of blood money that had built the base of his fortune and funded his takeover war chest. Always concerned with the worst-case scenario, he worried about becoming an object of scorn. He yearned for the respectability of the true entrepreneurs—the likes of Andrew Carnegie, Bill Paley, Tom Watson, Ross Perot—who had built enormous businesses and had become deeply engrained in the American folklore.

Equally important, annointing himself as the CEO of a major American company gave Icahn-the-management-critic ample opportunity to prove his theories regarding "reverse Darwinism" in the executive suite. With an owner rather than a professional manager at the helm, Icahn was convinced that he could create a paradigm for the new American corporation. If he was successful, even his critics would have to admit, "Carl can do it all."

.   .   .

From the very first days of his tenure as TWA's chairman, events would play havoc with Icahn's dream. In April 1986, just three months after Carl strutted around the office in his flight jacket, Arab terrorists hijacked a TWA jumbo jet. Icahn, scheduled to attend Drexel's annual junk-bond ball, had to forgo that event to deal with the crisis.

Later that year, President Reagan responded to the growing menace of Libyan-sponsored terrorism by ordering bombing raids on Maummar Qaddafi's outlaw state. As the fear of random violence spread throughout the United States and western Europe, traffic on TWA's cash cow transatlantic routes virtually dried up. For the first time in his career, Icahn was facing powerful forces he could not threaten, bully or buy out.

"Carl saw something with TWA," said Leon Black. "He saw the hatred the unions had for Lorenzo and that he could channel that hatred into concessions. He also saw that the airline was poorly run and he was insightful as to what he could do with the cost structure.

"But Carl overestimated what he could do on the revenue side. Too many things were not under his control in that industry, like oil prices, recessions, terrorism, and unions, once an initial agreement had expired."

All of this came as a rude awakening to a man who had run off a string of successes in the options business and subsequently as a corporate raider. When he acquired TWA, he assumed that those successes would continue.

"When Carl took over, he was very cocky," said Edward Gehrlein, TWA's former vice president of sales. "He loved the idea of running an airline. At one Christmas party the executive staff exchanged gifts. The staff gave Carl a leather jacket, a silk scarf, and a World War I aviator's helmet, and he paraded around the office like a combat ace. He ate it up.

"But he didn't understand the leverage in the business. He would sit there in the fall of 1985 looking at the projections for 1986, and he was amazed to see how a penny increase in fuel prices could cut earnings by about $14 million. And how a single additional passenger on TWA's planes could boost profits by $12 million or so. This kind of leverage really surprised him. He didn't have the experience in the business to understand it.

"Still, he was cocky. He believed his own gospel that the only problem with airlines was that they were run by stupid managers."

Integral to Icahn's initial strategy for revitalizing TWA, he was determined to expand on the wage concessions extracted from the pilots and machinists by slashing jobs and operational overhead across the board. A key part of the austerity program called for winning concessions from the flight attendants, the only major union that had failed to come to terms with Carl before his takeover.

Just why the flight attendants had been left out beforehand is a matter of controversy. As Icahn was negotiating with the unions in the summer of 1985, he demanded that the flight attendants grant concessions of 22 percent. But Vicki Frankovich, president of the Independent Federation of Flight Attendants, argued that the rank and file—who earned less than half the pilots' average pay of $90,000—could hardly afford to take deep pay cuts and refused to budge beyond the 15 percent concessions secured from the machinists.

There was probably room to negotiate on both sides, but Frankovich—a testy, hard-as-nails leader who clashed with Icahn at every turn—was repelled by Carl's go-for-the-jugular style. Over months of bitter and seemingly fruitless talks, she grew increasingly irritated at what she viewed as Icahn's one-sidedness and his insensitivity to the plight of her members.

The clash between the two reached a climax on an August 1985 weekend when leaders of the pilots and the machinists engaged in marathon negotiations with Icahn, leading to pacts with both of the unions. Frankovich, who was invited to the session, chose instead to fly to California to attend to personal matters. In her absence, Icahn tied down the two most powerful labor groups, leaving their weak sister isolated. Because Icahn had demanded that the pilots and machinists sign pledges not to honor the picket lines of other TWA unions, Frankovich was denied the leverage of calling for a general strike should that be the only way to retaliate against Carl's intransigence.

According to Frankovich, isolating and then bullying the flight attendants was Icahn's master plan from the start.

"When I went to California that August weekend, I gave Carl my West Coast telephone number," Frankovich said. "But he never called. Then, after my return to New York on Monday, he had the audacity to say that if I'd been at the meeting, I could have cut a deal at the same 15 percent the machinists accepted. But because I wasn't there, I would have to accept the 22 percent he'd been demanding all along.

"Nonsense. If the 15 percent deal was available on Saturday, why wasn't it available on Monday? This is typical Icahn. He creates diversionary tactics, finding a way to shift responsibility for his stubborn position from himself to those he is negotiating with. But the truth is, if I had camped out in Icahn's office for all of June and July it wouldn't have made any difference. He'd never made us a 15 percent or even a 17 percent offer, and he wasn't going to.

"Look, Icahn can charm you at the negotiating table. He talks about life, politics, his place in the world, his destiny. But all the while he is trying to slit your throat. We know he's a shark. We knew it from the first day. The question is, how do you protect yourself from a shark?"

From Icahn's perspective, the showdown with the flight attendants was based on simple economics. Unless he could reduce wages, he could not compete in the marketplace.

Squaring off with Frankovich on the Larry King television show, Icahn summed up his view of the matter this way:

"Other airlines we compete with have flight attendants working at $1,000 a month, or $12,000 a year. We pay $35,000. . . . You don't have to be Einstein to understand that we cannot exist on that basis."

As Icahn debated Frankovich before a national audience, a deep resentment of the 1980s financial manipulators bubbled to the surface. The first caller used the opportunity to lambast Icahn, expressing the pent-up hostility millions were experiencing as the biggest names in American industry were being ransacked by greenmailers and corporate raiders. This was the flip-side of the Roaring Eighties—the wide gulf between the elite who were accumulating wealth and the majority who were losing it.

"This is not a dispute between an employer and a union," the caller said. "This is an American dispute between unions and Wall Street raiders. This guy takes over an airline, wheels and deals it and puts a whole union out of business."

The flight attendants called for a strike to commence in the first week of March 1986. On the final day of a thirty-day cooling off period—after which the IFFA was free to strike under provisions of the Railway Labor Act—Icahn met with union leaders for an eleventh-hour session. But according to the IFFA's attorney Bill Jolley, Icahn had come to the meeting with a closed mind.

"He starts off the meetings saying, 'I don't know why I'm here. I have nothing to negotiate. You know what you have to give me. I need $110 million in cost savings. I can't take less. My credibility is at stake.'

"Why would his credibility be at stake? Because he's a guy who makes deals and once he said what he would do, he believed he couldn't be seen backing down."

When the union came up with an alternative proposal that would save an additional $15 to $20 million in direct salary reductions and work rule changes, Icahn again dismissed the offer out of hand. His chief negotiator, TWA executive Bill Hoar, directed the unions to come up with a better number.

Dutifully, the union leaders worked through the night, offering total savings in excess of $50 million. At the time, IFFA officials had a Salomon Brothers report that showed that $50 million in savings would make the airline profitable.

"But Carl insisted that this was completely unsatisfactory," Jolley says. "That's because he wasn't there to negotiate. He was there to get his way. Icahn goes into a room with a predisposition of what the bottom line should be and he won't change from that predisposition.

"His orientation is that of a poker player. Poker players

have a pot before them. Winner takes all. You don't play to divide the pot, you play to win it. That's what Carl does."

Judging by Icahn's treatment of the flight attendants' union, his ultimate goal was to cut their wages not by 15, 20, or 22 percent, but down to the $1,000 a month subsistence wage he had in his head. That this would bring severe hardship to 6,000-plus employees, creating a huge body of resentment within the company, was of less concern to Icahn than the fact that whole-sale salary cuts would have a positive impact on TWA's bottom line, and, in turn, on his personal investment in the carrier.

"I think of him as a reverse Robin Hood," Frankovich said. "He takes from the poor and gives to the rich. His financial wizardry is undeniable but it comes out of the pockets of the people who work for him. He is a modern day robber baron."

But the flight attendants saw more than greed in Icahn's move to slash their wages. To many in the union, forcing the only TWA labor group dominated by women to accept subsistence wages was a blatant case of sexism.

"He treated us poorly from the beginning," said Karen Lance, a former union vice president. "He called us 'girls.' He told us we could give up more because we had husbands who could pay our bills.

"He couldn't relate to people who weren't rich. He didn't understand that many of our people were single parents or that they were part of families that actually needed two incomes to make it. He told us, 'You should go out and marry rich men if you have a problem making ends meet.'

"At one meeting at TWA's New York headquarters, he went to a window, looked down, and said, 'You flight attendants are totally replaceable. I can get any girl off the streets down there and make her a flight attendant.' "

When the flight attendants went on strike on March 7, 1986, they believed this would disrupt the airline. But rather than bending to the pressure, Icahn used the opportunity to replace the strikers with $1,000 a month scabs. This threw oil on the fire, turning what had been a bitter stand-off into open hostility.

Enraged at what they considered to be slavemaster treat-ment by a Wall Street millionaire—and determined to generate public sympathy for their cause—the flight attendants' union produced a video starring Jesse Jackson, who took Carl to task as an enemy of the working man.

"What the Icahns of the world must face is that when these workers cannot buy food, cannot buy cars, the economy is being held hostage by a handful of greedy people. . . ." the video proclaimed. "Here is Icahn able on one hand to profit while workers are losing their jobs and their capacity to make a living at TWA."

In the midst of the strike, an angry crowd of flight attendants joined forces at the wrought iron gates outside the sprawling grounds of Icahn's Bedford estate.

At first Icahn remained sequestered within the safety of his manor house while the crowd picketed and shouted epithets across the wooded acres. But then, on the spur of the moment, Icahn waded into the enemy camp, convinced that he could use his formidable negotiating powers to turn the crowd's anger away from himself and on to archenemy Vicki Frankovich.

Dressed in a bulky ski jacket and casual slacks, Icahn moved into the thick of the crowd. As he started to speak, his words were drowned out in a cacaphony of hisses and boos.

"You come to my house on a Saturday," Icahn said, starting off with a lesson in etiquette. "I come out to talk to you. The least you can do is give me the courtesy of listening to me."

Quickly, Icahn claimed that Frankovich had fed her members misinformation. "The problem is," he charged, "that you are brainwashed."

Visibly testy and agitated, the crowd swarmed around Icahn, hurling charge after charge at him. After being vilified for failing to meet with Frankovich to negotiate a settlement, Icahn resumed the offensive:

"She says she wants me there, but I don't want to be there, because I don't like dealing with her. You can't force me to like someone. I have a whole group of people there qualified to deal with her. But she only wants me to be there and I don't want to."

When another picketer challenged Icahn's sense of decency, asking, "What does it mean to you that 96 percent of us are on strike?" Icahn tossed the hot potato back in the union's lap. "I think you're crazy," he said. "I'd tell Frankovich she's leading you over a cliff. You keep doing this and I'll have 10,000 applicants to take over your jobs."

With that, the boos and jeers rose to a crescendo. A flight attendant yelled out, "You and your buddy Lorenzo—you are two of the same."

"What? I fought Lorenzo," Carl retorted.

"No, you are two of the same!"

Charges and taunts erupted from the crowd. "Where is the money you got from concessions? Why is the airline losing money?"

Concerned that this mass of angry workers would lose control, Icahn retreated back through the gates and into the pastoral beauty of his estate. As he moved away, the picketers broke out into a loud chant: "Solidarity forever. Solidarity forever. Our union makes us strong."

In truth, though, the union proved to be a weakling. When the IFFA launched its strike, it counted 6,000 members at work on TWA flights. Slightly more than two months later, when the leadership called off the strike, the union had lost all but 198 of the jobs to nonunion replacements signing on at a minimum of $1007.50 per month. Under the terms of the union's unconditional offer to return to work, TWA was required to fill new positions with union members, but it would take more than three years for the IFFA to get all of its members back on the payroll, mostly by filling slots that opened through attrition.

In its battle with Carl Icahn, the International Federation of Flight Attendants clearly lost. But paradoxically, so did the man who seemed to beat them. Yes, Icahn managed to take an ax to TWA's salary structure. In doing so, however, he unleashed a groundswell of animosity among TWA's front-line employees. Ultimately, those union workers would be back on Carl's planes, serving not as goodwill ambassadors but as agents of hatred determined to retaliate against the man they saw as the devil incarnate.

"I was working the upper deck of a 747 flight bound for Tel Aviv," recalled an IFFA member, "when this woman followed me into the galley asking, 'You people were on strike, weren't you?' When I said, 'Yes,' she responded, 'Must have been terrible. What do you think of him—of Carl Icahn?' I said, 'I could cheerfully strangle him for all of the hurt he has caused. For the people losing their homes, for forcing me into bankruptcy.'

"As it turned out, the woman was a quality-assurance person and she reported that I seriously threatened to kill Carl. I had said it facetiously, the way you talk about someone who exasperates you. But they were out to get me. . . ."

A flight attendant's complaint is hardly going to get Carl Icahn's attention. But in this regard, he is myopic. By focusing almost exclusively on the numbers, he has failed to consider the human element that is the basic building block of quality service and that gives the top-notch airlines a critical edge in winning and retaining passenger loyalty. Although these "soft" issues are dismissed by Icahn, the numbers man and deal maker, taken together they have a powerful impact on load factor, one of the key components of airline profitability. Given Icahn's devout faith in financial engineering, as opposed to building a business brick by brick, he cannot see the connections among motivated flight attendants, quality service, and the bottom line.

"Icahn is a brilliant negotiator, but he has an Achilles' heel," said famed labor negotiator Theodore Kheel, who met with Icahn on behalf of the IFFA. "He is so bottom-line oriented that he can't see the big picture. There's no other way to explain the way he has squeezed the flight attendants. These people, who are his first line of contact with the public and who could be out there helping to build his business, are instead his enemies.

"You have to understand the man. Shortly after the flight attendants made their unconditional offer to return to work, I went to see Carl in Mt. Kisco, where I was ushered into his office. The place is spectacular, cavernous in size and decorated with expensive reproductions of English antiques. When I complimented Carl on this huge, opulent oriental rug, he made a point of telling me he got a good deal on it at a London auction. When I admired a spectacular table, he said he liked it so much he bought the company that made it. And when I remarked that a painting of an English judge in his red robes was extraordinary,

Carl remarked that the dealer wanted too much money for it and he wouldn't pay their price, so he was leasing it."

Kheel came away from the meeting convinced that Icahn lives by a strange and unattractive ethos.

"Icahn's bottom line: If you can't beat up on people and get things at a good price, then those things aren't worth much," Kheel said. "To him, possessions cannot be enjoyed unless they were acquired for a bargain."

With TWA on the verge of a losing year in 1986, Icahn took the opportunity to beat up on the pilots again. In spite of the substantial concessions the pilots had made at the outset, Icahn wanted more. Carl's contract with the union provided that he could sell TWA assets in a year the carrier suffered particularly heavy losses. Knowing that the pilots feared asset sales as the beginning of the end of TWA, Icahn capitalized on this fear to extend the pilots' concessions.

"His message is 'I can break up the airline,' " Kent Scott said. "But in classic Icahn style he waffles. 'I'm not saying I will [sell the assets], but I can. If I do, don't say I didn't tell you. I could but maybe I won't.'

"And he winds up saying, 'If you give me a contract extension, maybe, just maybe, I won't have to sell assets.' The message is give me labor peace and cost control and I'll protect you guys."

With the contract extension in mind, Icahn met with the pilots' master executive council at New York's Lexington Hotel in September 1986.

"Eighteen union leaders, all pilots, were in the hotel waiting to meet with Carl, who came in a good hour late," recalled Kent Scott. "That's his style—keep the mice quivering. Finally, he makes a grand entrance with his executives Bill Hoar and Mark Buckstein. Carl moves to the head of the table and immediately goes into his 'I might, I could, I didn't say I would sell the assets' spiel.

"Carl is masterful. His presence is commanding. He's six feet three, a billionaire, a crafty negotiator. He has the pilots spellbound. One of the guys even pulls out an Instamatic and asks Icahn to pose while he snaps his picture. When another pilot challenged Icahn, saying he, too, has run a business and so he knows where Carl has erred in running TWA, Icahn shredded the guy and dismissed him as a lightweight."

Icahn displayed an awesome combination of power and wealth and the pilots were mesmerized by him. "He stood there," Scott recalled, "holding TWA in his hand, like an egg he could squeeze at any time." Icahn knew every move to make, every word to say, and he did it all perfectly, creating a climate of apprehension. Had he gone into the meeting making a straightforward request for the contract extension, he would have been turned down. But Icahn knew better than to do that. Instead, "he creates the specter of World War III," Scott remembered, "that being the asset sales the pilots feared. He creates an entire Ben Hur epic, just to get the one issue he wants his way."

In the end, Icahn's move proved successful. The pilots capitulated.

In spite of the problems that plagued him in the early days of his TWA tenure, Icahn did make real progress. In short order he moved decisively to cut operating waste from a system that had tolerated it for years, realigned the route map to eliminate money-losing flights and capitalized on the carrier's strong hubs in St. Louis and New York's Kennedy Airport. Focusing on the last point, he saw the benefit of eliminating St. Louis's competitor Ozark Airlines, thus enabling TWA to dominate a major market along with the network of routes radiating from it. Although TWA's previous management had broached the idea of acquiring Ozark, the negotiations went nowhere before petering out with both sides further apart than when the talks began. But Icahn rekindled the idea and succeeded against all odds in consummating an acquisition for $237 million.

"The Ozark acquisition was the high point of our relationship with Carl," said Kent Scott. "The integration of their pilots with ours gave us real advancement for the first time in years.

Because most of the TWA guys were senior to our Ozark counterparts, we moved up on the seniority ladder."

In spite of the woes of the opening months, Icahn appeared to be making real headway in turning TWA around. Thanks to labor concessions and a fortuitous decline in fuel prices, Icahn cut the airline's overhead by roughly $600 million. With a virtual monopoly in St. Louis, Icahn raised fares and scheduled dozens of new flights, adding the best of the former Ozark runs to TWA's route map.

At this point, Icahn was believing his own daydreams, seeing himself as the baron of a vast airline empire. His theories were right, he believed: Running a major company would be as easy as launching a takeover raid. The critical prerequisites were toughness and intelligence, assets he knew he had in abundance.

Emboldened by the apparent success of the Ozark acquisition, Icahn's appetite was whetted for another, grander addition to his airline.

"Carl is very entrepreneurial—if he gets an idea in his head, he'll turn the ship around and pursue it in a matter of minutes," said former TWA executive Ed Gehrlein. "I remember once talking with him in his office about selling part of our reservation system, PARS. Suddenly someone else came in to talk to him and the subject turned to Delta Airlines.

"Suddenly, Carl jumped up and said, 'Why don't we buy Delta? Get me the numbers on Delta.' "

Within hours, Icahn's aides had generated reams of printouts on Delta's assets, cash flow, return on equity and capitalization, as well as data on the carrier's corporate structure and takeover defenses. As the picture began to take shape, Icahn and his aides saw the opportunity to buy Delta, and then to force TWA's lower wage costs on the carrier. If all went according to plan, Delta's profitability would soar, providing Icahn with the income flow to pay for the acquisition.

"The idea seemed promising, but there was a major hitch," said Brian Freeman. "Delta would never agree to a friendly takeover, and Carl didn't have the financing to launch a tender offer. Furthermore, he had a concern that there would be major political problems with the Atlanta politicians (where Delta is based), and there was also some concern that TWA's cost structure could not actually be imposed on Delta."

Still, Icahn's lust for a deal reflected the confidence he was feeling at this point in his tenure as TWA's top gun.

"Guys get into the airline business and they get mesmerized by it," Freeman said. "There's a glamour appeal to it, even a manhood issue involved. They get a lot of press and they think that by being smarter than the guys who ran it before them, they'll make lots of money. So they get sucked into it."

Determined to protect his market position from competitive assault, Icahn responded quickly and decisively to the announcement in February 1987 that U.S. Air and Piedmont were planning to merge. Calling U.S. Air's chairman Edwin Colodny on February 21, Icahn complained that the merger would change the competitive outlook of the industry, putting TWA in a vulnerable position. Drawing a line in the sand, Icahn warned Colodny that he would not allow the merger to go uncontested. Instead, he had another idea in mind: TWA should buy U.S. Air or U.S. Air should buy TWA.

The next day, Icahn called Colodny again, complaining that he did not want TWA to be "out there alone." Later that day, Icahn called yet again, saying that he could not wait any longer for a response and that TWA was prepared to make an offer of $50 per share for U.S. Air's stock.

Determined to block the U.S. Air/Piedmont deal, Icahn resorted to his familiar tactics. He would buy stock, using the leverage this gave him to threaten and frustrate his corporate opponents.

On March 4, while the Piedmont and U.S. Air boards were putting the final touches on a merger agreement, Icahn had the temerity to announce that he had become U.S. Air's largest single shareholder and to compound his adversaries' woes, he was now offering $52 a share to acquire the airline. This drove a stake into the heart of the merger, forcing the boards to retreat without a deal.

"With Icahn's offer on the table, the boards had to put the merger on hold until they analyzed exactly what Icahn was offering," said a U.S. Air adviser. "So they had their investment bankers and the lawyers advise them on the merits of the Icahn proposal. Two major findings emerged. One was that the deal didn't make sense. The Justice Department would quash it on antitrust grounds, and even if that wasn't a problem, there was great skepticism that Icahn had the money to consummate the transaction.

"Two, the feeling was that Icahn had no intention of acquiring U.S. Air but instead was in the game as a spoiler. He worried that the merged airline would be a formidable competitor and, equally important, that the merger would remove two of the best candidates to buy TWA. And selling TWA was his secret agenda from the outset. In fact, when Icahn started talking to U.S. Air at the time of the proposed merger with Piedmont, one of his suggestions was for a three-way combination between TWA, U.S. Air, and Piedmont."

To prevent Icahn from succeeding as a spoiler, U.S. Air filed suit in federal court in Pittsburgh, seeking a preliminary injunction enjoining Icahn from proceeding with his takeover bid.

According to the U.S. Air complaint, the purpose of Icahn's offer was to "disrupt the Piedmont/U.S. Air merger and to damage U.S. Air through an expensive and disruptive takeover fight. Icahn was fully aware that many experts believed that the government would not approve a merger of TWA, U.S. Air, and Piedmont. Thus by injecting TWA into a control position over U.S. Air, Icahn might be able to prevent or delay government approval of the Piedmont/U.S. Air merger. And as an experienced corporate raider, Icahn knew full well the devastating effect that a failed takeover attempt would have on a company. On the other hand, if Icahn is successful in aborting the U.S. Air/Piedmont transaction and in seizing control of U.S. Air, he would eliminate a competitor."

There is reason to believe that Icahn's move against U.S. Air was in part retaliation against a decision Colodny had made months before.

"I had been trying to sell TWA to get rid of Carl," said Brian Freeman. "From the beginning we knew that he might not be the right man to guide TWA over the long term. His entrepreneurial needs for a payback would lead him to squeeze rather than build the carrier. So I was talking to a number of potential buyers to step in and take Carl's place."

With this in mind, Freeman broached the idea to U.S. Air. "When I went to Colodny and asked him to buy it, he told me in so many words to back off—that the airline was a piece of shit.

"When I told Carl what I had done, he told me not to do that kind of thing. That I wasn't his agent."

Bad chemistry between Colodny and Icahn was virtually inevitable. As a straight shooter corporate type and an airline insider, Colodny had trouble relating to Icahn, who had come to the airline business as a financial opportunist. And on a more visceral level, he found himself repelled by Icahn's aggressive bargaining style.

As Icahn played his U.S. Air hand, he put that style on display, demonstrating all of his skills as a buyer and a seller simultaneously. By taking a big position on the verge of U.S. Air's merger with Piedmont, he stood to: 1. prompt management to buy his stock, 2. earn a profit if the stock rose, or 3. if the merger deal blew up, to acquire U.S. Air.

Ultimately, a federal court granted U.S. Air a preliminary injunction requiring Icahn to prove that his offer for the company was more than a charade intended to block the U.S. Air/ Piedmont merger.

"It was actually surprising that the judge granted the preliminary injunction, because in cases like this judges usually liked the natural market forces to deal with the issue," said the U.S. Air adviser. "But recognizing that Icahn's action could have a deleterious effect on a pending merger, the court was willing to decide in U.S. Air's favor, holding off Icahn with the idea that the case could come to a full trial, at which time Carl could seek to have the injunction lifted.

"But it never came to that. After U.S. Air got what it wanted in court, Icahn just went away. Obviously, he recognized the litigation had merit and this was one case he wasn't going to win.

"He tried to use the threat of breaking up the merger as leverage for selling TWA, which was his real agenda. When he saw that wasn't going to happen, he saw no reason to continue with the bluff."

By year-end 1987, Icahn was boasting that he had engineered a dramatic turnaround. The carrier was in the black, generating operating income of $240 million and on its way to $259 million for 1988.

Although the numbers looked impressive, a closer look revealed that a good part of the profits were based more on the financial engineering that came naturally to Icahn than on managerial prowess. Consider the use of more liberal depreciation methods that enabled TWA to extend the useful life projections on the carrier's wide-body aircraft, producing savings of $44 million. And note that TWA gained roughly $50 million from a long-standing law suit against Hughes Tool Co.

Subtract these and other extraordinary sums, including tax-loss carryforwards, and TWA's results would have shown losses. In spite of the decisive moves Icahn had made in cutting costs and acquiring Ozark, in spite of the fact that the numbers had improved under his command, TWA was still a wounded bird with an aging fleet, a weak management structure and tense labor relations.

In part, Icahn's problems could be traced to the corporate culture he created in his own image.

"Carl is surrounded by people who lead him to believe that he can get something for nothing," said airline consultant Bob Mann, who served as TWA's vice president of marketing from December 1988 through February 1990.

After the flight attendants' strike, the carrier launched an advertising campaign under the theme "The New TWA: See How Good We Really Are." This was designed to wipe away the memory of the strike, reposition the carrier, win back market share, and regain customer loyalty. In principle, it would be part of an evolutionary campaign. As service improved and share expanded, new advertising would come on stream in tandem. But the master plan came apart when service ratings actually deteriorated. That's because the appropriate and necessary capital investments were not made.

TWA executives led Carl to believe that he could borrow from Peter to pay Paul. Instead of improving service across the board, they would take from domestic service to improve the North Atlantic service. But what the experienced airline managers failed to tell Icahn, and what he should have known instinctively, is that you cannot get away with that gimmick for long. Domestic fliers will experience a decrease in service. And because the domestic service was critical for TWA, that strategy would be counterproductive.

"I think that some of the top executives who worked for Carl were less than intellectually honest with him," Mann said. "I think they told him what he wanted to hear."

Within Icahn's executive corps, competing factions emerged, lobbying the boss to pursue one of three strategies: 1. create a niche airline with strength in a limited number of key routes, 2. build TWA into a world-class carrier, 3. engage in short-term caretaker management until a sale of the business or the assets could be consummated.

Over time Icahn has used each of these strategies, zigzagging from one to another in search of an instant cure. But in his heart he favored number three. Carl knew better than anyone else that rebuilding TWA on a long-term basis, and revitalizing it as a major competitor in the air wars against American, Delta, and United, would require huge investments in aircraft, computer systems, employee perks and management talent. The payback would be slow—and in an industry subject to the roller-coaster impact of fluctuating fuel costs, cyclical consumer confidence, and terrorism—the returns would be uncertain.

From the beginning, Icahn's game plan called for turning around TWA and then selling it for a huge profit, bringing him greater wealth and newfound respectability as a greenmailer turned industrialist. The window of opportunity opened widest in the period between mid-1988 and early 1989, when the turnaround seemed to be for real. With this in mind, Icahn spoke with several would-be buyers, including Northwest Airlines co-chairman Alfred Checchi. Flying to Mt. Kisco to meet with

Icahn, Checchi sat down to discuss a deal only to discover that the talks would go nowhere. From Checchi's perspective, Icahn's price tag was too high, based as it was on an unreasonable assessment of the value of TWA's assets. In seeking to cut an exceptional deal at Checchi's expense, Icahn was demonstrating once again that he was willing to act on his terms and his terms alone. Clearly at this point, he felt no real urgency to sell TWA.

Still, as a man who viewed balance sheets in terms of selling assets rather than adding to them, and who entered every deal with a clear path to the exit door, Icahn found himself increasingly uncomfortable with the money he had invested in a beast that seemed difficult, if not impossible, to tame.

"Carl is a smart Neanderthal," said Marty Whitman. "He's a Neanderthal because he doesn't listen. He has fixed ideas. He doesn't see that you can make money by investing in a business. He only wants to cash out—to get cash flow. He doesn't understand that most of the great businesses built in this country were cash consumers. They used public markets and consumed cash to build fabulous wealth for their owners. But Carl just wants the cash-out approach.

"The characteristics that made Carl a great arbitrageur made him the worst guy to run TWA. He's demonstrated that he can't manage an operating business. He can't play the reorganization game with troubled companies."

As early as 1987, Icahn's focus on managing the airline was distracted by the urge to take major positions in potential takeovers. When Australian investor Robert Holmes á Court sought to sell his huge stake in Texaco after the October stock market crash, Icahn bought the stock, financing the purchase in part with TWA funds. Icahn also took a major position in USX.

Although Icahn had not yet fully abandoned the idea of building TWA into a highly profitable carrier—and making himself the new Lee Iaccoca, whose widespread praise Carl secretly envied—he saw a greater opportunity to enhance his personal wealth by continuing his takeover activities, funded in part by the airline.

On another front, Icahn—always careful to protect his downside—decided the time had come to withdraw his risk capital, staying in control of TWA while spinning the wheel with "other people's money." He would accomplish this feat of financial engineering by taking TWA private.

Under the terms of a privatization plan, approved by TWA's shareholders on September 7, 1988, TWA purchased all outstanding shares, including the majority block owned by Icahn, and then the carrier merged with a company controlled by Carl. In return for their stock, the public shareholders received $20 per share in cash along with a twenty-year, $30 face-value bond (due in 2008). The deal was embraced by the shareholders, who saw an opportunity to cash out at favorable terms. Those who sold the debt portion soon after the transaction did well indeed.

Icahn would also receive $20 a share for his stock, paid both in cash and in shares of Texaco and USX stock, then in TWA's treasury, along with a special issue of preferred stock (since known as the "Icahn preferred") valued at $196 million.

The privatization was funded by $660 million in junk bonds raised by Drexel. An earlier attempt to accomplish a similar goal had failed when Paine Webber, which had promised to do the deal at a lower cost, found itself unable to raise the capital. Adding insult to injury, Paine Webber had to pay Icahn a $1 million consolation prize—a fee he had built into the agreement just in case the would-be financiers could not perform.

The deal ultimately funded by Drexel's unparalleled junk bond network was just the kind of complex financial alchemy that appeared to turn dross into gold throughout the 1980s. In structuring the deal, Icahn was at the top of his game. When the documents were signed, the raider turned CEO wound up with $469 million, representing all of his initial investment, and a 19 percent profit (minus carrying costs on his initial investment). His equity stake in the company also increased, from 76 to 85 percent of TWA stock before the privatization to 90 percent after the deal was done. Although Icahn's initial risk capital was now removed, he remained in control of the company, capable of earning millions on the new issue of preferred stock (which was entitled to first dibs on the company's dividends) and free to use TWA's cash horde to continue making investments in Texaco and USX.

"When the privatization is complete, Icahn winds up with this great pot of cash at no cost to himself," Freeman said. "It's like he wants a bank and gets one for free."

But while the privatization was a Christmas gift for Icahn, it would saddle the carrier with an enormous debt load, soaking up capital better suited for reinvestment in operating assets. This downside of junk bond financing would weigh heavily on TWA, as it would on dozens of major companies whose fortunes reversed as the euphoria of the eighties collided with the realities of the nineties.

In the wake of the privatization, the unions were furious, charging that Icahn had leveraged the company to the point that its future was in jeopardy. Considering the carrier's staggering debt load, labor worried that TWA would be hard pressed to meet its obligations, much less to invest in the assets it would need to be a global competitor. Instead, they saw Icahn using the airline's capital for takeover attempts on USX and Texaco. As the machinists charged in a lawsuit over the privatization:

"The Plan has been characterized as an act of desperation by the defendant Icahn to 'extricate' himself from his TWA investment and to permit him to reemerge as America's preeminent 'corporate raider.' "

In another suit, the IAM went to the crux of the issue, charging that "TWA is already highly leveraged as a result of its takeover in 1986 by defendant Icahn. . . . TWA's fleet of airplanes is generally old. . . . TWA will have to incur major capital expenditures by the end of the decade. The flexibility of financing these required expenditures is severely limited by the financial impositions of the Icahn Plan. . . . The Icahn Plan will strip defendant TWA of any possible financial 'cushion.' . . . The net effect of the Icahn Plan is to cripple the defendant TWA financially, solely to permit the defendant Icahn to take TWA private and to pay himself a $450 million 'dividend' for his TWA stock. No benefit or consideration whatsoever passes to TWA in return for the assumption of a huge debt burden, which will leave the airline insolvent or with unreasonably small capital to carry on its business."

From Icahn's perspective, the unions' bashing of the privatization revealed them as ungrateful beneficiaries of his willingness to save the company from Lorenzo.

What's more, Icahn's initial agreement with the unions gave him the right to take TWA private. Anyone who doubted that he would do just that—and that he would do it sooner rather than later—didn't understand Carl Icahn's determination to keep the leverage, and the clout that goes with it.

In the course of a dinner at Icahn's house, Brian Freeman teased Carl that if he didn't stop riding roughshod on the unions, he would place pickets in front of Carl's house. When Liba looked concerned, Freeman said jokingly, "Don't worry, I'll keep them 100 feet away." To which Liba responded, "But that means they'll be inside the gates!"

Describing Icahn's rollercoaster relationship with the unions, former TWA pilots' chief Tom Ashwood said, "Carl is a financial terrorist who holds employees hostage. At first the employees suffer from the Stockholm syndrome, so they go through this period when they think their imprisoner is the only one who can save them. That happened at TWA, but fortunately the effects of the syndrome passed and the vast majority of the people recognized that Icahn was the last one who would save them from anything."

Privatization cemented the relationship between Icahn and Leon Black, since the latter served as an intermediary between Drexel's junk bond coffers and the takeover king. In part, their relationship was grounded in the common pursuit of profit. Black capitalized on his Icahn ties to promote his place in the Drexel hierarchy, and Icahn used his access to Leon to secure unlimited financing. Although they would fancy themselves as friends—playing tennis and chess, vacationing with their families—it was also a marriage of convenience.

"Carl and Leon hit it off for two reasons," said a prominent

New York attorney. "Both are very good with numbers. Very fast. Carl talks a kind of shorthand a lot of people don't understand. They can't pick up on what he is saying. 'Is this the great Icahn?' they ask themselves. He doesn't appear impressive. He seems like this Damon Runyon figure.

"But Leon can understand Carl's shorthand. He cuts right through the foliage and sees the scene Carl wants to paint. That brought them together. And always there was the fact that Drexel represented a huge pool of capital for Icahn. So he had a vested interest in getting close to a Drexel power who could unlock that capital for him."

Black is under no illusions himself. "Look, Carl and I like each other and respect each other. We are friends. But did the genesis of our relationship have to do with Carl's getting access to Drexel funds? Let me put it this way: Carl is no fool. Drexel in the 1980s was the premier source of capital. Plus we were the most credible threat in the takeover arena he played in.

"Carl is a billionaire today, and to become a billionaire you need access to billions."

The Drexel-financed privatization was a sweet deal for Icahn and, it appeared, for his fellow shareholders. Considering that TWA had teetered on the brink of financial disaster for years, they were delighted to be cashing in their chips.

But when a weak and degenerating company is able to make everyone rich while its problems mount and its market share tumbles, someone has to pay the piper. In this case the pilots and the machinists were convinced that the burden would fall on them.

"Carl's original agreement with the unions called for him to take TWA private at some point," said Ashwood. "We had supported this idea on the assumption that buying out the public shareholders would deepen Icahn's commitment to TWA.

"But we were shocked when we read Icahn's prospectus for taking TWA private. Instead of reaching into his own pockets, in part, to make it happen, he would get TWA to buy out the public shareholders. Instantly, we recognized that his plan had nothing to do with extending his commitment to the airline. Instead, he planned to take his money out of TWA two times, first on the sale of his shares and subsequently as an investment basket for other ventures. This left the employees who had counted on him with nothing more than an empty shell."

"The privatization was a clear case of OPM," said Alexander Greene, a managing director with Whitman Heffernan Rhine & Co., investment bankers specializing in the reorganization of troubled companies. "In effect, Carl arbitraged the union concessions for his own equity purchases."

Privatization would prove to be a watershed in Icahn's fragile alliance with organized labor. The Ozark acquisition, the revamping of the route structure and the initial turnaround in reported earnings led the unions to believe that they had made the right choice between Icahn and Lorenzo. Perhaps all the negative press about Icahn—the charges that he was a greedy Wall Street backroom wheeler-dealer—were nothing more than yellow journalism. Perhaps Icahn was, as he portrayed himself, a 1980s Renaissance man: part financial genius, part business builder, always a man of his word.

The optimism that prevailed during the honeymoon period, though, turned quickly to anger and pessimism as details of the privatization leaked to the unions. "When we heard his plans for the privatization, we knew Icahn's promises to turn TWA into a premier airline were bullshit," Ashwood said. "We knew Icahn's promises to upgrade the fleet were bullshit."

According to Ashwood, Joe Corr, TWA's president installed by Icahn, kept telling the pilots that Carl was going to build a better airline. That he was going to expand and modernize the fleet by acquiring sixty MD-80's (a McDonnel Douglas aircraft).

"At first, Corr honestly believed that it was going to be that way," Ashwood said. "But then he, too, recognized that Carl's promises were bullshit. He was honest enough to say that what he'd been telling us about Icahn's intentions turned out to be optimistic nonsense."

Corr agrees that Icahn had little stomach for investing heavily in TWA, but he sees it as a case of good intentions gone bad rather than a diabolical plot to rape the unions.

"When Carl expressed a desire to rebuild TWA, he wasn't lying," Corr said. "I think he did intend to do so. Then, for several reasons, he changed his mind. These included fear of overcapacity, massive investment requirements, and he predicted trouble with the unions. Most important, he felt he could make more money with other investments."

Relations reached a low at a meeting between Icahn, Bill Hoar, and leaders of the pilots' union. When Carl used the occasion to announce the good news that the board had approved a major capital expenditure that would boost the revenue side, the labor leaders found their spirits rising. Perhaps Icahn had seen the light and would begin to reinvest in a new TWA that was more than an empty promise in an advertising campaign. But as Icahn and Hoar continued to speak, the union's hopes were dashed. As it turned out, the major capital expenditure was for vacuum cleaners to improve maintenance on TWA planes as well as funds to fix a broken escalator at the Kennedy Airport terminal.

"The most amazing thing is that these guys were serious," recalled Kent Scott. "They touted goddamn vacuum cleaners as a genuine breakthrough. That was really going to take us to the top."

From Ashwood's perspective, those who trusted Carl to rebuild TWA were naive from the outset. "A leopard doesn't change his spots. Icahn was, and is, a financial engineer. He can't run a business. He can't run a corner deli. If he ran the deli and the freezer broke, he wouldn't fix it. He'd try to sell the spoiled milk rather than have the freezer fixed."

Through his financial engineering, Icahn had created a Frankenstein monster of ill will within his own organization. Soon after the privatization, vicious slurs were scrawled on the walls of TWA hangars, and an oven in a jumbo jet's lower galley read, "Hey, Carl, this one's for you." As employees vented their animosity, cruel jokes swept through the airline's cockpits and ticket counters. Two of the favorites:

"Carl and one of his aides are walking down the street when a young blonde passes by. The aide says to Carl, 'Hey, why don't you screw her?' Carl replies, 'Out of what?' "

"Saddam Hussein looks in the mirror and asks, 'Mirror, mirror, who's the meanest, most detestable son of a bitch in the world?'

" 'What! Who the hell is Carl Icahn?' "

ICAHN VS.
TEXACO

Another Year, Another $500 Million

"When you negotiate with Carl it can seem as if he is just going around in circles. But the way to see where Carl is going is to keep your eye on the money. Carl always winds up where the money is."
—Dennis O'Dea, partner with the law firm of Keck, Mahin & Cate

A year before Icahn purchased TWA, a corporate confrontation of enormous proportions had begun to take shape in the Texas/Oklahoma oil patch, pitting huge, hidebound Texaco, Inc., against smaller, feistier Penzoil.

The battle began when the two petroleum companies locked horns in an ugly tug-of-war over the rights to acquire Getty Oil, then blessed with rich reserves of valuable crude. As events unfolded, Penzoil celebrated what it thought was a firm deal to acquire Getty, only to watch Texaco make an eleventh-hour bid that snatched victory away from a stunned and furious Penzoil.

The losers in the M&A contests of the 1980s were wont to

cry foul when the other guy won, but Penzoil's cantankerous CEO Hugh Liedtke was determined to do more than the requisite whining. He sued the White Plains, New York–based oil giant for "tortious interference" with Penzoil's agreement to buy Getty.

But this was only the opening salvo. Texaco, founded as the Texas Company in 1902, had grown to become of the most arrogant and anachronistic companies in the United States. No way, management thought, could this gnat from Houston hurt the big red star of the American highway. This arrogance only intensified when Penzoil's hired gun, Houston attorney "King of Torts" Joe Jamail, convinced a Texas jury that Penzoil had suffered enormous damages. Texaco was faced with a staggering bill for $10.5 billion, plus an additional $600 million in prejudgment interest by the time the judgment was entered.

Initially, high and mighty Texaco assumed that legal appeals would overturn the decision. With this in mind, Texaco moved on two fronts, seeking a preliminary injunction preventing Penzoil from seizing its assets in accordance with the judgment and simultaneously pursuing an appeal to reverse the judgment.

At first Texaco hit paydirt by securing a preliminary injunction from the U.S. District Court in the Southern District of New York. But then events turned against the company as a Texas court rejected Texaco's motion for an appeal in February 1987, and in April of that year the U.S. Supreme Court lifted the temporary injunction, thus leaving Texaco's assets vulnerable to seizure. To prevent that, the once mighty oil titan—its pride crushed, its viability threatened—saw no other option but to file for bankruptcy on April 12, 1987, thus voiding the need to post a multibillion dollar bond as it pursued a number of strategies, including an ultimate appeal to the Supreme Court on the judgment itself.

Thus would begin a long, drawn-out process throughout which Texaco's fate would hang in limbo. With uncertainty over the Penzoil claim clouding its prospects, Texaco stock took a drubbing in the October 19, 1987, crash, its share price falling to $28 from a high of more than $41 in early October. Sensing opportunity, Icahn ordered TWA (acting through a subsidiary called Swan) to begin making open-market purchases of Texaco. Between October 2 and October 23, 1982, 4,347,500 Texaco shares were acquired through this arrangement at an average price of $33.95 a share. With Texaco stock coming under more pressure in the wake of the Crash, Icahn resumed his purchases (through TWA and Swan) accumulating an additional 1,537,500 Texaco shares between November 6 and November 13.

It was at this time that Icahn, on his way to Martha's Vineyard to scout a vacation house, noticed a newspaper headline referring to the financial woes of Robert Holmes á Court. Pressed by wary bankers, the story read, Holmes á Court would have to sell off chunks of his substantial assets, including a huge block of Texaco shares, representing about 10 percent of the company's outstanding stock. Icahn, who had been buying Texaco as a value play, saw an opportunity to seize a massive stake from a highly vulnerable owner.

Placing a call to Holmes á Court as soon as he landed in the Vineyard, Icahn played a shrewd hand, presenting himself not as a vulture, but as a fair-minded buyer who could help the soft-spoken Australian out of a jam.

Icahn opened the negotiations with a candid assessment of Holmes á Court's weak position.

"Robert, I have been reading that you are having financial difficulties," Icahn said.

"Yes, I do," Holmes á Court responded a decibal or two above a whisper.

"I would like to make you an offer," Icahn continued without missing a beat. "The stock is selling for $29. I'll buy your entire position for that price. I'm not going to try to steal it from you for $26 or $27. I'm not here to play games. By the same token, I don't want you to come back and quote me $31, or $30 or even $29⅛."

Knowing full well that Holmes á Court, a crafty investor in his own right, would shop the offer before responding, Icahn gave him forty-eight hours to make the deal or to let it pass. Knowing that British investor James Goldsmith was buzzing around Texaco, and was likely interested in snaring the Holmes á Court block for his own account, Icahn saw the Brit as his major competitor. But that's why his market price offer was savvy. Given Goldsmith's penchant for driving a hard bargain, Icahn assumed that he would bid the $26 or $27 Carl had already sworn off. As Holmes á Court beat the bushes for a deal, Carl's preemptive offer would look too good to pass up.

Within twenty-four hours, the Australian called back, confirming a deal at $29, for 12 million of the total 24 million Texaco shares Holmes á Court owned. As part of the deal, signed on November 25, Icahn secured the voting rights to all of Holmes á Court's stock, and was granted the right of first refusal on the balance of Holmes á Court's shares.

"I'm impressed with the way Carl acquired the Texaco stock," says Robert Lange, a one-time member of Texaco's shareholders committee, formed when the company was in bankruptcy. "He gets wind that Holmes á Court is leveraged to the hilt and that his bankers are putting in the screws to sell assets. That's when Icahn strikes.

"This is a tremendously adroit thing to do. Vintage Carl. He waits until someone is so stretched out and in need of a deal that he can come in and buy under the most favorable terms."

With that, Icahn became the largest shareholder in a beleaguered company facing life-threatening litigation. But in this environment of uncertainty Icahn spotted opportunity. Given his talent for viewing situations from a holistic perspective, he saw room to operate, to create value, and ultimately to turn adversity into enormous profit.

Suddenly, Texaco's management, led by CEO James Kinnear, faced a dual threat: In addition to the $10.5 billion Penzoil claim, the most notorious takeover bully in America was now its largest shareholder. Unlike the unwary CEOs Icahn had tangled with at an earlier stage in his career, Kinnear, installed as Texaco's chief executive on January 1987, knew from the start that Icahn was not going to remain idle. From the moment he decided to buy Holmes á Court's stake, Icahn was determined to inject himself into the Texaco/Penzoil battle, forging a compromise between the two companies. This done, he was convinced the shares would soar, making the Texaco purchase the shrewdest gamble of his life. Quickly, Icahn began calling the principal parties involved in the case. He called the creditors' committee, the equity committee, Texaco's bankruptcy attorney (Weil, Gotshal partner) Harvey Miller, Kinnear, and Liedtke. Each time he called, he was most interested in the probability of a settlement between Texaco and Penzoil.

"Carl said there had to be a settlement," Miller remembered. "He wanted one badly. He thought most any settlement would have a positive impact on the stock. He said, 'We could settle for $4 billion.' I said, 'A chimpanzee could settle for $4 billion; the actual settlement could be for much less.' But you sensed Carl wasn't interested in a billion here, a billion there."

The opposing sides appeared hopelessly deadlocked. Claiming that it had suffered at the hands of Texaco and that its legal position had been vindicated, Penzoil insisted publicly on settlement in full. Experienced observers took this for the poker-faced bluff that it was—an effort to put pressure on Texaco. It was also clear that given a reasonable offer—estimates ran from $3 to $5 billion—that Liedtke and his boys would settle.

Stodgy and imperious Texaco, however, would behave like anything but a reasonable adversary. Rather than admitting they had been beaten, Texaco's senior executives indicated that they were determined to take their case to the Supreme Court. Until they lost there, they wouldn't pay Penzoil a dime.

It was a John Wayne stance that would make the Texaco roughnecks proud. But this strategy amounted to an all-or-nothing crap shoot. If the Supreme Court refused to grant certiorari, thus denying the appeal, or if the justices granted certiorari and ultimately ruled in favor of Penzoil, Texaco would have no other option but to pay Penzoil perhaps twice as much as a precourt settlement—a sum that could easily drive a stake into Texaco's heart, killing off what had been a pillar of the business community.

That was a holocaust that Icahn the self-proclaimed "activist" was determined to prevent. To this end, he appointed himself as a mediator. On one hand, he pressed Texaco to come down from its pedestal and negotiate; on the other, he challenged Liedtke to set a reasonable price as the basis for a deal. Determined, as usual, to bring fear and uncertainty to his adversaries, he purchased a substantial block of Penzoil shares, claiming 2 percent of the company's stock. Without a word of the block ever passing between them, Liedtke understood the implied threat: Just as Icahn had emerged as Texaco's largest shareholder, capable of mounting an effective battle for control of the company, he could do the same at Penzoil. The move to keep Liedtke off guard and respectful of the raider's power was pure Icahn.

On the surface, the interaction between Liedtke and Icahn made for a comic clash of personalities. A rumpled character from the streets of New York was clashing with a bear of an oil man from the Southwest. Even Icahn's aides wondered if he would lose patience with Liedtke, writing him off as an impossible hick. But the fact is, Icahn had greater rapport with Liedtke than with Texaco's play-it-by-the-book managers.

"There was really not this jarring clash of backgrounds between Icahn and Liedtke," says Dennis O'Dea, a Chicago-based attorney who represented a committee of Texaco shareholders. "Liedtke was presented as this romantic figure from the oil patch, but the Ewell Gibbons image that grew around him was based more on marketing and theatrics than on reality. He went to school at Amherst just as Icahn went to Princeton, and he was a smart and thoughtful man in his own right."

Emotionally and intellectually, Icahn understood Liedtke. Here was a man who had defied the odds, taken on a giant and beat it in the courts. With a $10.5 billion judgment in hand, he had the leverage to make Texaco squirm, which was precisely what he intended to do as he angled for a rich settlement— exactly the way Icahn would play the hand.

Texaco's response was another matter. That professional managers, none of whom had substantial equity in Texaco, were able to put the company in jeopardy at the expense of the shareholders elicited the sense of outrage that had infused Icahn ever since his father railed against robber barons. That Kinnear and his cohorts would even consider risking his money for the sake of macho pride left Icahn livid.

At one point he asked Kinnear what he would do if he couldn't make a deal with Penzoil. According to Icahn, Kinnear responded, "Well, I can just go fishing." When Carl pressed further, asking, "What happens if there's no company when you come back?" Kinnear is said to have answered, "Well, I'll still have my fishing pole."

To Icahn, this apparent nonchalance about shareholders' assets was unforgivable. In an interview with *Newsweek* Icahn vented his spleen. "Kinnear might have his fishing pole, but what would all the other shareholders have? The other shareholders wouldn't even have a fish. There's something wrong with a system where management and a board can make a decision to bet the ranch without even allowing the shareholders to be involved. In this case, it might well be that management and directors would have allowed this company to go straight down the path of destruction."

As Texaco remained mired in the quicksand of Chapter XI, committees of the company's creditors and equity holders tried to structure a settlement with Penzoil that Kinnear and the board would approve. But with both sides clinging to irreconcilable positions, the committees were striking out. Determined to break through the logjam, Icahn gravitated toward the equity committee, viewing it as the ideal vehicle for achieving his goals. His master plan called for approaching the committee as a force capable of achieving real progress, dominating the membership and reshaping the body in his image. But from the start he ran into a group unwilling to be intimidated by him, takeover king or not.

"The committee was a colorful group, dramatically different from Carl in style and background," recalled Wilbur Ross, who as a senior managing director of Rothschild, Inc., served as adviser to the committee. "Our chairman, Robert Norris, was a great grandson of a Texaco founder, his mother had been the largest Texaco shareholder and his father the company's longest serving director. So he went way back with the company. And did he look the part. A rancher by profession, he had actually been picked as the original Marlboro Man."

Powerfully built, leather-skinned and a friend of John Wayne, Norris was the living embodiment of the Old West.

Other members of the equity committee included a retired
Texaco executive whose family had inherited a large block of
Texaco shares, a retired hourly worker who served as a lightning
rod for mom-and-pop shareholders and representatives of state
pension funds that had multimillion-dollar investments in Texaco stock. As a whole, the group knew that they didn't want or
need Icahn to play God. In fact, when Carl sought membership
as the first step in his broader goal to dominate the body, he was
stopped cold.

"We told Carl that he would only be admitted to the committee if he signed a restrictive agreement prohibiting him from
continuing to trade in Texaco stock," Ross said. "We insisted on
this on the grounds that as a committee member he would be
privy to confidential information. When Carl refused to sign
anything that would limit his options, we opted not to invite him
to join the committee."

In secret deliberations, the equity committee had come to
the conclusion that the Texaco/Penzoil settlement should fall
around the $3 billion mark. As committee members maneuvered
between the parties, though, they came to believe that the Texaco
forces were dug in. One school of thought was that Texaco
chairman Alfred DeCrane, Jr. was inclined to settle with Penzoil
but that Kinnear, a starched-shirt Annapolis graduate who had
served in the navy during the Korean War, was more inclined to
tough it out in court.

"It was clear to me that Kinnear had decided to go for broke
with a Supreme Court appeal," Ross says. "If he wasn't out for
that, he was the world's worst negotiator. Behind the scenes,
Texaco executives were saying that they would pay $1.8 to $2
billion, but that was more of an insult than a legitimate offer.
Penzoil would accept that only if they believed they didn't have
a prayer in court, but Liedtke and Jamail knew that just the
opposite was true.

"We had done our homework and we were sure that Penzoil
did theirs. When you figured out the math, the odds were in
Penzoil's favor. The Supreme Court hears only five percent of
the certiorari petitions presented to it, but even if we gave Texaco
the benefit of the doubt and said they had a 50/50 chance of

getting before the court to make their case, and a 50/50 percent chance of having the court decide in their favor, they only had a 25 percent chance of winning. We didn't think those odds were good enough to bet the company's fate."

A break in the logjam came in December 1987 when Judge Howard Schwartzberg of the U.S. Bankruptcy Court of the Southern District of New York became frustrated with Texaco's intrasigence and gave the creditor and equity committees the right to strike a deal with Penzoil and to file their own plans for settling the stalemate with the bankruptcy court.

At first, Schwartzberg indicated that he would entertain a plan worked out by Penzoil and the creditors, apparently excluding the equity committee from the negotiations to end the impasse. Determined to prevent this, Dennis O'Dea assembled the committee members and marched them into the court. Asking the judge to reconsider, he noted that if anyone deserved to play a role in this settlement, it was the shareholders.

Driving home his point with a bit of legal dramatics, he introduced the members one at a time, making it clear people on the committee had financial interests in Texaco tracing back to the company's founding.

"I introduced Bob Norris and Henry Campbell, both whom were the direct descendants of Texas Company founders," O'Dea said. "My point was that these weren't schleppers off the street. They were people with genuine economic interest in the company and thus deserving of a voice in structuring a settlement.

"At that point, the judge said he never intended to exclude the equity committee, and that yes, we could negotiate directly with Penzoil."

When Texaco lost the exclusive right to file a plan with the court, the picture changed dramatically—more than Kinnear, DeCrane, Icahn or anyone outside the equity committee's inner circle recognized. Unbeknownst to the rest of the world, Norris, Ross, and O'Dea had made a pact that if the judge cut them in, they would fly to Houston the next day to put an offer before Liedtke.

In a private telephone call to Norris, Liedtke had invited the equity committee to make an offer substantial enough to end the stalemate. Sensing that a deal could now be struck, Norris asked how much Liedtke had in mind.

"He said, 'In excess of $3 billion,' " Norris recalled. "I asked him to be more specific, to give me a number, but again he repeated, 'In excess of $3 billion.' "

Clearly, Liedtke had put a floor on the deal; the ball was now in Norris's court. Proving himself to be a shrewd negotiator in his own right, the one-time Marlboro Man contacted his fellow committee members, suggesting they make a formal offer of $3.01 billion. Although most were skeptical that Penzoil would agree to an offer so close to the floor, Norris insisted that they had a shot.

On the evening before they departed for Houston, Norris and Ross dined with Icahn at New York's Parker Meridien Hotel. Ironically, Carl had called the meeting to boast that he was making progress in his Penzoil-Texaco shuttle diplomacy and that the amateurs on the committee should back off and let a pro take charge.

"Carl was there with his lawyers, his boys," Norris remembered. "He went through this song and dance about how he handled other companies—how he intimidated his opponents by pushing them into a corner and coming on strong.

"He said to me, 'Goddamn it, Norris, why don't you go back to your ranch? I don't tell you how to raise your cattle. Don't tell me how to deal with companies. What do you know about it?' "

"Well, I told him, 'It's never too late to learn.' "

Ross had come to the dinner to make certain, without giving away their plan, that Icahn would accept a $3 billion settlement. The last thing he wanted was to cut a deal with Liedtke, only to have it explode because Icahn refused to support it.

"I felt confident we would have Carl's support, because during the dinner meeting he made it clear that he would be willing to settle at a higher number," Ross recalled. "As far as I was concerned, it was mission accomplished."

Playing "I've got a secret" with Icahn may have been amusing, but the prospect of dealing with Liedtke, and possibly coming away empty-handed, left Norris on edge. That night he slept poorly. "When we got to Houston, I don't mind telling you I was sweating," Norris recalled. "Certain stockholder groups threatened to sue if we screwed up the deal."

Orchestrating their presentation one last time, the triad met for breakfast at the Four Seasons Hotel. At the session, it was decided that Ross would open with an overview of the financial issues, O'Dea would follow quickly with the legal/structural side and then Norris would deliver the settlement number. The way Norris put it at the time, Ross and O'Dea would do the blocking so that he could run through with the ball.

With the strategy set, the men left the Four Seasons for the Penzoil Tower. Norris, Ross, and O'Dea were ushered into a conference room handsomely decorated in a southwestern motif. Liedtke sat at the head of a long table, flanked by a pair of Penzoil lawyers. "When we arrived at Penzoil, O'Dea and Ross met with Liedtke alone for a few minutes," Norris recalled. "Then I came in and said, 'I'm here to give you our number. Not to negotiate. You say no and I'm out the door. We're prepared to offer you $3 billion, $1 million.' "

At first Liedtke sat motionless, expressionless, as if he hadn't heard what Norris said. Ross, the most experienced of the group, didn't know what to make of it. Was Liedtke insulted? Was this the silence before the storm? Would he erupt in a rage?

Finally, after what seemed like an eternity, Liedtke spoke. "Bob," he said, "I can live with that."

When word of the deal reached New York, Texaco's management was incensed. Their power had been usurped and their strategy derailed by unwelcome intruders—who just happened to own the company. With Texaco, the press, Icahn, and Penzoil trying to reach Norris, O'Dea thought it best to keep him under wraps until the deal was put to ink. A major concern was that Penzoil, which wanted to add interest payments to the $3.01* billion settlement, would try to get Norris to change the terms of the agreement. To prevent anything from blowing the deal at this

*The extra $1 million was dropped from the settlement when the papers were drawn up.

critical juncture, O'Dea hid Norris at the Plaza Hotel, registering him under the pseudonym of Tom Cross—a reference to Norris's T-Cross ranches.

In a December 11, 1987, press release on the "Reported Agreement Between Penzoil and Equity Committee," Texaco charged that "a more economic single-number settlement could have been achieved with Penzoil if the equity committee had not acted unilaterally. Texaco advised the equity committee that Texaco was continuing to negotiate with Penzoil and believed that such negotiations could have been fruitful."

This was the company's public reaction. Behind the scenes, management was crazed, wounded, searching for villains.

"Texaco went crazy," Ross said. "The day after the settlement was reached, they summoned O'Dea and I to a board meeting held in a huge room at the company's Westchester headquarters.

"It had all the trappings of a star chamber. Picture a cadre of Texaco lawyers from Cravath and Weil Gotshall, Texaco's investment bankers from Morgan Stanley, and the company's directors seated in a horseshoe engulfing O'Dea and I. Call us the accused. The proceedings smacked of a trial or worse than that, a witch-hunt."

As O'Dea walked in, he recalled, Texaco's attorney David Boies "turned his back on me. He refused to say hello."

When Ross and O'Dea took their seats, they were greeted by a chilling silence.

Quickly, Kinnear launched into a half speech, half tirade, berating Ross and O'Dea for making a deal when the company was allegedly in striking range of a $2.5 billion settlement—a claim that appeared to be a distant stretch for a company that was playing hardball with Penzoil to the end.

"From my perspective, Texaco had no interest in a settlement," said Joel Zweibel, attorney for the creditors' committee. "They made no effort to make that happen. Every time we asked Kinnear to pick a number for a settlement, he would pull out his cassette speech about the immorality of the Penzoil case. To say that management did anything positive to move the talks off center is absurd."

After vilifying Ross and O'Dea in closed session, Texaco decided to publicly embrace the deal. Just eight days after issuing its press release slamming the equity committee for settling for $3 billion, Texaco made a dramatic about-face, declaring in a follow-up release:

"In view of all circumstances, including the reduction of Penzoil's demands to $3 billion, we have determined that the best course of action, and the best business judgment available to us on the part of our shareholders and employees is to remove the legal shackles that have restrained our company.

"This settlement provides the assurance our stockholders, employees, creditors, and business partners need that Texaco's competitive future will not be curtailed by either the massive judgment or the settlement at a higher, crippling price."

A senior Texaco adviser even said in private that Kinnear had used Icahn as a pawn, encouraging him to keep whittling down Liedtke's demands to an acceptable range. The way this story goes, Icahn convinced Jamail to settle for $3.5 billion, only to have Kinnear send him back to Houston to get some more.

"All excited about the $3.5 billion offer, Carl barged into Kinnear's office demanding that he not only grab the deal but that he lay down on the floor and kiss his feet for bringing it about," said the Texaco adviser. "But Jim told Icahn, 'You've already saved $500 million. Think how much you can save if you try a little harder. Let's talk again when you get another billion.' "

Although Icahn insists that this was part of a plan on his part to strike a deal at $3 billion or less by moving incrementally, insiders agree that he would have been pleased to make a deal at $3.5 billion to $4 billion. And although he was angry at Ross, Norris, and O'Dea for keeping him in the dark the night before they made their pact with Liedtke, indications are that he was surprised and delighted to have the case closed for $3 billion.

With the framework for a Penzoil deal in writing, Icahn was halfway toward his goal of increasing the value of his Texaco stock. But at this point a prominent buyer stepped forward to make a bid for the shares.

Armand Hammer, aging chairman of Occidental Petroleum, asked for a meeting to discuss Icahn's Texaco stock. The
session, attended by key advisers who huddled at Icahn's estate,
took on comical proportions.

Feeble and hard of hearing, Hammer started off the meeting
telling Icahn that he was a rich young man, and with the offer he
was about to make, Carl would be a lot richer. As a source in
attendance recalls it, setting the stage, he warned Icahn that he
knew nothing about the oil business and that if he were wise, he
would take his profits and wash his hands of Texaco. With that,
a senior Occidental executive who accompanied Hammer announced that they were willing to be very generous, offering $45
a share for Icahn's stock. "This is a great price, a terrific offer,"
he told Icahn. "We shouldn't do this, but we want to make a
deal, so we are willing to go all out."

When Icahn shrugged this off as being nowhere close to a
good number, Hammer's associate turned up the volume, saying,
"Okay, okay. I don't know why we are doing this, but we'll go
to $50 a share. That's ten points over the market. My God, what
an offer. You'd better grab it, Icahn. We couldn't go a penny
more. Even this is crazy. But I said it, so we'll do it. We'll do it."

Hammer, who could barely hear what his executive was
saying, kept smiling at Icahn as if he was the recipient of some
wonderful news. But when Hammer sensed that Icahn was not
responding the way they had hoped, he piped up, blowing all his
aide had been working toward.

"You're a fool, young man," Hammer said. "Fifty-five dollars is a wonderful price."

It was indeed a good price, but Icahn was uncertain as to the
sincerity of the offer. What's more, he wanted to proceed with
step two of his plan, to implement fundamental changes in Texaco before selling his shares. As one of the most anemic perform-
ers in the oil patch, Texaco was in dire need of massive
restructuring. Icahn's master plan called for stripping away lay-
ers of costly bureaucracy and selling off valuable assets. Confident that he could succeed, Icahn purchased the additional block
of Texaco stock still held by Holmes á Court.

Once again Icahn regarded the equity committee as the

ideal forum for achieving his goals. Considering his mastery of balance sheets and his keen sense for selling off corporate assets for a profit, he was the ideal man to take the lead at this juncture. With this in mind, he moved again to influence and perhaps dominate the equity committee. Immediately he lobbied committee members to dump Wilbur Ross and Dennis O'Dea. As knowledgeable and experienced advisers, both men posed a threat to Icahn's plans to bend the committee to his will.

"Carl's strategy, at the outset, was to destroy the smartest opposition he would have to face," says committee member Robert Lange, senior vice president of the Lindner Fund, then a Texaco shareholder. "That meant getting rid of Dennis and Wilbur. With those guys out of the way, Carl believed he would go unchallenged in his dealings with the committee.

"But there was absolutely no sentiment on the committee to fire either Ross or O'Dea. The consensus was that they were doing a fine job and that we would do well by their counsel. So when Carl suggested that we fire them, the committee's response ranged from anger to amusement to 'get the hell out of here, Icahn.' "

Although he lost this first round, Icahn forged on in his relentless style. His next obstacle was committee chairman Bob Norris. As Carl bid for control, the two clashed openly. Icahn's in-your-face approach was anathema to Norris.

Norris was never the one to instigate a row, but neither was he the kind to back off from one. As Carl kept pushing and Norris's back stiffened, a nasty confrontation was only a matter of time. The blow-up occurred when a rumor surfaced that Texaco had offered Norris a seat on the board.

Norris remembered, "I had no interest in the offer and I told Dennis to pass the word to Texaco. The whole thing smelled wrong. It was as if Texaco was trying to influence me. I wanted no part of that.

"But the next day Carl went after me in the *Wall Street Journal*, saying in effect that I was a self-serving so-and-so, that I wanted to be on the Texaco board and that I was angling to have Dennis O'Dea serve with me."

Just what was going on behind the scenes is a matter of

controversy. According to Dennis O'Dea, a Texaco lawyer called him to say that two board seats were opening and that they would be open to Norris and a designee. But considering that Texaco never officially offered Norris a seat, and the fact that Norris was adamantly opposed to accepting one were it offered, there is speculation that Texaco was seeking not only to discredit Norris by having him appear to be pursuing his own agenda, but also to create friction between Icahn and the committee. Those who see dirty tricks at work charge that Icahn was informed of the Norris "offer" by a Texaco source shortly after O'Dea took the call from the Texaco attorney. Icahn then took the bait and brought the story to the *Journal*.

Stung by the *Journal* article, Norris flew to New York to attend an equity committee meeting, knowing full well that Icahn planned an all-out assault on the chairmanship. The meeting was held at the Plaza's presidential suite, the very hotel Norris's great uncle "Bet a Million" Gates had built. The atmosphere was highly charged as Icahn, accompanied by Kingsley, took a place at the head of the table and began to complain that the committee had fouled up everything. Rather than addressing the committee in a traditional sense, he scolded the members, declaring that as the company's largest shareholder, he should have a greater voice in the committee's work. His goal was to intimidate the committee members, but to his surprise and consternation, no one was buckling. In fact, as Icahn surveyed the committee members sitting before him, he saw a united show of force. Whatever intimidation he was trying to achieve was being thrown back at him.

As Icahn went on the attack, Norris unveiled an imposing Swiss army knife that he liked to use as a makeshift gavel. This time he unsheathed the biggest blade and stabbed it gently but methodically on a mound of papers. As Carl was busy playing little Caesar, the committee members could see him following the motion of the knife out of the corner of his eye. This was Norris's shorthand for saying, "No way are you going to intimidate me, Icahn."

"Carl may be a fearsome guy to accountants and lawyers, but Norris is a fearsome guy to all men—physically fearsome," said O'Dea. "He is incredibly strong and fit and lives out on a ranch in the part of the country where a man learns how to take care of himself. As Bob stabbed that knife on the table, you could see Carl's eyebrows twitching. He was genuinely frightened."

Still, with hundreds of millions of dollars hanging in the balance, Icahn was not going to let frontier machismo come between himself and his money. Convinced that he could use the committee to further his interests, he confirmed the worst-kept secret in town. Staring eyeball to eyeball with chairman Norris, he told the former Marlboro Man that he wanted his job. As one of the members recalled, "It was the first attempt I'd seen to conduct a hostile takeover of a committee."

For a few tense moments both men stared at each other in stony silence. Just what would happen next was uncertain. Icahn leaned across the table awaiting a response; Norris sat erect, the veins in his forehead twitching. Just as the tension was about to erupt, one of the committee members intervened, speaking in a deep, clear voice.

"Mr. Icahn, we already have a chairman!"

Without need of a vote, Icahn realized that with that one line he had heard the consensus. The committee chairmanship would remain with Norris. But just when the issue seemed to be put to rest, another point of contention flared. Still livid over the *Wall Street Journal* story, Norris ripped into Icahn. "Who told you I was going to serve on the Texaco board? And that I was going to ask Dennis O'Dea to join me?"

"I heard it on the Street."

"Bullshit. Who said that about me?"

"I told you, I heard it on the Street."

At this point Norris blew up, all of his animosity toward Icahn bubbling to the surface.

"I wanted to crawl across the desk and get at him," Norris recalled. "I warned him that next time he had something to say, he had better run it by me first. 'Call me on the phone, goddamn it, and settle it with me personally. I'm not going to take this from you.'"

Beaten down at a forum he had hoped to dominate, Icahn slinked out of the meeting, his head handed to him.

"When Icahn first surfaced as the owner of the Holmes á Court shares, there was a sense of excitement in the committee," recalls attorney Steven Felderstein, a committee member representing the California Public Employees Retirement System (Calpers), which was a major Texaco shareholder. "Carl had been in the news a great deal. He was a true business star. When he walked in the room, some of the members lined up to shake his hand.

"But in twenty-five minutes he managed to turn all of that goodwill into bad blood. He offended everyone the way he demanded that he be given control. This was an incredible miscalculation on his part, especially so because the committee was eager for his help and for the clout he could deliver by working with us."

Norris, who had found himself repelled by the brash New Yorker from the outset, was convinced that the public confrontation had poured salt on wounds that would never be healed. But then Icahn revealed a side of himself Norris had not seen before. Ten minutes after he left the Plaza meeting, Icahn called Norris, who was still in the Plaza suite, to apologize for the *Journal* story.

"There I am listening to Icahn say he's sorry and I'm totally stunned by it," Norris recalled. "He said he'd been frustrated by the committee's action with Penzoil, but that didn't excuse his action. He admitted that he should have called me on the phone and settled the issue together. I'm sure that was hard for Carl to say and I appreciated it.

"More than that, it left me with another view of Icahn: He's a heavy hitter, as aggressive as you can get, but in his own way, he's fair."

Those who viewed Icahn's clash with the equity committee as a classic power play failed to understand that power for the sake of power has never motivated him. Nor does he sulk or hold grudges. Although Norris and his supporters might have taken Icahn's bellicosity on a personal level, to Carl there was nothing personal about it. All that counts is the winning, and the money that comes as its reward.

"People say Carl is an emotional man, but just the opposite is true," said Wilbur Ross. "He is an economics man. The only thing that matters is the numbers. He hasn't the time or the inclination for emotions."

The December after the Texaco battle, Ross hosted the annual Christmas party at his apartment in the Dakota. Even though he had been at odds with Icahn over Texaco, he decided to extend Carl an invitation. Although Ross's friends were betting that Carl would send regrets, he accepted, mingled, proved to be a convivial guest. "You'd never know there'd been any tension between us," Ross recalled. "Carl's just not the kind of man to hold a grudge. He probably views it as a waste of time."

With or without the support of the equity committee, Icahn was determined to serve as a lightning rod for systemic change that would transform Texaco from a plodding giant to a leaner oil machine. In typical fashion, he couched his next attack in the now familiar populist spiel:

"Profit isn't the only thing that interests me," Icahn told *Newsweek*. "There's outrage. It really annoys the hell out of me. It's an insult to shareholders. Management has their planes, their perks, their limos. And they are in control, with no stock. And you look at them and say: But wait, you've done poorly. You got the company into bankruptcy. You almost destroyed us. And then you say, OK, fellows, we'll give you another chance. We'll still let you run the company, but don't you think you should be held accountable if things get messed up again? And they look at you and say: 'No. Trust us.'

"To me, that's unconscionable. It's time to stand up and say, 'We're fed up.' " As he continued to paint a picture of Texaco's senior management as a bumbling, inept group, Icahn grated on the nerves of company man Kinnear, who after more than three decades with the oil giant had undying loyalty to the Texaco star. That Icahn would present himself as some kind of righteous force made Kinnear livid. In a letter to Icahn, he vented his anger.

"From the moment that you became involved with Texaco, you have proven again and again that you are the champion of only one Texaco shareholder: yourself."

Behind Icahn's soapbox appeal to the shareholders lay a calculated strategy to boost shareholder value quickly and dramatically. Clearly, Texaco could benefit from a determined catalyst for change. At the time Icahn had purchased the Holmes á Court shares, Texaco's performance was at the bottom of the oil barrel. Return on equity languished at an anemic 5 percent, less than half the industry average. Kinnear was said to favor restructuring as well as awakening the sleepy, arrogant Texaco culture, but it appeared that his goals and timetable were evolutionary as opposed to Icahn's plans for quick and radical change. Knowing that every dollar he added to Texaco's value added to his personal fortune, Icahn was determined that his blueprint for change would prevail.

His approach was classic Icahn. For openers, he would file his own plan for Texaco's reorganization with the bankruptcy court. As his plan noted, he would put an end to restrictive voting covenants that required the shareholders to gain an 80 percent super-majority of the votes in order to have their way on major corporate actions. This effectively put all of the power in management's hands. He also called for dissolving the company's poison pill, which insulated management from market forces. With the pill removed, a number of positive options could materialize. Would-be acquirers could bid for Texaco, thus driving up the value of its stock. Icahn himself could be a principal force here, mounting a takeover drive designed to put the company in play or to seize control. Equally important, the psychology of fear would take hold. As Icahn had long understood, if corporate management is allowed to remain entrenched and protected, shareholder values often stagnate. But tie the CEO's fate to performance, and suddenly change comes fast and furious. As Icahn viewed it, creating a climate of fear would force Kinnear's hand. From the beginning, Icahn warned that the company "must be seriously restructured or sold."

To give both reorganization plans a hearing, the equity committee invited Icahn and a Texaco contingent (including chairman Al DeCrane and attorney Harvey Miller) to Keewayden, a tiny

island south of Naples, Florida, that had been owned by the
Norris family since 1944. Expecting the usual lavish setting for
a high-powered corporate gathering, the attendees were shocked
to find themselves in a rustic setting with all the charm of a Boy
Scout camp.

"You had to take this tiny little ferry from the mainland to
the island, and I still remember seeing Icahn in the boat as it
chugged, chugged along," recalled a committee member. "He
looked out of place, like an overgrown kid standing in a toy boat.
And he had this look on his face, as if to say, 'What the hell am
I doing here?'

"But when Carl got off the boat, he surprised me by his
ability to instantly adapt to the place. More than that, he had this
beguiling curiosity. He wandered around, asking questions,
more like a child with a hyperactive brain than the threatening,
table-pounding egotist I'd seen in the past.

"In contrast, the Texaco guys, with their suits and ties and
briefcases, just couldn't blend in with the scenery. All the while
they were on the island they looked hot under the collar, annoyed
as hell, as if someone had forced them out of the world they knew
and into this primitive bivouac."

Compounding matters, the Texaco group was furious that
the equity committee would weigh their plan versus Icahn's. The
way Kinnear and DeCrane saw it, the committee had virtually
forced the initial plan on Texaco—after cutting the deal with
Liedtke—but was now changing the rules in midstream. Like a
nightmare come true, they found Carl's plan catching fire with
the committee because it contained the very shareholder governance provisions Texaco was opposed to.

"As the Texaco equity committee began exploring the two
reorganization plans, Carl's point that all shareholders should
have a say in the governance of the corporation gained a favorable reception among our members," O'Dea said. "Why, they
asked, shouldn't shareholders with a longstanding financial interest in the company, have a greater voice in governing Texaco?"

At Keewayden, Icahn was at the top of his form, driving
home the governance issue with the zeal of an evangelist. In a
shrewd move, he also abandoned his confrontational approach.

"Carl was Mr. Conciliatory," said Lange. "He said, 'If there's anything I can do to help you, if I can put my lawyers at your disposal, please let me know.' He turned from a fire-breathing dragon to a guy who was offering us warm milk."

A day after the Keewayden session broke up, Norris received a surprising call from Icahn. In a rare bout of introspection, precipitated by a harrowing plane ride back to New York through a vicious storm, Carl mused aloud about his peculiar lifestyle as a wealthy man so trapped in the 1980s money-making frenzy that there was no time in his life to smell the roses.

"Goddamn it," he told Norris, "I've got to say something. You're sitting there in the sun. Liedtke is off in a duck blind somewhere. My wife is off skiing. And I'm sitting here in my office fussing over Texaco. Something's wrong."

The next equity committee meeting, held in a conference room at Texaco's offices, proved to be a marathon affair, stretching from noon to nearly daybreak. Although the group had left Keewayden tilting toward Icahn, Texaco moved quickly to narrow the gap on the governance issues, conceding a number of key provisions, including removal of the poison pill within a year, changing the requirements for successful shareholder votes from 80 percent to two-thirds and adding a ban on the payment of greenmail.

As the session wore through the night, Icahn, who could have addressed the meeting in person, preferred to work the phones from his office and his home. Placing calls to various members, he lobbied relentlessly, trying to influence the course of the voting in his favor.

"Carl was so eager to get the committee's blessing because he knew it would give his plan the legitimacy it needed to carry weight with the bankruptcy court," O'Dea said. "Without it, he would look like a self-interested raider scheming to put a plan— any plan—in place so that he could buy the company on the cheap. Even though our plan contained some important governance issues, Carl preferred his own version because it went further, making it easier for the shareholders to call meetings and to vote as a group on corporate matters. You could think of Carl's plan as a corporate governance wish list."

When the committee voted, the first tally resulted in a tie with two members abstaining. The group apparently deadlocked, it was up to Norris—who, as chairman, had also abstained on the first go-round—to break the tie. At first Norris resisted, throwing the decision back to the committee by asking the others who had abstained to cast their votes. But the members balked, preferring to have Norris set the direction.

Norris found his sympathies tilted toward Texaco. This was understandable. His great uncle, John "Bet a Million" Gates had been a Texaco founder and his father, Lester Norris, had served as a Texaco director for forty-five years. Considering this lineage, the family had a personal as well as a financial stake in the company. But Icahn, always focused on the numbers, found that difficult to fathom.

"At one point, Carl said, 'Why don't you like me?' " Norris recalled. " 'I never said I don't like you,' I answered. 'We both have similar desires for change in corporate governance rules, but we have different bottom lines. Texaco has 52,000 employees and I want the company to remain viable, in part for them. But you'll come in here and rape the company.'

"Carl answered: 'I'm not going to do that. If that's what I wanted, I'd have to raise $13 billion and that would take me months.'

"That, more than anything else, showed me how Icahn lives in a different world. He plays with money. It's a game to him."

Ultimately, Norris would vote on the side of Texaco.

After the vote was taken, Dennis O'Dea began to draft a press release announcing the news on behalf of the committee. Ironically, he found himself in a conference room with Texaco's outside PR gun, Linda Robinson, the reigning publicity queen of the Roaring Eighties. Discovering that Robinson was drafting a release of her own for Texaco, O'Dea asked if she would apply her professional talents to write a draft for the committee as well. But after the bruising proxy battle that saw Robinson working the media relentlessly on her client's behalf, the request ran into a buzzsaw.

"When I asked for her help, Robinson gave me this real pointed look as if to say, 'No way I'm going to do a damn thing for you.' "

Icahn, who had filed his plan with the bankruptcy court, had hoped to have it approved for submission to the creditors and the shareholders along with the Texaco plan. This would be the subject of a bankruptcy court hearing the morning after the equity committee voted. But once the court learned that the committee was not supporting Icahn's plan, and that it deemed an alternative plan unnecessary, the Icahn option was locked out of the voting by the shareholders.

Moving on another front, Icahn pressed Texaco to engage in substantial asset sales. Although management had agreed to sell $5 billion of the company's assets—a move that would slim down operations and provide for a cash distribution to the shareholders—Icahn argued that this fell far short of the mark. Going for the jugular, he insisted that the company put its crown jewels, Texaco Canada and Caltex Petroleum, on the block, raising billions more.

Not surprisingly, management resisted Icahn's demands, insisting that a go-slow approach on asset sales was the more prudent course. Rebuffed, Icahn announced that he would launch a proxy battle to elect his own slate of candidates to the board, both as a prerequisite for restructuring the company and for implementing the governance provisions included in his now defunct reorganization plan. Icahn's slate included himself, Kingsley, TWA vice chairman Joe Corr, Kurt Wulff, and Edward Downe, Jr., a private investor. They would be pitted against the Texaco slate of Kinnear, former Prudential Insurance CEO Robert Beck, Chase Manhattan CEO Willard Butcher, Apollo Computer CEO Thomas Vanderslice, and former chairman of PPG Industries, L. Stanton Williams.

At first, Icahn viewed the proxy contest primarily as a pressure tactic. But as the campaign progressed, and gained momentum, Icahn began to broaden his focus, believing that he could actually go the distance and defeat Texaco. This budding confidence was due, in part, to encouragement from Icahn's proxy solicitors, D.F. King & Co., which after careful analysis of the shareholder blocks (and how they were likely to vote) told Icahn that the voting would be close, and that he had a solid chance of winning. Fueled by this, Icahn became obsessed with the prospect of victory and was seen keeping track of the projected voting on scraps of paper, dinner napkins, and milk cartons.

Were he to succeed in getting his own people elected, Icahn knew he would be in a stronger position to exert his influence on Texaco. "Once you get activist directors on the board," said Dennis O'Dea, "they can stir up a fuss and make the other directors feel uncomfortable by charging they are not acting in the shareholders' best interests. They worry about shareholder suits charging a breach of fiduciary duty.

"Carl knew all of this when he proposed his slate and it scared the hell out of Texaco. The company knew that once a camel gets his nose under your tent, it's hard to get him out."

As Icahn proceeded with his proxy challenge, Texaco used every tactic at its disposal to convince him to back off. Because Kinnear and his corporate boys knew they were out of their league in dealing with the flamethrower from Queens, they dispatched attorneys Joe Flom and David Boies to meet personally with Icahn. They were supposed to use their negotiating skills to get the raider to rethink his proxy challenge.

During a dinner at La Cremaillere, a Banksville, New York, culinary outpost just minutes from Carl's Bedford estate, Boies—on this occasion accompanied by Kinnear—outlined the company's position. As Carl toyed with his food, he heard the following reasons why he should drop proxy contest: 1. You cannot win a proxy fight; 2. In trying to win, you may be making charges and representations which are not true—such as the ability to raise the financing for a $60 per share offer—and we will sue you for that; and 3. We have strong indications that

Kohlberg, Kravis & Roberts, the big leverage buy-out firm that holds about 5 percent of Texaco's stock, will side with us in a proxy showdown.

Once the Texaco braintrust laid out this bleak picture, warning Icahn that his every move had been anticipated, his every path blocked, they rested their case. And then they waited for some sign of capitulation or of room for compromise.

For a moment there was silence. As Icahn moved the food around his plate, he appeared to be deep in thought. Perhaps a breakthrough was at hand. Perhaps the Texaco contingent had knocked some sense into the takeover king.

But just as Texaco's hopes were rising, Icahn gently placed his utensils on the table and crushed his adversaries with a clear and unyielding assessment of their advice.

"You all think I'll lose," Carl said. "I think I'll win. Your advisers are being paid by Texaco. My advisers are being paid by me.

"I think I'll listen to mine."

Seeing that Icahn was determined to stay the course, Texaco made a last-ditch attempt to arrange a backroom settlement. On May 16, 1988, the company announced that it was negotiating with Icahn to solve their differences without proceeding to a proxy battle. At the time Texaco went to great pains to state that "any resolution of the differences will not include consideration for any shareholder that is not equally available to all Texaco shareholders." In other words, no greenmail.

For days Kingsley and Icahn lawyer Gary Duberstein squared off with Boies and Joe Flom in a series of acrimonious meetings that shifted from Icahn's home and office to Texaco's headquarters and back again. The negotiations centered around a proposed standstill agreement that Icahn would have to sign, barring him from making additional purchases of Texaco stock for the standstill period and limiting his ability to sell his existing block. This limitation irritated Icahn.

"I couldn't sell my stock to anybody except if he were the

Pope or something. He would have to be Mother Teresa to buy the stock."

Throughout the negotiations Icahn's proxies demanded a sweetener in the form of immediate stock dividends based on massive asset sales, but Texaco would not agree to move at Icahn's pace as the price for peace. In litigation that would arise after the talks, Texaco charged that "Icahn repeatedly demanded that Texaco engage in a restructuring program that would enable Icahn to dispose of his shares in proportions greater than those available to other shareholders and also enable Icahn to avoid certain liabilities applicable to him but not to other shareholders."

According to Texaco, Icahn employed his patented pistol-to-the-head tactics, repeatedly threatening "to make a bid for Texaco unless Texaco yielded to Icahn's demands."

But this was Texaco trying to shift all the blame to Icahn. The fact is, the talks revolved around the problem of producing a standstill agreement that would assure Texaco of a moratorium in its battle with the raider and would still give Icahn the flexibility to maximize the value of his shares. Although Icahn agreed in principle to a standstill, every time Texaco put the terms in legalese, he found the proposed contract impossible to live with.

In this contentious environment, with both sides blaming the other for the impasse, the shaky truce was called off.

On May 25, Kinnear marked the collapse of the talks by taking a public swipe at Icahn:

"Texaco has negotiated tirelessly, in good faith and with an open mind over the last several weeks to avoid a time-consuming and expensive proxy fight and end the uncertainty Icahn's actions have caused our shareholders and potential business partners. But we simply could not structure a transaction that would satisfy Icahn's demands without violating our pledge not to provide consideration to him that was not available to all our shareholders or threatening Texaco's economic future. *While the various transactions proposed by Icahn may not be technically greenmail, they would in Texaco's view benefit Icahn at the expense of the best interest of the company and its shareholders generally.''*

In turn Icahn charged that it was Texaco that had sought to pay him greenmail, offering to arrange for a third-party buyer, First Boston, to purchase his shares at a premium. The offer allegedly came during the course of a dinner meeting at New York's Il Tinello Restaurant.

At the Il Tinello powwow, attended by Icahn and a Texaco contingent including Cravath's David Boies, the Texaco side allegedly came up with a plan for a third party to buy Icahn's shares, with the understanding that Texaco would stand behind the purchase. But Icahn claimed he rejected the proposal on the grounds that it would amount to greenmail.

Texaco advisers insist, however, that the negotiations— which extended beyond the restaurant to a curbside conversation between Icahn and Boies—were designed simply to find a way to restructure the company in a way that would be of maximum benefit to Icahn (as the biggest shareholder), without being detrimental to the average stockholder.

Once the backroom negotiations broke off without a deal, Texaco hoped that labeling Carl as a self-interested wheeler-dealer would antagonize the rest of the shareholders, thus taking the steam out of Icahn's takeover drive.

But instead Icahn increased the pressure by floating a bid to take over the company for $60 a share, a bid that would be financed in part by selling $5.3 billion of Texaco's assets. Texaco responded that Icahn was seeking to "raid the assets of the company," turning Texaco into the "corporate equivalent of an instant lottery ticket." When management refused to put Icahn's offer to a shareholder vote, the confrontation reached new levels of acrimony.

In a June 6, 1988, advertisement in the *New York Times*, Icahn played to shareholder interests, charging, "the Texaco board of directors fears the result of a stockholder vote on our

---

*Texaco later clarified this charge, noting that "while the transactions proposed earlier by Icahn would have been made available for all shareholders, the form, content and timing of such transactions were designed to meet Icahn's particular needs and interests and were not as favorable to other shareholders as they were to him."

$60 cash merger proposal. We believe they know that given the choice, stockholders will reject their so-called restructuring program and approve our $60 cash merger proposal."

Immediately, Texaco retaliated, countering that Icahn's "so-called offer" was merely a ploy to get the company to agree to a sweetheart deal. Management based its charge on the claim that Icahn lacked the financing to consummate the tender.

"There is no basis to believe that Mr. Icahn can arrange the financing for a transaction of approximately $20 billion—including the purchase of the shares he doesn't own in Texaco and the payment of debt and other obligations that would have to be satisfied in connection with his proposal," Kinnear charged. "If Icahn's proposal were anything more than an effort to create a platform for himself and his hand-picked nominees in their proxy contest, one would expect that he would have provided more information and more than 48 hours for Texaco's board of directors to pass on a $20 billion transaction."

Still, Icahn kept the heat on, taking out tabloid-style advertisements headlined: "Texaco Stockholders: Why won't they let you vote for $60 in cash?" In the highly charged text, Icahn claimed that if the "Texaco Stockholders Committee nominees are elected to the Texaco Board, you will then have the best chance to vote for $60 because we believe we can persuade three other directors to support our proposal. It's up to you to decide if you want a 1982 dividend level and business as usual or the right to vote for $60."

Incensed by Texaco's advertising—that impugned his ability to raise the capital—Icahn moved on another front, secretly hiring a private investigator to sniff out dirt on Texaco's senior executives. Specifically, he was looking for evidence that management was misusing corporate funds, aircraft and hunting lodges. Evidently, Icahn hoped to find a smoking gun that would turn shareholder sentiment against the company, though no evidence of wrongdoing was found.

Interestingly, on the other side of the battle front, Texaco was equally busy trying to dig up scandalous material on Icahn. Operatives from Kroll Associates, the white-collar private detective firm that in the wild and wooly 1980s functioned as Wall

Street's FBI-for-hire, were set loose to look for evidence of wrongdoing at TWA and in Icahn's earlier takeover conquests. But much as they snooped around the ariline and looked into SEC files, the Kroll gumshoes came up with little fodder for Texaco's anti-Icahn ad campaign.

"We couldn't find a smoking gun," recalls a senior Texaco adviser. "What we did find was that Icahn ran a pretty clean, tight ship."

Addressing a meeting of security analysts on June 2, Icahn fielded tough questions concerning his ability to finance the deal. In the midst of an intense session, he charmed the generally skeptical crowd. Asked why he didn't have a Drexel Burnham "highly confident" letter to back up his plan, Icahn responded, "I think I have more capital than most of these investment bankers."

In dismissing Icahn's offer as little more than a negotiating tactic, Texaco's executives were acting on the assumption that the raider in their midst was bluffing. But these straight-arrow climbers of the corporate ladder had little experience with a wily adversary; in dismissing him out of hand, they were underestimating his determination to win.

Behind the scenes, Icahn was conducting a series of secret meetings with deep-pocketed sources interested in playing a role in financing his bid. In a two-week period beginning in late May 1988, private jets carrying potential Icahn partners were landing at Westchester Airport, just minutes from Foxfield. The executives—including senior management of Gulf Canada Resources Ltd. and Husky Oil—were picked up at the airport by Icahn's driver and whisked to his home for dinner and discussions until the early hours of the morning.

The most promising discussions were held with Gulf, which indicated a willingness to participate in a friendly buy-out by putting up $4.1 billion, mostly for the purchase of Texaco Canada. Were Gulf to put up the capital, Icahn was led to believe that Citibank (TWA's bankers) would provide additional financing. Although the prospects of a deal looked promising at first, Icahn worried that he would be selling Texaco Canada at a fire-sale price, and Gulf was reluctant to make such a major investment on short notice.

In another series of closed-door meetings, Icahn huddled with Sir Gordon White of the UK-based Hanson PLC. At their first meeting, Icahn met the British executive at his New York apartment, followed by a private dinner at a Manhattan restaurant. Beginning with this meeting and continuing over the course of subsequent telephone conversations, the outline for a deal began to emerge, whereby Icahn and Hanson would make a joint offer for Texaco. Discussions progressed to the point that Icahn, accompanied by Kingsley and his in-house counsel Gary Duberstein, met with Hanson's investment bankers at Rothschild & Co. in New York. Ultimately the talks were suspended when Hanson's lawyers raised concerns on technical grounds related to a foreign company taking ownership of Texaco's maritime fleet.

At one point, Icahn also explored the possibility of joining forces with Boone Pickens in a joint venture similar to the Hanson proposal. The men had first talked about Texaco soon after Icahn's Holmes á Court purchases became public knowledge. Pickens, who vaguely remembers the conversations, says that he might have been interested in buying the Holmes á Court block from Icahn.

"He had called me initially . . ." Icahn recalled, "and mentioned to me . . . that Texaco was of great interest to him and if I was ever interested I should call him about it."

With Icahn exploring various options for financing a Texaco acquisition, he took Pickens up on his offer, calling him to discuss the possibility of a partnership arrangement. Although Pickens appeared at first to be interested, one of his senior aides called back Icahn soon after to say that their "plate is too full."

Throughout, the Street remained skeptical of Icahn's ability to back the $60 offer. This disbelief was reflected in Texaco's share price, which remained at $50, proving that sophisticated investors had no faith in their ability to cash out at the higher number.

Still, Texaco was increasingly concerned with Icahn's proxy challenge. In an effort to court big blocks of stock, management lobbied hard to win the support of the company's institutional shareholders.

Just days before the date of the annual meeting, Texaco demonstrated its commitment to restructuring by announcing the sale of its German subsidiary, Deutsche Texaco AG. On another front, Texaco enticed the institutions by offering them the opportunity to consult on the selection of board members.

Icahn was busy politicking too. Pressing for every vote he could muster, he made an extraordinary appeal to Wall Street's major brokerage firms, asking for a platform to address their salespeople. This was a calculated plan to win over the brokers and, in turn, their small investor clients, who collectively controlled millions of Texaco shares.

At times the battle turned surreal, with Texaco warning opera buffs that Icahn might halt the company's long-standing sponsorship of the Metropolitan Opera radio broadcasts and Icahn, the fearsome raider, suddenly posing as a patron of the arts.

"I love music," Icahn said. "I give a lot to Carnegie Hall."

The proxy contest would come to a head at Texaco's annual meeting at Tulsa's Westin Hotel on June 17, 1988. Icahn kept up the pressure until the last minute, announcing that if his slate of directors was elected and the board still refused to put his $60 offer to a vote, he would consider using his TWA and ACF stock to raise capital for a hostile tender offer.

Once in Tulsa, the Texaco and Icahn contingents set up headquarters to plot last-minute strategy. Texaco's army of executives and advisers occupied the Westin; Icahn's much smaller contingent worked out of the Doubletree Hotel. As the deadline for the voting approached, the outcome was up in the air. A number of major shareholders—some initially favoring management—had moved into the Icahn camp, disgusted that Texaco would bar them from voting on Icahn's $60 offer. James Ullman, a trustee of Battermarchy Financial Management, which controlled more than a million Texaco shares, justified his firm's support of Icahn on the grounds that "the shareholders, not the board of directors, own this company." And New York City's comptroller Harrison Goldin, who voted the city's pension funds, said of Texaco: "This has been a poorly run company. The existing men at the top of Texaco come from the culture and bowels of that corporate bureaucracy." Other major shareholders, even those who supported Icahn on an ideological basis, remained skeptical of his ability to fund a $60 buy-out. In this camp, most favored giving management the opportunity to continue its restructuring.

Arriving at the Westin on the day of the meeting, Icahn found himself deep in the oil patch—hostile territory for a Wall Streeter attacking a mainstay of the region's economy. Reflecting the local sentiment, a spray-painted sign on a local garage read ICAHN GO HOME. The city of Tulsa, home to more than 800 Texaco employees, declared this to be "Texaco Day," and in the spirit of this love fest, shareholders were presented with big red and white buttons reading TULSA WELCOMES TEXACO.

In every way possible, Texaco used the home court to its advantage. When Icahn arrived at the hotel, he was met in the lobby by an armed security guard, who insisted that he queue up at the sign-in table, going through the same procedure as retired employees with 100 shares of stock.

"Texaco stage-managed the event beautifully," recalled Wilbur Ross. "The night before they held a dinner for Texaco retirees. These people detested everything Carl stood for: Wall Street, ethnicity, financial engineering.

"On the day of the meeting, the retirees and the other dyed-in-the-wool Texaco supporters had big sections of the room roped off for them. In sharp contrast, Carl was relegated to a little corner off to the side. You could tell just by the lay of the land that he was going to have a rough time there. If ever Icahn was out of his element, this was it."

As the meeting was called to order, Kinnear, dressed in a gray suit, white shirt, and blue rep tie, got right to the point: Icahn's $60 buy-out proposal had not been sent to the shareholders for a separate vote "because that proposal wasn't and isn't real. . . . In the opinion of Morgan Stanley, it could not be financed. The more we have learned about the plan, and Mr.

Icahn's statements about it, the more strongly that analysis has held up. Despite contact with a wide number of banks and potential partners, the Icahn group still has no financing, no partners of substance."

Kinnear played to the Texaco loyalists whose presence dominated the room. Finally, he had Icahn in a controlled environment where he could squeeze him, make him feel vulnerble. It would be the corporate equivalent of a frontier lynching.

Following Texaco's choreography, the mom-and-pop shareholders who ranked the company right up there with God and country were brought to the microphones. "I feel that the comments of Carl Icahn, Boone Pickens, and the other raiders are full of deceit, hypocrisy and pretense," said one. Another said, "If we give the company to Icahn it will be like giving a Stradivarius to a gorilla." Still another declared that Bob Hope— that great arbiter of corporate performance—was on Texaco's side. "I spent a day a couple or three weeks ago [sic] with Bob Hope. We talked about this and Bob Hope said, 'I will stick with the man who wears the star.' "

Much as management would have loved to pull the plug at this point, it had to let the other side speak, giving vent to those shareholders who believed Texaco had been victimized by ineffective and irresponsible leadership.

"I think it is time for you people to explain yourselves," said one angry voice from the crowd. "Explain how you got us into a position where we had to pay Penzoil $3.2 billion.

"You know, I think the Texaco management is very analogous to a guy who is the father of six children, got a wife, got a home in the suburbs, but he is also a compulsive gambler. Well, he racked up a hundred grand in gambling debts and now he's got to sell the car, the house and the vacation home and the rest of it."

When Icahn's turn came, he approached the microphone tentatively, intimidated momentarily by the setting. Whereas management sat on a dais elevated above the crowd of 1,000 shareholders, Icahn was forced to speak at floor level, near the back of the room. As he launched into his speech, Kinnear—bitter at the prospect of Icahn invading his turf—stared at the floor, refusing to acknowledge Icahn's presence.

Fumbling with a prepared text written by his aides to check his tendency to ramble, Icahn started to read verbatim. But then halfway down the first page, he had a change of heart. Folding the paper and stuffing it in his suit pocket, he ad-libbed as he went along. Instantly he felt in control, confident that he could make an impact on the assembled, no matter how the deck might be stacked against him.

The brunt of Icahn's remarks focused on the issues of corporate democracy and shareholders' rights. Why, he asked, if he was willing to offer $60 a share for the stock, couldn't the stockholders—being the legitimate owners of the company—have the right to vote yea or nay?

To drive home his point, Icahn drew the analogy of an estate owner who feels he hasn't gotten full value out of his property. "When a visitor says, 'You have beautiful apple orchards above the estate, why can't you sell?' the owner replies, 'I'd love to but the caretaker, he is partying all the time. He is having a good time down there and he won't let anybody come on the grounds. He has, in fact, put a machine gun on the gate and he wouldn't allow anybody to come on these grounds to buy the apple orchard or indeed to buy the estate. . . . '

"And you look at that person and say, 'I don't understand. Why don't you get the police and throw the caretaker out?' You sort of shrug your shoulders and the person shrugs his shoulders and doesn't have an answer.

"And that is the problem we have in America today. There seems to be no answer, no answer whatsoever as to why we are in the position we are in corporate America."

Icahn proceeded to the heart of his antimanagement philosophy, linking the ineptitude of America's corporate management to the nation's broader economic malaise.

"What happened with Rome, what happened with Portugal, what happened with Spain, all through history, is that these countries went into decline when they could not produce because a large part of the population of their middle class stopped working.

"But we are even worse than that because we have a corporate welfare state where numbers and numbers of vice presidents and bureaucrats have developed. . . . It would be better to have them on the golf course. But they are working and they are working with papers, with bureaucracy, with problems that make the line worker stop."

As Carl espoused his theories about reverse Darwinism in the corporate hierarchy, his barbs stuck in the craw of the dozens of Texaco company men in attendance. Aware that he was touching a nerve, Icahn stepped up his attack. Suddenly DeCrane, somber in a black suit and white shirt, informed Icahn that his ten minutes had expired and that he would have to yield the microphone. This set off a chilly exchange.

Icahn retorted, "I think, under the circumstances, I should have the right to talk for a couple of more minutes. You can talk as long as you want. That's fine with me."

DeCrane answered, "We have an agenda that we have to follow in order to be fair to all the other people who have propositions to come before the meeting. I certainly feel that you can have a minute or two to wind down your comments."

"Perhaps this is the manifestation of inflexibility that has caused the proxy we have today."

With that, catcalls rang out from the mostly pro-management audience.

As with modern political conventions, the Icahn/Texaco presentations were perfunctory. Most of the proxies had already been received, and most hands recognized that Texaco would win, having convinced the institutions that management would act decisively to sell assets and otherwise restructure the company. Still, the margin was known to be close and a wild card hung in the balance. Icahn's only chance was to control a block of stock owned by Kohlberg, Kravis & Roberts.

Before the annual meeting, Alan Greenberg, chairman of

Bear Stearns, KKR's broker, had called Icahn to tell him that a 4.95 percent block of Texaco's shares were for sale. Although Greenberg failed to identify the owners, Icahn—who had studied the whereabouts of virtually every share of Texaco stock—likely knew that it was KKR. Tempted by the offer, Icahn was nevertheless hamstrung by Delaware law, where Texaco was registered, which required that a buyer acquiring 15 percent of a company had to rapidly boost his stake to 85 percent or be barred from merging the company or selling its assets for a three-year period. Since he already held 14.9 percent of Texaco stock, Icahn's acquisition of the KKR shares would put him across the 15 percent threshold.

Still, determined to lock up the voting power that the KKR block represented, Icahn spoke with Canadian investors Sam and Marc Belzberg. Quickly they hatched a plan whereby the Belzbergs would form an investment group to buy the Bear Stearns block. This was done with the assumption that the Belzberg group would support Icahn if he was successful in snaring the shares. As Kingsley said at the time, "We knew that Belzberg was in our camp." But with the Belzbergs determined to play hardball in the negotiations, and with Bear Stearns equally determined to hold the line on price, the deal fell apart over ⅛ of a point per share, a disappointment that left Icahn fuming.

Icahn says he made a last-ditch attempt to buy the shares directly from Henry Kravis.

"I told him that I need your vote. I said I assume you want to enhance your value and you would be crazy not to vote for me. He said he wants good value and he would like to see the stock go higher. . . .

"We were talking back and forth and I said, 'Henry, the stock is 50, 51, would you sell it here?' He said he thinks it's going higher. He said 55 to 60. I don't know if that was an offer, but I said, 'Would you sell it here? I would be interested in buying it right here.' His answer was no."

Although the block was sold to another party, KKR remained very much in the Texaco picture. Because the buy-out firm owned the stock on the April 11 record date for proxy voting, it retained the right to exercise the voting rights reflected in the stock. As the date of the Texaco annual meeting neared, just which way KKR would vote was the biggest guessing game on Wall Street. Arbitrageurs, who had bought the stock with the hope that Icahn's slate would win a seat on the board, were praying Carl could push the shares toward $60. With this in mind, they were pressing KKR to vote with Icahn.

But KKR, which some believed was hoping to participate in a management-led leveraged buy-out of Texaco, and would support the company in order to win points with it, kept its options open to the last minute, waiting to vote its proxies in person at the Texaco annual meeting rather than handing them over to a proxy solicitor. When the time came, an agent acting on KKR's behalf dropped its proxy in the ballot box and mysteriously left the room, without a clue as to how it had voted.

When the proxy voting was counted, the Icahn slate received 41.3 percent vs. Texaco's 58.7 percent. Texaco's victory margin, although hardly a landslide, was substantially in excess of the KKR vote.

Icahn had expected an uphill battle, but the defeat, and the personal attacks that accompanied it, left him in a foul mood. As the warring factions of lawyers, investment bankers, and corporate executives streaked back to New York in their Gulfstreams, a Texaco adviser crossing signals with Icahn's cellular telephone, eavesdropped as Carl told an aide, "Goddamn it, those sons of bitches were all lined up against me. Even when those guys farted, everyone applauded."

Before the voting, Icahn had said on several occasions that were he to fail to elect his slate, he would sell his stock and put Texaco behind him.

But for Icahn, backing off would be wildly out of character. He always took the offensive, and sure enough, he started saying in his usual "Maybe I will, maybe I won't, I'm not sure what I'll do" manner that he was mulling over the possibility of a hostile tender. As one analyst said at the time: "I'd rather go to Vegas than speculate on Icahn's next move."

This determination—some say compulsion—to stick with a

deal, to find new ways to make it work, and to hang tough regardless of the firepower his adversaries threw at him, made Icahn the most forceful and credible raider of the decade.

Clearly, Wall Street was betting that Icahn still had cards to play. Although Texaco's stock dropped nearly two points after the proxy vote, it started to recover the lost ground almost immediately. Incredibly, as far as the arbs and the analysts were concerned, the company was still "in play." Speculation centered around an Icahn-led hostile tender.

Icahn used every opportunity to keep the threat alive, not as a precursor to a hostile tender, but as a means of keeping Kinnear on edge, looking over his shoulder at this rambling, threatening raider with a huge block of stock and a wildly unpredictable streak. Although Texaco's executives worked mightily to frame their victory as a landslide, privately they were shocked at how close Icahn had come to taking over the company. Nothing in their up-the-corporate-ladder backgrounds had prepared them for the day that a lone wolf could take on the big red star and nearly wrest it away from them. As much as they detested Icahn, secretly they feared him. In a series of closed-door meetings, management plotted strategy. How would they keep the menace from regrouping and striking again?

Quickly a battle plan emerged. Imitating Icahn, Texaco would move on two fronts, holding out a carrot and a stick. On one hand, Texaco's lawyers from Cravath, Swaine & Moore threatened massive legal action. But as the club was raised, they agreed to offer Icahn a peaceful settlement by moving, inch by inch, toward his demands to sell assets and increase shareholder value.

For months Icahn and Texaco engaged in secret negotiations. Then in January 1989, Texaco formally announced that it would pay its shareholders two special dividends totaling $8 a share. This concession reflected the power of Icahn, who through his perseverance had forced the company to sell and redeploy $7 billion in assets. To reward the "friendly" institutions for supporting management in Tulsa, and to discourage them from throwing their weight to Icahn in another proxy war, Texaco's management team had engineered the sale of once prized subsidiaries including Deutsche Texaco and Texaco Canada. Although the company's spin doctors couched this asset sell-off as part of a restructuring that was unrelated to Icahn, to observers watching from the sidelines, that was a laugh.

At the same time Texaco announced the shareholder dividends, the company also revealed that it had signed a standstill agreement with Icahn. Under its terms, negotiated primarily by Kingsley in a marathon session that stretched throughout the last weekend of January 1989, litigation between the parties was dropped, Icahn was barred from buying additional shares of Texaco stock, he would vote his shares proportionately with those of the other shareholders (except with respect to dividend payments) and he would define the manner in which he would dispose of shares when he decided to sell. In return, Texaco agreed to settle all outstanding litigation against Icahn.

For management, this was an opportunity to rid itself of a tenacious and potentially dangerous foe. For Icahn, signing the standstill was a pleasant way to put the wrappings on the biggest deal of his life, knowing he would be free of the lawyers and risk of costly and time-consuming litigation.

"Icahn first bought the Holmes á Court stock as an arbitrage play," said Dennis O'Dea. "In classic arb fashion, he hoped to buy low and quickly sell high. When the opportunity to do that came along—albeit at a much later date than he originally thought—Carl took his profit. Forget all the proxy battles and the like, that's what he was after."

On June 1, 1989, the largest single trade in the history of the New York Stock Exchange—Carl Icahn's sale of his Texaco shares at $49 each—crossed the wire. With three prominent investment banks—Shearson Lehman Hutton, Salomon Brothers, and Goldman Sachs—handling the transaction, a sum total of 42.3 million shares changed hands for a dollar value of $2.07 billion. Nineteen months after acquiring Holmes á Court's stock, Icahn was cashing in his Texaco stake for a profit of more than $500 million including dividends.

For Texaco, the sale came as a great relief. Because Icahn had bought the stock at a bargain price that would likely never be seen again, the odds of another raider assembling so huge a position was remote.

As for Icahn, the Texaco transaction was undoubtedly his finest hour. Not only had he gained a windfall profit, which even in the context of the outsized eighties was an awesome amount, but also he had served as a positive force in transforming a hidebound, imperious company into one more responsive to its shareholders. Although Texaco apologists claimed that change was inevitable under Kinnear's regime with or without Icahn, this was simply the old guard's reluctance to admit that a New Yorker who couldn't tell sweet crude from Log Cabin syrup could have a positive impact in the oil patch.

As he had done in virtually all of the prior deals leading up to Texaco, Icahn kept management and its brain trust of lawyers and investment bankers off balance by threatening, cajoling, demanding, and refusing to buckle no matter what Kinnear or the collective might of Texaco loyalists threw at him. Throughout, Icahn followed the rule that had guided him since the late 70s: If you own the stock, you have the leverage.

"Carl wasn't the only one putting pressure on Texaco, but he may have been the only one the company was listening to," said Robert Lange. "That's because he was the only one with a gun to its head."

Viewed in hindsight, Icahn's encounter with Texaco was a bravura performance. Even those who had clashed with him during the Texaco settlement came away from the process impressed by Icahn's unique and extraordinarily effective modus operandi.

"Carl is a one-man operation," said Dennis O'Dea. "He doesn't really need a lawyer. He doesn't need advisers. He has a great grasp of everything himself. All the issues, legal or business, he sees each one and how they interrelate. And most impressive, he sees them all instantaneously."

Perhaps the most significant tribute to Icahn's role in the remaking of Texaco came from the man on the equity committee who loved the company best. "Carl got the shareholders the dividend from Texaco," said Bob Norris. "I tried to get it, but

Texaco had this or that excuse. Carl got it done. All the credit goes to him.

"The Thanksgiving day after we got the money, I called Carl at his home. I said, 'I'd just like to thank you on behalf of the shareholders for getting the extra dividend for all of us.'

"Well, Carl didn't expect my call and he just about fainted. He said, 'Goddamn, would you put that in a letter? I want to hang it on my wall.' "

Icahn's ability to win the respect—and even the grudging affection—of Bob Norris is testimony to the fact that he can be personally appealing and engaging on a human level. He is a splendid conversationalist, well versed in history, music, philosophy, and politics. Culturally, his tastes are eclectic. In literature, his favorites range from *Grapes of Wrath* to the spy novels of Le Carré and Ludlum; in film, his top ten list includes *Breaker Morant* and *Tunes of Glory*. Unlike the Ivan Boeskys of his era, there is a learned, intellectual quality about the man that transcends his mastery of mathematics and finance. At the dinner table munching on the simple home-cooked fare he favors, he can be a charming host, regaling guests with behind-the-scenes anecdotes of the heavyweights he has encountered in the course of his exploits, offering guests amusing glimpses at such legendary characters as Armand Hammer, Ivan Boesky, and Donald Trump. Buoyed by the laughter of his small but appreciative audience, he can be an engaging performer, a borsht-belt comedian on loan from the Concord Hotel.

One of his favorite stories recounts a conversation with Trump: "One day Trump invited me to a football game at the New Jersey Meadowlands. We fly over in Trump's helicopter, accompanied by this absolutely beautiful young woman. A knockout.

"Right in front of her, Trump says, 'Isn't she gorgeous, Carl? Have you ever seen such a beauty? And there's more to her than looks. Everyone knows I'm having some business problems now. You know it. She knows it. But does that matter? I'm down to my last $500 million and she's still sticking with me. Is that a woman, Carl? Is that a woman?' "

In recent years, Icahn has begun to divide his private life between Bedford and the Long Island community of East Hampton, where he purchased a 5.2 acre beachside estate.

East Hampton is the only place where Icahn, the round-the-clock deal maker, ever comes close to relaxing. In this chic village by the sea, Icahn likes to walk the beach and to hold court at The Palm, an east-end outpost of the famed Manhattan steak house. Surrounded by a clique of cronies from New York's premier law firms and investment banks, Carl is at the top of the pecking order. But even here, Icahn reveals an apparent compulsion to turn everything he touches into a money-making proposition. On one occasion, marking the formal unveiling of his East Hampton home, Icahn held a cocktail party orchestrated by his Uncle Elliot Schnall, who had introduced him to the Hamptons and who compiled the guest list and fussed over the details.

"I suggested that Carl have the party on the Labor Day weekend of his first year in the house," Schnall remembered. "But he said, 'I don't want one of those goddamn dinner parties. I hate them.'

"So I said, 'Make it a cocktail party—just for two hours. Everyone wants to see your house.' So we held it from six to eight. I gave Carl a list of people and he scratched some names, added others. Everyone in the Hamptons wanted an invitation but we limited the list to about seventy-five to eighty people and it was a great success."

Or was it? Some who had their first peak into King Icahn's private life came away feeling cheated.

"Carl's home is beautiful—the land, the setting, the structure—but there is something missing," says a well-known investment banker. "Call it soul. Call it finesse. Call it the kind of panache one would expect to find in the home of one of the world's wealthiest men. There's a void there.

"Consider the so-called art works. The paintings are pleasant enough but they look like the kind of mass-produced knock-offs you'd find in a Hilton Hotel. I know art. I collect art. And I can tell you with authority that what Carl has there isn't art. It was Muzak for the walls.

"There was something third-rate about the whole experience at Icahn's house. There was Carl giving these tours of the place, going to great lengths to point out the quality of the woodwork. Don't get me wrong, the craftsmanship was quite good, but this was more here than a proud guy showing off his house. It turned out that Carl owned the woodworking company and as you put two and two together, you got the feeling he was selling, trying to get you to sign up for a new bookcase.

"Talk about tacky!"

If the Icahn estate-by-the-beach lacks the patina of the old-money mansions in the WASP citadel of Southampton, the lady of the manor could hardly care less. The antithesis of the Park Avenue social butterflies who make a career out of hosting dinner parties and attending Sotheby's auctions, Liba Icahn is disarmingly simple in her homegrown tastes and her understated beauty. In her travels around Bedford and Southampton, she is given to drip dry hair styles, tennis warm-ups, and little or no makeup. When she complains to Carl it is not for jewels or cars or a lavish wardrobe, but to limit rather than expand their lifestyle. Although they appear to be kindred spirits, where Carl is often driven by a miserly streak, Liba's tastes gravitate toward the simple without regard for economics.

In December 1990, the Icahns moved out of their main house in Bedford to begin extensive renovations on the former O'Neil mansion, then in dire need of new plumbing, air-conditioning, and heating. To house the family while work was in progress, Carl had Bayswater Realty and Capital Corp. (a firm he launched to pursue real estate interests) build a modest two-story home on the Foxfield estate. The plan was for the Icahns to move back across the property into the main house once the renovation was complete.

But when Liba settled into the "temporary" housing, she

found herself happier than she had been in the mansion. The simple but comfortable quarters, the lack of pretension, the modest scale of the place suited her style and temperament much more than the stone fortress. And so the Icahns shifted their view of the "temporary" house to a more or less permanent abode.

"Almost any other woman married to a wealthy guy like Carl would be bitching and moaning about living in a 'development house,' but Liba likes it," said a close friend of the family. "She used to hold these beautiful Christmas parties in the mansion. The house would glow, the food was wonderful, it was all very special. Like a Christmas storybook. But Liba, like Carl, is not much of a party animal and even those parties got to be too much for her. The 'development house' is too small for that kind of entertaining—she hasn't thrown a Christmas party since they moved in—and I think that's one of the things she likes about staying right where she is.

"The idea that they would ever move out of the new house was flawed from the start. The way they planned it, when the plumbers and carpenters were done with whatever they had to do, the family would move back into the mansion and the other place would be a guest house. The problem is the Icahns never have sleep-over guests. It's never been their thing."

Even when she travels to Manhattan, to the ballet (which she adores) or to an occasional society affair (which she abhors), one of the wealthiest women in New York forgoes couturier clothing and the museum quality jewelry that are the badges of her peers.

"Some years ago, Carl gave Liba a gorgeous diamond and emerald necklace," said the family friend. "Any other woman would have glued it to her neck, but Liba never wore it. Never.

"Then one time, knowing that the Icahns were scheduled to attend a gala performance of the New York Philharmonic, a girlfriend called Liba, suggesting that she wear the necklace. This, the girlfriend assured her, would be the right occasion.

"And sure enough she brought herself to wear the necklace and it was truly drop-dead. A magnificent piece of jewelry. But you could tell from the moment that Liba walked in that she was uncomfortable with it. At first, she went to the ladies room and put a scarf around her neck to camouflage the thing as if it were a wart. Then, when the scarf wasn't enough, she took off the necklace and slipped it in her purse. That's the last anyone's ever seen of it."

Although the Icahns appear to have a workable marriage, built around love for their two children, Carl's great obsession is his work and his pursuit of ever-greater wealth. Whether he is at his desk or by the pool with the kids, a telephone console is by his side, the lights flashing, the calls flowing in like the jets stacked up at La Guardia. When Liba retires for the evening, Icahn storms into the second phase of his day, fielding calls and holding meetings well into the wee hours. When he takes a break, it is to eat a light dinner and watch an old film, alone in his comfortable reading room. Often work is an invisible wall separating Icahn and his family.

"Liba would like to get more of Carl's attention—you know, the little things women like," said a Bedford neighbor. "But Carl's mind is always someplace else. Off on some gibillion-dollar business deal that makes everything else seem so pedestrian.

"Liba used to keep this sweet little ceramic dish, dotted with hearts, by her bed table. For three years running she wrapped it up and gave it to Carl for Valentine's day. And each time he acted surprised and appreciative, never even realizing it was the identical gift she'd given him over and over again."

COLD
STEEL

USX and the End of an Era

*"Carl makes management of companies nervous because noth-
ing in their experience ever led them to deal with someone like
him. These managers have great resources at their disposal.
They can snap their fingers and have fifteen PR people or
twenty lawyers in the room. But Carl still makes them nervous.
He has this wild look in his eyes and he intimidates them."*
—A MEMBER OF THE TEXACO EQUITY COMMITTEE

In his nonstop search for diamonds in the rough, Icahn believed
he could capitalize on the struggles of another stumbling corporate behemoth, USX. Although this odyssey began in the mid-
eighties, it would stretch out well after the Texaco chapter was
closed, taking Icahn into a new decade—one that would bring a
sudden halt to Carl and his fellow raiders' ability to "control the
destiny of companies."

Established as U.S. Steel in 1901 through a patchwork of
mergers engineered by J.P. Morgan and steel tycoon Judge El-

bert Gary, the company—the first billion-dollar corporation in the world—grew enormously over the decades, providing a critical resource for an increasingly muscular American industry that required steel for cars, washing machines, trucks, factories, and oil rigs. For generations United States manufacturing was the envy of the world, and steel was at the core of this industrial juggernaut.

But in the 1950s, the tide began to turn as long and acrimonious strikes and the emergence of cheaper alternative sources led domestic customers to look overseas for steel. This reversal of fortunes, coupled with the maturation of American industry, transformed U.S. Steel from a high flyer into a cyclical giant.

To reduce its dependence on the mercurial steel industry, the company acquired Marathon Oil in 1982, consummating the second-largest merger in U.S. history. Four years later, the steel/oil conglomerate expanded its energy component with the $3 billion acquisition of Texas Oil & Gas, a larger producer of natural gas. In that year, the company underwent a fundamental restructuring under chairman David Roderick. Four independent operating units—Marathon Oil, Texas Oil, U.S. Diversified Group and U.S.S.—were established under the parent corporation, now renamed USX.*

At the time of the restructuring, the company was essentially a two-headed mutant composed of the tired and lackluster steel operation suffering heavy losses and a vital energy business whose profits were also suffering temporarily due to a sharp decline in crude oil prices. A heavy debt of more than $6 billion (assumed, in part, to fund the energy acquisitions) further depressed the bottom line. Add to this Wall Street's long-standing aversion to hybrid stocks, whose fate is tied to more than one industry, and shares of USX languished below book value. This gap, a cause for consternation among the company's investors, drew Icahn to the stock. Viewing it as an opportunity in disguise, he accumulated a substantial block in the summer of 1986. With USX's market price at about $6 billion, and securities analysts estimating that the company's energy assets could fetch $7 to $12

*The *X* had been the company's New York Stock Exchange symbol since 1924.

billion, there seemed to be little downside risk but substantial upside potential in acquiring USX shares.

Still, considering the depth of the problems plaguing USX, insiders wondered if the takeover artist hadn't picked a target that would prove immune to his financial wizardry.

"We couldn't fathom why anyone who wasn't forced to buy our stock would come within one hundred feet of it," says a former USX executive who came to the company via the Marathon Oil merger. "Inside the bowels of this place, we looked around and saw nothing but unsolved problems. Not your garden-variety problems but boulder-sized headaches that defied easy solutions. At the corporate level, we had hundreds of lawsuits hanging over our heads, many of them concerning serious environmental infractions with huge financial liabilities.

"And the steel business—well, that was like being sucked back into the eighteenth century. The mentality was that of the early Industrial Revolution. Bureaucratic rules and procedures were embedded in every corner of the place. Company policies covering the simplest matters went on for twenty pages, and for every job that needed one person to do the work, they had five. Visitors would whisper that the company reminded them of the army, but those of us who were here long enough to look beneath the surface knew that it was much worse.

"That Icahn would want any part of this place shocked us."

But to Icahn and a flock of raiders, including Robert Holmes á Court, Boone Pickens, and Irwin Jacobs, then circling the company like so many vultures, how USX conducted its business was irrelevant. All that mattered were the assets, steel and energy. Icahn dreamed of spinning off steel and allowing the energy unit to reach its true high-water mark. Although Icahn was not the first or the only observer to see the potential inherent in such a spin off, he alone would make it a cause célèbre.

Determined to emerge as a force management would have to reckon with, Icahn and an investor group headed by him purchased 9.8 percent of USX stock for prices ranging from $17.50 to $26.25 a share in the late summer and fall of 1986, and then turned up the heat on October 6 by making a "friendly" offer to buy the balance of the company's 259 million outstanding shares for $31 each, for a total of about $8 billion. Were it consummated, the acquisition would be the third-largest takeover in U.S. history. Icahn claimed that he could finance the massive purchase in part through his own resources (including $1.6 billion from ACF and TWA) and furthermore that Drexel was confident it would raise more than $6 billion from its sources.

As usual, Icahn's timing was impeccable. USX, then in the midst of a crippling strike by 22,000 steel workers, was losing nearly $100 million a month. Angry shareholders were demanding action. Roderick, who had imposed an October 20 deadline for announcing plans to boost the company's anemic stock price, found himself pinned to the wall by the Icahn offer. As Icahn declared at the time, if he was not pleased with Roderick's plan, which rumor had it would include stock repurchases and limited asset sales, he would proceed with actions of his own. Should he take this independent route, Icahn suggested that his plan, as well as management's strategy, be put to a vote by the shareholders. With arbs and other speculators holding big positions in USX (based on takeover scenarios) Icahn believed that a substantial body of shareholders seeking rapid gains would vote in his favor. In effect, he would be tapping a built-in constituency that would maximize his leverage for either taking over the company or forcing management to act decisively in boosting shareholder value. Similarly, taking a page from his successful battle for control of TWA, Icahn suggested he might seek to negotiate a deal with the striking steelworkers, offering limited equity in USX in exchange for wage concessions. With TWA performing well during the early stage of Icahn's stewardship, he could present himself to labor as an enlightened miracle worker, and as an appealing alternative to current management. Whether Icahn really intended to take over USX or, as many speculated, he was simply out to force management's hand in boosting shareholder value, building bridges to the unions would give him more clout as he squared off against the company.

To this point, the script read like so many other Icahn assaults on his corporate prey. But in the case of USX, there would be a new and unexpected twist. Unlike the other CEOs who had barred Icahn from the inner sanctum, USX's chief executive, David Roderick, invited Icahn to engage in man-to-man negotiations. It would be one of the few occasions in the Roaring Eighties when a raider and the management he was pursuing would engage in extended, generally civilized dialogue, without the legal saber-rattling that typically inflamed such encounters.

Icahn's civility could be traced, in part, to a series of events that would serve as an ominous backdrop for his meetings with Roderick. In May 1986, Dennis Levine—a rising-star Drexel Burnham managing director—was arrested and charged as the mastermind of a pervasive insider-trading scheme that would shock Wall Street. Shortly thereafter, the fast-talking Levine (who by coincidence had advised the Icahn team on the Phillips Petroleum battle) would implicate Ivan Boesky, with whom Levine had struck an illegal deal to sell inside information. Ultimately the firm of Drexel Burnham would fall victim to the widening scandal.*

Although the events would take several years to unfold, the arrest of Boesky—who was wired one way or another into hundreds of Wall Street's most powerful figures—ignited a quiet panic in the law firms and boardrooms of the financial community. With once prominent men being led from their offices in handcuffs, and with SEC enforcement chief Gary Lynch determined to track down illegal practices at the highest levels, scores of the eighties M&A jackpot millionaires wondered and worried who would be next.

Considering his dealings both with Drexel and Boesky, Icahn had to be concerned. In an effort to court favor with the prosecutors, and thus to limit his own punishment, Boesky told of their joint meetings with Gulf & Western chairman Martin Davis. Although Icahn insisted from the start that he had nothing to hide (and a subsequent investigation of his dealings bore this out, failing to find illegal activities of any kind), merely

---

*Drexel Burnham pled guilty to securities law violations in December 1988 and filed for bankruptcy in February 1990. Milken, also caught up in the widened scandal, was indicted on charges of racketeering and securities fraud in March 1989 and sentenced to ten years in prison in November 1990.

being sucked into the scandal had to have a chilling effect. Clearly, the market regulators and the public would be less tolerant of the brash takeover artists who had manipulated the capitalist system for their own advantage. What's more, with rumors concerning a Drexel investigation filling the air, Icahn had to worry that his pipeline to billions of dollars in junk bond capital would be closed off.

In fall 1986 and early winter 1987, Icahn and Roderick began huddling in closed-door negotiating sessions at the USX's Pittsburgh-based executive offices, in the CEO's sixty-first-floor suite. Roderick, the son of a Pittsburgh postal employee, who had started his career at Gulf Oil and then climbed the ladder in U.S. Steel's accounting department, had presided over the company since 1979. Although the CEO and the raider were far apart philosophically, they did share some common ground. Both were the superachiever offsprings of working-class parents, and, as an observer to the talks noted, "both were blood-and-guts guys who got right to the heart of the issues without the usual small talk."

From the start the men were outwardly cordial, but at the same time suspicious of the other's goals and what they would do to achieve them. Although they were willing to camouflage their true feelings under a veil of civility, Icahn and Roderick detested what the other stood for. Privately, Roderick, who was fond of reading and quoting from the Bible, viewed Icahn as a nemesis of American industry, and Icahn viewed Roderick as the archetypical company man.

From the start a pattern developed: Icahn would challenge Roderick to perform radical surgery on USX, releasing the value of the energy assets by breaking up the company. But Roderick, much like Texaco's Jim Kinnear, insisted on a steady-as-you-go approach that called for piecemeal assets sales without dismantling USX. When investment bankers presented USX with a strategy for selling off the diversified businesses by putting them in a kitchen sink and selling them as a package, Roderick rejected the idea.

"I used to talk to Roderick about his meetings with Icahn," said Andrew Gray III, a securities analyst with Donaldson, Lufkin, Jenrette's Pershing division. "He would tell me that indirectly, Icahn was trying to accomplish similar things for the company that management was trying to accomplish, but that 'We intend to accomplish it at our own pace, not his.' "

The initial talks revolved around Icahn's $31 per share friendly offer and management's pledge to announce its own plan for boosting shareholder value by October 22. As the deadline approached, Icahn threatened that if the plan failed to satisfy him, he might proceed with a hostile takeover. In that case, speculation ran high that he would offer only $26 per share. But the deadline came and went without a hostile bid from Icahn.

Clearly, he was operating under the mistaken assumption that he could intimidate USX. In confronting Roderick, he was facing a Napoleonic character—short in stature but with a bull-dog personality and iron will. Throughout their talks, when the air would be filled with rumors that Icahn was on the verge of making big new purchases of USX stock, or that a European conglomerate was interested in buying Icahn's shares as part of a takeover plot, Roderick remained steadfast, refusing to give in to the kind of management paranoia that had enriched Icahn in his previous forays. Having substantially reshaped the company (known in the steel industry as "The Corporation") during his tenure, Roderick was determined to keep the USX he created intact, having it serve as a legacy of his management tenure. No way would he allow a raider to dismantle "The Corporation" before his eyes. Before that would happen, he would have USX's investment bankers at Goldman Sachs and First Boston comb the world for a white knight. Says a former USX strategic-planning executive who worked closely with Roderick, "Whatever Icahn said, or did, or threatened to do, Roderick refused to panic. Keep in mind that he was an ex-marine platoon sergeant who saw World War II action in the Pacific. In his life, whenever it came to fight or flight, he chose to fight."

Icahn, also a fighter, recognized, however, that he could not win round one. On January 8, 1987, he called off his offer to acquire USX for $31 a share. Behind the scenes, he was struggling to secure the financing to mount a viable threat, a task complicated by USX's calculated decision to redeem $2.9 billion of its notes, using a cash horde (previously available to a raider) to consummate the transaction. This was a blow to Icahn, but in classic fashion he made it clear that rather than retreating, he was simply regrouping, thus keeping his options open for a subsequent and perhaps more tenacious attack. In an SEC filing, he noted that his group might pursue new tactics to control USX, and in a letter to Roderick, he warned that he would be keeping a close eye on USX and that he would consider engaging in a proxy contest to put his own candidates on the board of directors.

As his talks with Icahn proceeded into early 1987, Roderick played mind games of his own, suggesting various options to boost USX's stock price but always pursuing his own agenda. At times he announced discussions with third parties (including British Petroleum Company) about a possible sale of USX energy assets. On other occasions he declared that management and the board were employing restructuring strategies. But as Icahn watched and waited, USX failed to take the drastic steps he had demanded from the start.

Roderick's hold-the-fort position dovetailed with his long-term strategy. An agent for change in his own right, he had transformed USX from a steel-dependent dinosaur into a more balanced steel and energy hybrid. Taking a sword to USX's sacred steel cow, he had closed down inefficient plants, slashing steel-making capacity by more than 50 percent over the course of his tenure. Tackling the company's mountainous overhead, he installed broad cost-saving measures including cutbacks on executives' salaries. These moves had helped USX to withstand downturns in the steel business better than its leading competitors. Since analysts were predicting improved sales in steel and energy, Roderick was convinced that his master plan would begin to pay off handsomely in the waning years of the 1980s and into the coming decade. The company's $219 million profit in 1987, coming on the heels of a $1.8 billion loss the year before, gave him all the confirmation he needed that he was on track.

As much as Icahn believed he was getting his way in having regular access to the chief executive, thus applying pressure for change without having to launch a hostile bid, there is reason to believe that in appearing to placate the raider in his midst, Roderick was actually manipulating him.

Within USX, Roderick was known as a cagey tactician who would hear out his lieutenants, giving them the illusion of considerable influence with the boss. This was his way of creating the impression of team building and empowerment. But for the most part these sessions were window dressing: When the time came to make a decision, the only counsel Roderick heeded was his own.

Adds a former USX executive, "Roderick's style of management was of the school that says, 'If it's not my idea, it's not a good idea.' He may have talked about consensus building, but in his heart of hearts, he had no respect for it. He was the kind of guy who believed a leader gets paid to lead, not to listen.

"This style of doing business carried over into his relationship with Icahn. Although he maintained a dialogue with Carl— which led to widespread speculation that they had achieved some kind of extraordinary bonding—the truth is Roderick would meet with Icahn and then go about his business as if Icahn wasn't there."

"Roderick always listened, paid attention but never agreed to anything Carl wanted to do," says attorney Steve Jacobs, who represented Icahn in the USX talks. "He was never arrogant in disagreeing, just firm. Roderick handled Carl intelligently. You must treat Carl as a man of respect. If not, he is not immune from emotion. He is inclined to be hostile to people who are hostile to him."

Apparently, Icahn had launched his offensive against USX on the premise that management would cave in to his one-two-three punch of threats, demands, and flirtations with the unions. But when Roderick proved to be a tougher rival than he anticipated, and when Drexel got caught in the muck of the ugly Wall Street scandal, Icahn found himself boxed in. On one level, the idea of bailing out of USX was appealing, but Icahn feared that his credibility as a raider who perseveres and wears down management like a Chinese water torture would be damaged. What's more, he still believed that there was money to be made in USX. As he would put it, something in his mind still went "click."

But there was a price to be paid for this optimism. At this point Icahn had invested $670 million in USX, much of it with borrowed funds, and the interest meter was ticking. Every day he stayed with USX, his debt service (offset partially by USX dividends) grew. What's more, if Icahn sought to increase his leverage by boosting his USX holdings, he would run into the sticky wicket of the company's poison pill, which enabled shareholders to buy more stock at half price once an acquirer's stake reached 15 percent of the outstanding shares.

In one of the few times in his career, he found himself betwixt and between. Although in public statements he put on a brave show, in the privacy of his office he agonized over what to do. For the time being, he elected to stay with the investment, fearing that the cost of cashing in his chips would be greater than the risk of holding his cards and waiting for a new opportunity to strike.

Icahn's patience was influenced in part by Roderick's performance as well as by the widening insider-trading scandal. Just as the CEO had projected, his steady-as-you-go restructuring began to have a snowball effect on the bottom line, with profits soaring from $219 million in '87 to $756 million in '88. The stock reflected this turnaround, rising from a low of $14½ per share in 1986 to a high of $34⅜ in 1988.

But in spite of this improved financial environment, the more or less gentle tug-of-war between the raider and USX came to an abrupt end in the spring of 1989. In late May, Roderick, then sixty-five, retired as USX chairman after ten years at the helm, and was replaced by Charles Corry, a younger executive with a different view about the propriety of negotiating with Icahn. Two days after this changing of the guard, Icahn sold his Texaco stake, replenishing his war chest and fueling speculation that he would launch a drive to take over USX.

As soon as Corry assumed power, Icahn found that the welcome mat to the company's executive office was rolled back. Having worked in Roderick's shadows for years, Corry was determined to put his own stamp on the company. The last thing he wanted was for a New York financial engineer to be perceived by Wall Street as a major force in the company's decision-making.

Corry and Roderick were radically different personalities. Whereas Roderick was gregarious, loved to be in front of an audience, and was determined to make key decisions single-handedly, Corry was a soft-spoken, determined team player who turned to his senior managers for advice and consent on the broad range of managerial issues. Shortly after Corry took the reins from Roderick, a senior executive, finding himself back in the decision-making process, said, "I haven't enjoyed working here this much for years."

Roderick had enjoyed sparring with Icahn, but Corry detested it. From all indications, he believed it had been a mistake for Roderick to consult with Icahn on a regular basis, in part because it was "beneath" the CEO to do so and in part because it would be viewed as a sign of weakness by Icahn and his fellow corporate raiders.

By the time Corry came to power, Icahn's plan for restructuring USX had evolved as a proposal to divide the company in two by spinning off 80 percent of the steel component into a separate corporation, which Icahn claimed would then trade on the market for roughly $9 a share. What's more, by releasing the company's energy component so that it could be treated as a pure gas and oil play, Icahn predicted that this entity alone would trade for $39 a share. Presto! Through a single stroke of financial alchemy, a security trading in the low $30's would rise, simply by freeing its component parts to trade independently, to $48.

Icahn claimed that his plan would work because it would unleash the hidden value locked up in USX. But Corry was of two minds about the idea. On a conceptual level, he saw merit in spinning off the steel unit.

"Corry knew from historical data that for every dollar invested in steel, he might get a return as high as 12 percent," Gray says. "And he also knew that by taking the same dollar and drilling a discovery well, he could earn many times that. So he would think, 'Why put $300 million in a highly automated continuous caster steel operation, when I can put $300 million in the North Sea and have the chance of hitting a grand slam?' "

Although Corry's numbers-crunching view of the company differed somewhat from Roderick's whose tenure dated back to steel's glory days and who remained somewhat nostalgic about it, he agreed with his predecessor that change should be gradual. He had agreed to sell diversified assets, as well as certain oil and natural gas reserves, but balked at the more sweeping proposals put forth by Icahn. Convinced that the depressed value of steel's assets would rise significantly in the early 1990s, Corry argued that an immediate spin-off would be shortchanging the company on two fronts: It would fail to secure top dollar for the assets, and it would squander $900 million in tax-loss carry-forwards (remnants of the years of red ink) that could be used to limit taxation now that USX had returned to profitability. Like Roderick, Corry preferred to nurture the company's businesses, building profits and values before putting steel on the block.

To the Icahn camp, Corry's opposition to an immediate restructuring was based more on a determination to flex his muscles and to thwart Icahn than to protect the best interests of the company. Some of Icahn's supporters viewed this as an arbitrary and destructive power play.

"Roderick's and Corry's slow-as-you-go-approach was just an excuse—a delaying tactic," charges securities analyst Kurt Wulff, who worked with Carl in the Texaco and USX incursions. "If you are going to spin off the entities, it doesn't matter when you do it. 1989 would have been a great year because of the strength of the energy stocks. 1990 was a less favorable climate, but it still would have been good. But management didn't care about any of this. The only timing issue that mattered to them was that they create separate entities on their own terms, not on Icahn's or anyone else's.

"At a quarterly meeting of securities analysts, Corry was asked about my analysis that showed the benefits of creating two separate units. He said it was 'flawed.' But when I asked if he'd read the full seventeen-page report, he said no. So he was responding to a critical issue without making it his business to learn all the facts.

"Do you need more proof that he was more interested in

protecting his prerogatives than in giving our proposal a fair hearing?"

Determined to take the issue directly to the shareholders, Icahn succeeded in scheduling the matter for a non-binding vote, the results of which would be announced at the USX annual meeting on May 7, 1990.

In the months leading to the event, Icahn—who at this point was the company's largest stockholder with 13.3 percent of the shares—kept hammering away at the magic of a spinoff, claiming in press interviews and paid advertisements that his proposal was a quick and viable means of enchancing share-holder value.

But as he proceeded with this $10 million campaign to sell the institutional shareholders (who controlled 46 percent of USX stock) on the wisdom of his concept, he ran into a legion of skeptics who believed he had overstated the value of the USX components.

"Where Icahn saw a rise of about $15 a share for USX after the spinoff, from about $33 to $48, I saw only about a $2 to $3 rise," says Jeffrey Miller, an analyst with Duff & Phelps. "In effect, Icahn was saying that by lighting a torch to the steel company, he could get substantially more value from Marathon, because the oil portion alone would go from $33 to $38. If you use this reasoning, steel had a negative value of minus $5. No way was that true. Even Carl himself didn't believe that because he assigned a positive value to steel of about $9.

"Icahn said the market was terribly inefficient in the way it valued USX. And it was inefficient, but not to the extent that he indicated."

Icahn and Kingsley were both keen appraisers of corporate values, so were they indulging in wishful thinking? Did they see something the majority of analysts and institutional shareholders failed to see? Or were they, as one school of thought now holds, using the spinoff alchemy as a means of keeping the pressure on management, hoping, in typical fashion, that Corry would buckle under the pressure and buy out the raider's shares for a premium?

Whether or not Icahn was fishing for a sweetheart deal (which both Carl and USX now deny), Corry clung to his case for building asset values before a major sale was made. And when the shareholders voted on the issue, Icahn lost by a substantial margin.

Much as Icahn's raid on Phillips Petroleum had been a watershed event of the Roaring Eighties, marking the Drexel-junk-bond-takeover alliance at the height of its powers, USX was a harbinger of the decline of the takeover bullies. By the time of the USX vote, Drexel Burnham—devastated by the insider-trading scandal—was in liquidation. In this context, Icahn's loss must be attributed, in part, to his diminished credibility as a raider.

"On the day it was announced that Boesky was going down, I was negotiating with USX lawyers about the terms of a possible agreement that would give Carl the opportunity to have access to USX's financial information," Steve Jacobs recalls. "This presumably would facilitate Carl's ability to make a bid because Drexel needed the information. But when the announcement came about Boesky, you knew the transaction was not going to fly."

In the past Icahn had succeeded in intimidating his adversaries by convincing them that he had the resources to make good on his threats. In most cases, that meant buying stock until he controlled or appeared capable of controlling the companies he attacked. But once Drexel was laid low and the pipeline of takeover capital had run dry, Icahn's options were limited. In a critical transition, USX's lawyers and investment bankers started treating Icahn as a major stockholder rather than as a raider capable of acquiring the business.

Still, Icahn had cards to play. He is fond of saying that his money is his army and that it gives him power others don't have. Although Drexel was gone, Carl had his own war chest, now flush with the profits from his Texaco shares. Leveraging on this capital, he could continue to accumulate USX stock and in turn to put pressure on Corry, who was in a vulnerable position. In convincing the institutions to support the company in the Icahn voting, Corry had held out the prospect of improving shareholder values, a pledge he would now have to honor.

"Corry knew that he could go to the institutions once and ask them to stick with him, but if he did nothing to get values back up, watch out about going back to them," says a former USX planning executive. "They would have said, 'Carl is right. The company should be dismantled.' "

In the months after the USX annual meeting, the consensus on the Street was that Icahn would wait for the right opportunity to pounce again.

And although Icahn made noises about mounting a counterattack, nothing came of it. By this point the once irrepressible raider was so bogged down in the TWA fiasco and so weakened by the collapse of Drexel that he had difficulty focusing on USX with the kind of obsessiveness he had applied to his previous forays.

Instead he worked behind the scenes to cut a deal that would promise Corry peace in return for restructuring the company along the lines Icahn had been calling for.

The idea of pacifying Icahn in any way was anathema to Corry, but behind his stoic pose he worried about the unpredictable raider, confiding to associates that Carl "is a mystery man" and "a puzzle I can't figure out." Driven by the unknown, and by a passionate desire to rid himself of the Icahn plague, Corry would accelerate the timetable for restructuring USX.

In January 1991, USX announced a plan to issue a new common stock for the steel business, effectively splitting USX into separate securities for energy and steel, much the way General Motors had issued separate stock for its Hughes Aircraft and Electronic Data Systems subsidiaries. Under the proposed plan, steel would remain under the control of USX management, which still hoped to raise steel values before a sale of the assets would be consummated.

This mirrored a standstill agreement USX had been quietly

negotiating with Icahn. Dated January 31, 1991, it clearly presents the restructuring as a quid pro quo for an Icahn peace. No matter how much USX claims it followed its own agenda, the agreement speaks volumes for corporate management's determination to tie up the raider.

Among the provisions, the company agreed to submit to the shareholders a proposal to establish a new class of common stock "representing the right to receive dividends only with respect to the company's steel and diversified businesses (the 'Steel Stock')." These shares would be distributed to the holders of the company's common stock on a pro rata basis.

With this, management would essentially buy Icahn's backing, even to the extent of requiring that any public statements that he made about the proposed restructuring would have to express his support. What's more, USX management, determined to choke off further interference with its plans, prohibited Icahn from making "any public statement or announcements, including without limitation to any securities analysts or institutional investors, in opposition to or denigration of any nominee of the company for election to the board of directors of the company at the 1991 annual meeting."

On the market side, where Icahn had always had his greatest leverage, USX forbade him from purchasing additional USX shares with voting rights and blocked him from supporting others in the purchase of such stock. In addition, management sought to remove every vestige of the Icahn threat by forbidding the raider from: 1. proposing or otherwise supporting any type of shareholder proposal; 2. seeking election to the board, seeking to place a representative on the board, or seeking to remove any member of the board; 3. calling for a meeting of the shareholders; 4. engaging in any attempt to control the destiny of USX through mergers, takeovers, or similar actions. All of these prohibitions would apply for a period of seven years.

On May 6, 1991, stockholders officially ratified the company's restructuring, and on the next day trading in USX was replaced by trading in two separate entities, USX—U.S. Steel Group and USX–Marathon. This marked the end of an era for USX, which as a result of the split was removed as a component of the Dow Jones industrial average, replaced by the Walt Disney Co.

For Icahn, the USX outcome was bittersweet. On the plus side, he had managed to take on one of the behemoths of the corporate establishment and reshape the company. No matter how much Corry crowed that this was a route he intended to take anyway, the truth is that Icahn had exerted enormous influence on the company. Ever since he began accumulating USX stock, he had been a powerful goad to senior management. Ultimately, he had forced Corry to vastly accelerate the timetable for a spinoff.

On the other hand, his was a Pyrrhic victory. About a week after USX shareholders approved the issuance of dual securities, Icahn sold his stake in the company for $1.02 billion. The trade consummated by three Wall Street powers—Shearson Lehman, Salomon Brothers and Goldman Sachs—brought Icahn only mediocre rewards. After he had held the USX stock for five years, his gross profit on the trade was only about $183 million. From this, he had to take deductions for his costly proxy battles and for interest on his margin purchases over the term of the investment. Even when the USX dividends are factored in, he would have fared better by investing his money in T-bills over the same period of time.

"Profit is the only way Carl scores himself," says the president of a Wall Street investment firm. "And with USX, the score wasn't very high. Not by Icahn's standards."

Throughout the eighties, Icahn created fear and confusion in America's corporate suites and then thrived in this unsettled environment, picking apart his corporate adversaries. But in the case of USX, he found himself swept up in a vortex of events beyond his control. Toward the end, he couldn't decide whether to hold on to the stock, or to sell.

As Icahn struggled with the issues, Al Kingsley began to push for a sale. Fearing that the economy was headed down, that the market was set for a nosedive and that a modest profit was better than no profit at all, Kingsley kept up the pressure to bail out. For weeks, Icahn flip-flopped, one minute embracing Kingsley's view and the next deciding that he would tough it out until the stock rose to reflect the benefits of the spinoff.

Once Icahn decided to sell out he used Kingsley as a scapegoat, complaining that his alter ego had pushed him prematurely out of the shares.

One evening, while dining on a roast chicken dinner cooked by Liba at their Bedford estate, Icahn wondered aloud why he'd listened to Kingsley. But in his heart Icahn knew the answer. As he surveyed the Wall Street landscape in the new decade of the nineties, he saw carnage, defeat, and despair where just a few years before there had been boundless opportunity and staggering profits. Just like that, Drexel Burnham was gone. Ivan Boesky was gone. Michael Milken was gone. Dennis Levine was gone. Trump's empire had come unglued. Once rich and arrogant lawyers and investment bankers were scrounging for clients.

Increasingly, Icahn talked of the dangers of an economic catastrophe. He made a point of reading *The Great Depression of 1990*. In private, he speculated that real estate and the stock markets might well be on the verge of collapse. All at once he realized he had seen the end of an era. The change hit home on a deep, personal level. With Drexel just a memory, the big banks on their knees and the capital to finance takeovers all but dried up, Icahn's incredibly successful decade of corporate intimidation had come to an end.

There is reason to believe he'd seen the end coming for some time. "Carl used to keep this framed letter from Ivan Boesky on his office wall," said Brian Freeman. "The letter congratulated Carl on some deal that he'd done. One day I noticed that the letter was gone. You couldn't miss it because there was a discolored spot on the wall where it had been hanging. When I asked Carl where the letter was, he shrugged it off and said, 'What letter? What are you talking about?' I said, 'Carl, there was a letter here from Ivan Boesky. He was one of your best friends. Who are you kidding?' That's when Icahn responded, 'Boesky, he was a bad guy. He was no friend of mine.' "

The time had come to distance himself from Boesky.

On another occasion that symbolized the decline of an era,

Icahn called Freeman to share some thoughts on TWA, only to find that Freeman was busy writing a character letter to Kimba Wood, the judge in the Mike Milken trial.

"Teasing Carl, I told him I was writing a letter for him too," Freeman said. "When he objected, saying he hadn't done anything wrong, I told him I was keeping it on the side, just in case.

"With that, I started reading to him: 'Dear Judge, Carl Icahn's problems are very simple and easily understood. He cannot control his greed. He is a bottom fisher who will take no risk and believes others should provide value to him to make him wealthier. He believes that all value created belongs to him. . . . He has become effectively a financial nymphomaniac.'

"Of course, it was all in jest, but Carl couldn't take the joke. He called me a son of a bitch."

ALL THE KING'S HORSES AND ALL THE KING'S MEN...

"Carl can't understand why people don't have a burning desire to make him rich."

—JOE CORR, FORMER TWA PRESIDENT

As the Roaring Eighties faded into the history books, the infamous raiders of the bygone decade receded from the headlines, opting for less exposure and more traditional business pursuits. Saul Steinberg turned his attention back to his Reliance Insurance holdings and to the Park Avenue social whirl embraced by his wife Gayfred. Irwin Jacobs focused on his Minneapolis-based yachting business and Sir James Goldsmith, once the most flamboyant of raiders, took his fortune and virtually disappeared.

As much as Carl Icahn might have liked to perform a disappearing act of his own, transforming himself from a high-profile raider into a behind-the-scenes investor in troubled businesses, the continuing saga of beleaguered TWA kept him in the spotlight. Although he had regretted purchasing the airline for years, the worst was yet to come. Soon, he would wish he had never heard the name TWA. To his shock, his tenure at the helm would threaten the fortune he had amassed while terrifying corporate America for more than a decade.

Over the years, the TWA unions confirmed their view of Icahn as a parasite who lived on the fat of their wage concessions, siphoning capital out of the airline without engaging in the rebuilding program they had believed would follow his defeat of Lorenzo.

To Icahn, however, the decision to hold back on massive investments in aircraft and personnel in an era when the industry was already struggling with too many seats and too few passengers to fill them was a simple bow to the laws of supply and demand. Spending billions on a major fleet expansion was, from his perspective, throwing good money after bad. He prided himself on being the first airplane CEO to see things for what they really were and to halt the knee-jerk response to buy, buy, buy. If the smooth-talking airplane salesmen thought they could manipulate Icahn into buying more of what he felt he didn't need, he would show them the difference between dealing with Carl Icahn and dealing with a CEO who had risen to a level of incompetence.

On one occasion, a representative of an aircraft leasing company called on Icahn with the idea of selling him fuel-efficient jets. Taking a hard-sell approach, he launched into his pitch with the unequivocal statement: "Carl, you have to buy these planes," Icahn recalls. "Then he lays out charts and graphs projecting robust growth in passenger miles and airline revenues. Based on these rosy projections, he insists, there's no way to go but up. More people will be flying, more planes will carry them and more dollars will come in to pay for the planes."

That's when Icahn rained on his parade. " 'Wait, I say. What if there's a recession?'

"The guy freezes. 'There can't be a recession,' he says, as if there's some law against them.

" 'Why not?' I ask. Because, he says, 'The government will take care of that.'

"I'm supposed to accept that. Maybe it's not so stupid to think that I would. Because that's the way these airline guys behave. They're willing participants in a Ponzi scheme. They keep buying planes and adding seats, but there's no one to fly on them."

On another occasion, the airplane salesman tried to convince Icahn to buy a new generation of jets on the premise that glasnost would bring a surge in Russian tourism and that the aircraft would transport Russians from Moscow to Paris an hour earlier. If the salesman thought he had built a convincing case, he had to be crushed by Icahn's response. "You're talking about Russian peasants on the Volga River. Why the hell are they going to go from Moscow to Paris? And if they have to go, what the hell do they know or care if it's an hour faster?

"You're talking about peasants who don't even fly."

Icahn's tenure at TWA has shown him at his best and his worst. On the positive side, he is a savvy investor, attuned to the worst-case scenario, deftly extracting his risk capital from the company while simultaneously increasing his control. In arranging for the financing, in tilting the rewards to his column, he is masterful.

His prodigious intellect and striking analytical ability are counterbalanced, though, by a shortsightedness. Icahn's determination to put the screws into TWA employees and vendors left many who came in contact with him feeling cheated, angry.

"Carl's strategy is to squeeze you and see how far you'll go," said an executive with Young & Rubicam, TWA's former advertising agency. "He takes wild flings. He says, 'Cut the fee by $3 million. You can't? Then cut it by $2 million.' He tries things on for size. Comes up with an insultingly low offer and sees what happens.

"We resigned the TWA business because we couldn't possibly make money on the lower fee structure Icahn was proposing to us. He told us to find a way not to lose money, but we couldn't.

"He's an impossibly demanding client."

.   .   .

"Icahn's cheapness is extraordinary," said Tom Ashwood. "We had a dinner one night at the Waldorf Astoria to honor TWA's best employees. Carl gave this rambling speech, economics 101, according to Icahn. He rambles about the world economy and how wrong it is to borrow money. Strange advice for the world's greatest borrower whose company is up to its ass in junk bonds.

"After his embarrassing speech that no one there could relate to, Carl takes me aside with Kingsley to talk business. He dismisses his wife and sends her off. But then Kingsley's wife stops by and says to him, 'Good night, honey. I'm tired and going upstairs to sleep.'

"As she walks away, Carl erupts at Kingsley. 'You're staying here? At the hotel? What the hell are you doing that for? These rooms cost me $170 apiece.'

"After Carl left, I asked Kingsley if he'd been serious. 'Oh sure,' he said. This from a guy who made Carl $500 to $700 million."

After the privatization was complete, Icahn pursued an exit strategy that called for selling the carrier as a going concern by merging it into another airline.

But as Carl maneuvered to engineer a mega deal, his compulsion to go beyond a "fair price," citing figures that would make fools of prospective buyers, blew up in his face.

"Carl has been a pig," said Kent Scott. "He tried to sell the airline to Northwest, America West, and others, but he has always wanted $200 million more than it was worth at any given time."

When TWA president Joe Corr assembled an investment group to buy the airline from Icahn, he too found Carl unwilling to make a reasonable deal.

"When I expressed an interest in buying TWA, Carl told me to pursue it. This was in the summer of 1988. I lined up financing on company time and Carl would check on my progress.

"Eventually, I got most of the financing together, and I was highly confident that I could do the deal, but that's when Carl said no. I offered $425 million and he wanted $450 million. What really bothered me is that he then took my financing plan, which involved foreign airline participation, private investors, and route sales, and asked his friends to overbid me. I thought that was disgraceful. It angered me terribly, and it led, ultimately, to my departure from TWA."

In the spring of 1990, the machinists union presented Icahn with a proposal to buy the airline. As the author of the proposal, Brian Freeman couldn't resist taking a pot shot at Carl's penchant for turning off prospective buyers: "Employee ownership will facilitate transactions with other investors and airlines, some of which appear to have been chilled by their perceptions of your high above-market return requirements and/or your desire to capture all value."

In a May 31, 1990, letter to Icahn, Freeman charged that the unions' painful concessions to Icahn, made in the spirit of rebuilding the airline, had been mostly squandered:

"Viewed both objectively and from the employees' longer-term perspective, the substantial opportunity to improve TWA's medium to long-term situation that was created and subsidized by the massive employee investments from the IAM- and Air Line Pilots Association-represented employees (as well as those imposed on others) has been ignored and probably dissipated to a large degree. The remaining opportunities will continue to erode unless a fundamental change occurs. . . .

"Since your acquisition, you have largely sold, stripped, leased, and leveraged the assets and operating cash flow of the airline in order to repay yourself your original equity investment, increase your percentage ownership of TWA and create a cash horde for investment purposes. The employee investments have allowed you to strip the airline, and fund deteriorating operations while avoiding investment."

Under the terms of the proposed employee buy-out, a new

corporation would be established, bearing the name TWA. All of the airline's operating and related assets (other than aircraft), plus $300 million in cash from the airline or from Icahn's other resources, would be sold to the new TWA, which would be owned by the employees. The new company would be mostly free of the former TWA's debt load, but would agree to lease from it all existing aircraft and would assume the old entity's pension obligations.

By freeing the new TWA from its crushing debt, and by ridding it of its one-time "savior," labor believed it would be buying a new lease on life, giving the employees the opportunity to capitalize on the carrier's existing strengths, including its routes and landing slots. In this context, the union would contemplate making additional wage concessions, knowing that these savings would accrue to their own benefit, rather than to Icahn's.

Although the buy-out made good sense from the IAM's standpoint, the benefits to Icahn were not as clear. Under the terms of the plan, he would retain cash and other assets (including the aircraft) held by the old TWA. This company could then be retained, taken public or sold, after, as Freeman put it, "an additional period of operation and further financial engineering." Were Icahn unable to convince the company's creditors to take a haircut on the outstanding debt, he could tank the old TWA, wiping his hands of the carrier without the pension liability (which would come to haunt him) hanging over his head.

At the time, Icahn discounted the benefit of the pension-liability shift, and claimed that the deal offered him little in hard benefits. When labor retorted that he didn't deserve any more than he was being offered, Icahn, in typical fashion, held fast, demanding an additional cash payment of as much as $200 million in order to look favorably on the proposal. After a series of meetings in the spring of 1990, the machinists reluctantly agreed to consider sweetening the offer as Icahn demanded, provided the pilots bore a share of the costs. But when Freeman took up the idea with ALPA, he ran into a wall of resistance. With a powerful clique of ALPA's leadership convinced that TWA was doomed, the idea of making additional payments seemed like pouring more money into a black hole. Ultimately, the deal fell apart.

Icahn's hard bargaining on a possible sale of the airline to any number of potential buyers was based, in part, on the lingering belief that he could profit more by liquidating the assets. Although he has had limited success in this approach, mostly in the sale of transatlantic routes, here too Icahn miscalculated the complexity of the airline business.

"Carl kept thinking that if he couldn't sell TWA as a company, he could do an orderly liquidation of the business," said Kent Scott. "But in the airline business, there is no such thing as an orderly liquidation. One plane can be worth $7 million but try to sell fifty and they are worth $3.5 million each. Also, Carl doesn't want to be in the position of having to sell a load of planes to a buyer like American's Bob Crandall if Crandall knows Carl has to sell."

As Icahn vacillated from strategy to strategy, each time certain that he could find a profitable exit from TWA, the airline's financial condition continued to deteriorate, along with employee morale and passenger tolerance for slipshod service and filthy planes. By 1990, TWA had become for Carl Icahn what Vietnam had become for Lyndon Johnson.

"After the airline started to bleed money, Carl let his hair down with me one day," said Jim Freund. "He said, 'I was a schmuck. I let my loyalty to the pilots sway me.' I got the distinct impression that he regretted not letting Lorenzo take the company when he had the chance."

Working long into the night, holding exhaustive meetings with his TWA management team, a tired and uncharacteristically downtrodden Icahn—his eyes bleary, his hair disheveled—looked beaten, trapped for the first time in his life in a puzzle he couldn't piece together.

Icahn had no one to blame but himself. By trying to push every negotiation to a win/win outcome, he had squandered the opportunity to sell or merge TWA when the window of opportunity was open widest. What's more, Icahn let ego get in the way of intellect, telling himself over and over again that he could find a way to fix the problem. But the more he planned and strategized, the more he found himself stymied at every turn.

"I don't know who really won the contest between Carl and Lorenzo over TWA," said Ed Gehrlein. "Because Carl got stuck with TWA—a business he didn't understand. That took a toll on him, and I don't know if you can call that winning."

Clearly, the man who delighted in attacking corporate management found his words coming back to haunt him.

"Icahn has been a great critic of the management of American industry," said Theodore Kheel. "When he took over TWA he said, 'I'll show you how to do it.' But he's fallen flat on his face. He's done a miserable job of running the airline."

Throughout the last two years of his tenure as TWA's chairman, Icahn attempted, repeatedly, to deal with the monumental problems of a debt-ridden, demoralized, miserably inefficient carrier saddled with an obsolete fleet by engaging in the only process—financial engineering—he truly respects. Now and then he would imagine himself as a marketing whiz whose latest promotional scheme would lift TWA out of its doldrums. Encountered in TWA's Mt. Kisco offices during late evening brainstorming sessions with the executive staff, Icahn would wax poetic about his latest scheme to lower fares, streamline routes, capture the loyalty of the business traveler. Even for a street-smart billionaire with a skeptical view of the world, hope sprang eternal. Time and again he would pull isolated statistics out of the air, citing them as evidence that his marketing tactics were working. When a visitor expressed skepticism that TWA could overcome its horrendous image and antiquated fleet, Icahn—confident that he could outsmart the system, any system—would anoint one of the assembled executives as his alter ego, proclaiming support for whatever assertions the king was making.

Much like Lyndon Johnson's myopic determination to win the war in Vietnam, Icahn kept betting that the next strategy, the next tactic, would turn the tide. Again and again he believed he saw light at the end of the tunnel. No way the airline business was going to prove too great a challenge for a man who had run roughshod over the corporate establishment for more than a decade.

In the midst of his smoke-and-mirrors odyssey, Icahn found another shrewd investor, Beverly Hills–based billionaire Kirk Kerkorian, poking his nose under his tent. In an attempt to buy TWA by forging a pact with the carrier's unions, Kerkorian— who was convinced that all of TWA's London routes were critical to the airline's viability and to the prospects of engineering a turnaround—lobbied to block a proposed sale of the routes to American.

Under the Kerkorian plan (put forward by Tracinda Corp., Kerkorian's privately owned investment vehicle), machinists and pilots would provide a total of $177 million in wage concessions in exchange for a 33 percent equity stake in TWA. Kerkorian would claim 50 percent of the equity, and the creditors would get the remaining 17 percent. Preferring this proposal to anything Icahn would offer, labor pressed political leaders to quash any route sales to American on the grounds that Kerkorian's plan was known to be predicated on retention of all U.S.–London routes.

As Kerkorian maneuvered around the fringes of TWA, Icahn seethed. In a bitter irony, another strong-willed and powerful entrepreneur was poised to capitalize on a CEO's failure—in this case Icahn's. Instead of tendering for TWA's devalued stock (which Icahn held), Kerkorian would tender for the distressed emotions of TWA's unions and their supporters on Capitol Hill.

But the threat was short-lived.

On April 25, 1991, the Department of Transportation effectively foiled Kerkorian's plan by approving the sale of three of TWA's U.S.–London routes—Boston, New York, and Los Angeles. Although DOT Secretary Samuel Skinner (who would soon follow John Sununu as George Bush's chief of staff) announced that three of the six requested route sales (London to Baltimore, St. Louis, and Philadelphia) were rejected on the grounds that they could inhibit competition, American Air's CEO Bob Crandall knew that he had succeeded in acquiring the choice routes. As did Kerkorian, who, without these prized assets, was no longer interested in TWA.

Icahn's original deal with American called for a purchase price of $445 million for the six routes. With the deal restricted to three routes, American geared up for a new round of negotiations on a substantially reduced price. Crandall, being a reasonable man reared on the rules of fair play, assumed that Icahn would likewise be reasonable. But he was shocked to discover that the king of leverage was unwilling to reduce his price by as much as a dollar. For the three routes Icahn demanded the same $445 million.

Learning of this, Crandall placed an urgent call to Icahn, insisting—in an unusually emotional declaration—that the failure to reduce the price to reflect the limited dimensions of the deal was unconscionable. Crandall apparently believed that he could appeal to Icahn's sense of fairness, convincing him to shave a minimum of $100 million from the transaction price. But Icahn recognized that Crandall's overriding objective from the start was to secure the three trophy routes that DOT had approved. When Crandall balked—his management team insisting at first that they would not pay the full price—Icahn boasted that advance summer bookings to London were up and that he would keep the routes for TWA. Inherent in this strategy of brinkmanship was the blunt realization that American's CEO would pay anything within reasonable parameters to walk away with his prize. As it turned out, Icahn was right. Crandall would accept the outrageous terms. He would bitch and moan and cry foul, but in the end he would take out the corporate checkbook and fill in the required numbers.

Throughout TWA's prolonged slide, Icahn kept thinking, in typical fashion, that he would profit on the mistakes of others. As the ranks of beleaguered airlines appeared to grow by the month—with such carriers as Pan Am, Continental, Braniff, and America West teetering at the edge—Icahn saw his salvation in bottom fishing, buying planes and related assets cheaply as competitors collapsed in a sea of red ink. The way the thinking went, by leasing planes at fire-sale rates, Icahn would reduce his operating costs and—coupled with an upturn in the travel market he was forever certain was just around the corner—TWA would rebound and begin the steady march back to profitability. But in this uncharacteristic bout of self-deception, Icahn failed to see (or refused to admit to anyone, including himself) that TWA was not going to stage a comeback based on the rubble of obsolete aircraft.

"Carl approaches everything like a securities trader," says former Pan Am chairman Thomas Plaskett, who tangled with Icahn over a proposed merger of their airlines. "Everything has a bid and asked. He thought he could run an airline like a trader."

To chairman Icahn, the need to invest in modern, fuel-efficient aircraft, to upgrade substantially what was often embarrassingly shoddy service, and to mold TWA's rank and file into a motivated work force still seemed like Harvard Business School nonsense. But at this juncture his management myopia was a moot point. With most of TWA's cash and borrowing power depleted, Icahn's window of opportunity for rebuilding TWA into a financially strong carrier had long since passed.

The staggering debt load TWA had assumed as part of the infamous privatization weighed heavily on the carrier, soaking up a lopsided portion of its revenues. As Icahn struggled to give the airline breathing room until one of his dream-a-day marketing schemes could hit paydirt, he sought to lighten the debt load by offering bond holders debt for cash at a fraction of their original investments. He also sought to trade debt for equity, coming up with a series of plans to restructure the carrier on these bases.

As Icahn tinkered with his restructuring scenarios, his opponents in organized labor and on Capitol Hill feared that he would sell off TWA's assets and abandon the carrier, leaving its underfunded pension plan—and, in turn, the employee beneficiaries—in the lurch. Since Icahn, personally and through an investment group, controlled more than 80 percent of TWA stock, he was deemed to be part of a "control group," meaning his liability for the pension funding extended to his other businesses. But powerful forces—including Missouri Senator John Danforth—worried that if his equity stake in TWA were to drop below 80 percent in a reorganization, Icahn would be free of his obligation. An outspoken foe, Danforth had once said, "There are some people who shouldn't be allowed to run airlines, and I don't want to name names, but his initials are Carl Icahn."

In an effort to lock in Icahn's liability, Congress passed legislation, in the form of an amendment to the Dire Emergency Supplemental Bill, that would keep Icahn on the hook for TWA's pension liabilities even if his stake in the carrier dropped below 80 percent. In effect, this meant that Icahn's prized assets, from ACF to champion thoroughbred Meadow Star, could be seized to pay for pension beneficiaries.

"This amendment is narrow, simple, and straightforward," Danforth proclaimed. "Narrow in that it applies to this one unconscionable proposal to reduce Icahn's equity stake below 80 percent. Simple in that it says if Mr. Icahn controls TWA, either through ownership of the airline or by directing its management, he is liable for the pension obligations. Straightforward in that it provides the Pension Benefit Guaranty Corporation with the type of protection any private guarantor would receive in a similar situation."

In a letter to President Bush, Danforth summarized his feelings this way: "Do you believe that Carl Icahn should be able to take a business he now owns, continue to run it, but through a slick legal maneuver insulate his financial empire from liability for perhaps close to $1 billion in unfunded pension obligations, and turn over this liability, ultimately, to the federal taxpayer?

"If not, then support this amendment."

The "get Icahn" amendment—passed by the House on November 27, 1991, by 303 to 114 and by a voice vote in the Senate hours later—marked the beginning of the worst year of Icahn's life. Suddenly a financial lone wolf, a takeover king who had been careful to weigh the downside before making any moves, found himself blindsided by an act of Congress. With estimates of TWA's unfunded liability ranging up to $1.2 billion, his entire fortune hung in the balance.

Learning of Congress's action in his limousine en route to a Manhattan theater, Icahn was stricken with fear. Could everything he had worked for be taken from him? Could the wide-

spread resentment of corporate raiders finally be coming home
to roost? It seemed as if the establishment he had thumbed his
nose at for so long had risen up to break him.

As his mind raced, he wondered how he had fallen into this
quagmire. As did Icahn observers up and down Wall Street. One
school of thought held that Icahn, caught up in his optimistic
projections for TWA, believed that the carrier would remain
viable, that there would be plenty of cash to fund the pension
plan, and as such, that underfunding would never emerge as a
threatening issue.

Another theory took an opposite position, arguing that
Icahn had purposely crossed the 80 percent threshold in order to
arrange for a consolidation between TWA and ACF, thus using
the carrier to shelter taxes generated by ACF and Icahn's myriad
investments.

Wilbur Ross, who has tangled with Icahn in a series of
complex financial transactions, including the Texaco episode and
Icahn's emergence as the major debt holder in Donald Trump's
Taj Mahal casino, is uncertain why Icahn crossed the control
group threshold, but there is no arguing, he says, that it was a
"gigantic error."

From Icahn's perspective, the error was not his but that of
his lawyers who performed due diligence on the transaction. His
side of the story holds that the only actuarial assumptions he was
privy to placed his maximum liability at $120 million, figured by
projecting 9 percent earnings on the pension funds' assets. Ostensibly, Icahn was unaware that the Pension Benefit Guaranty
Board, a federal agency that insures and oversees more than
80,000 privately run pension plans including TWA's, could use
a 5 percent projected rate of return (thus boosting his liability to
$500 million) and furthermore that the government agency had
the power to terminate the pension plans, thus activating early
retirement clauses that could drive his liability to more than $1
billion.

The full threat of the pension liability emerged as TWA filed for
bankruptcy in January 1992. Concerned that the carrier would

fail while in Chapter XI, or soon after the airline emerged from bankruptcy through a court-approved reorganization, the PBGC was determined that Icahn—rather than the agency—would have to fill the potentially huge gap in the pension funding. From the beginning, PBGC deputy executive director Diane Burkley, who had made a name for herself as a nimble and tough-minded negotiator in private law practice and previous PBGC cases, made clear that she would not give her support to a reorganization that failed to address adequately the pension liability. Specifically, she was determined that Icahn—through his extensive business assets (which the agency tallied at close to $1 billion)— pay a hefty share of the tab.

As negotiations between Icahn and Burkley commenced in earnest in the summer of 1992, the PBGC talked publicly of the need to cover a potential $1.2 billion shortfall while at the same time it was indicating through back channels that if Icahn loaned TWA $200 million to keep the carrier afloat as it reorganized and signed $350 million in current-value notes payable to the PBGC, a settlement could be reached. In this way the carrier could emerge from Chapter XI, and Icahn would be free of the threat of a fortune-crushing billion-dollar settlement. Considering that the operating loan would be collateralized, Burkley believed that she had put a fair offer on the table. Granted, Icahn would have to pay a heavy price for the TWA fiasco, but he would still walk away a very wealthy man.

But to Icahn the offer was totally out of the question. Rather than agreeing to this enormous settlement, he would launch into the highest-stakes poker game of his life. His opening bid—to make TWA a collateralized loan and to pledge certain TWA assets to the PBGC—was about as close as he could get to telling Burkley to "go screw herself."

Icahn's macho gambit was based in part on the conviction that the PBGC would have to accept his loan on any terms or risk the political fallout of an airline failure coming on the heels of the collapse of Eastern and Pan Am. He figured that she would be wary of a full-fledged shoot-out that could jeopardize TWA's ability to emerge from bankruptcy.

In thinking this way, Icahn underestimated Burkley's negotiating abilities and her resolve to extract a pound of flesh from the erstwhile raider. Although the petite, stylishly coifed forty-year-old attorney-turned-pension enforcer had to be concerned with the political ramifications of another airline collapse (triggered, in part, by the PBGC's refusal to accept Icahn's financing), a countervailing mandate was to protect the PBGC (already $2.5 billion in the hole) from the kind of huge losses suffered by its banking equivalent, the Federal Deposit Insurance Corporation. With this mandate in mind Burkley responded to Icahn's opening offer with a flat-out refusal to even discuss it. If Icahn was going to play hardball, Burkley was determined to pursue him for the full $1.2 billion.

Up to this point, Icahn relied on his lawyers to do much of the negotiating. But when he realized that the steely and intelligent Burkley was not just another bureaucrat who could be bluffed with standard scare tactics, Icahn assumed personal responsibility for the negotiations.

He made the move reluctantly. Ensconced in his East Hampton beach house for the month of August, he yearned to walk the shoreline, to play tennis and poker, relieved, after years of misery, from the pox of TWA. But the problem refused to disappear, and he knew that unless he accepted the bitter pill and employed all of his negotiating skills, the fortune he had amassed over a tumultuous decade was in jeopardy. It was then his strategy shifted from an attempt to avoid payment to a more realistic goal of limiting the amount he would have to pay. For openers, he made a a lowball offer to pay $5 million a year for ten years. When Burkley stated that she would not begin to negotiate until Icahn put real money on the table, he proposed a settlement whereby he would make the $200 million collateralized loan plus payments of about $100 million to the pension plan and guarantee the plan's so-called "minimum funding" provisions allowing for benefits to be paid on a business-as-usual basis.

What appeared to be the first sign of substantive progress wound up having a negative impact on the negotiations. With Icahn believing that he had demonstrated good faith, and Burkley insisting that he was still light-years away from a realistic number, the tension that had simmered between the adversaries exploded. In a series of marathon telephone sessions (some, initiated by Icahn, placed in the middle of the night) and face-to-face encounters, Icahn and Burkley tangled on a personal level, their emotions boiling to the surface. At times Icahn accused Burkley of grandstanding, seeking to bring down the wealthy raider in a poorly veiled attempt to propel her own career. One night Burkley was so angered by the charge that she hung up on Icahn, only to have him call back to proclaim that no matter what she did or said, she would never bring him down.

The battle between them was waged on two levels. On the surface were complex legal and financial issues. But equally important, two bullheaded negotiators—both given to histrionics—were determined to make the other blink first.

As an observer to the talks noted: "This may have been the first case where a man and woman were negotiating and the goal was to prove who had a bigger pecker."

As much as the PBGC dismissed Icahn's insinuation that the case against him was a Burkley-inspired witch-hunt based on personal career motives, the agency was concerned enough to have executive director James Lockhart step in as a major participant in the negotiations. The idea behind this calculated move was to demonstrate to the media, the general public, and most of all to Icahn that Burkley's tough stance was not one woman's vendetta but instead reflected the resolve of the entire agency.

As the PBGC negotiations became increasingly acrimonious, Icahn found some of the old energy that had deserted him during the years of the TWA debacle. For a born gambler this was the game of a lifetime. On the one hand, he could lose his fortune; on the other, he could preserve his wealth and prove once again that he was among the world's master negotiators.

In classic Icahn style, he set out to confuse Burkley thoroughly, moving away from the typical linear negotiating style she was accustomed to—"I'll give you this, if you give me that"—to his Columbo-like routine, making dozens of simultaneous offers, some reasonable, others absurd. To complicate matters, he would toss Burkley curve balls that would leave her perplexed as

to her adversary's true intentions. At one point Icahn appeared
to capitulate, saying that perhaps he should let Burkley take
all of his assets. This, he teased, would relieve him of the problem
of bequeathing great wealth to his children without sapping them
of the work ethic. Still toying with her, he asked that if he did
surrender, he be allowed to keep his beloved beach house and
that Liba, who had never been fond of the Hamptons, be left a
modest home of her own.

All of this was just a diversionary tactic designed to set up
Burkley for the leverage that Icahn is a master of employing. In
this case it would be his willingness to make the $200 million loan
to a capital-deprived TWA. As the shouting match with Burkley
appeared to stall—the adversaries hundreds of millions of dollars apart—Icahn threw down the gauntlet. He would make
the loan only if his pension liability were limited to a present
value of slightly more than $100 million. This would be his best
offer.

In drawing the line this way, Icahn appeared to be taking an
enormous gamble. Should the PBGC succeed in securing the
TWA financing from another source, it would strip Icahn of the
leverage he held as the carrier's would-be savior, a repeat performance of the role he had played in the battle with Frank
Lorenzo. Although there was substantial risk in his position,
Icahn—who had intimate knowledge of TWA's finances—was
fairly confident that no one in his right mind would step forward
as an alternate source of capital. And as a backup position, he was
advised that if the PBGC terminated the pension plan and pursued him for the underfunding, he could litigate for years, perhaps winning his case or settling out of court for a fraction of the
$1.2 billion the PBGC claimed was at stake.

With the parties apparently deadlocked, Burkley attempted
an end run around Icahn by seeking to strike a deal with TWA's
unions and creditors. The way she planned it, Icahn would be
locked out of a TWA reorganization. As the plan was put forward, the creditors would trade their debt for a 55 percent equity
stake, and the unions would grant concessions in return for 45
percent of the reorganized company. TWA would agree to make
$300 million in payments to the pension underfunding, and once

the deal was set, the PBGC would terminate the pensions and pursue Icahn for the shortfall.

Conceptually, the idea was brilliant. But in practice, the need for the $200 million loan to keep the carrier operating through the winter of 1992–93 proved to be a major flaw. Without this capital infusion, the creditors—and even more so the unions—feared that the carrier would go belly-up, leaving them with nothing but the satisfaction of watching Icahn lose his leverage with the PBGC. Although Icahn had few sympathizers in the pack, they preferred to protect their financial interests rather than to join the PBGC in a get-Icahn scheme. In fact, just the opposite occurred. In one of the great ironies of the TWA episode, the same unions that had cursed themselves for having supported Icahn's original takeover were back in his camp, pressing the PBGC—as well as the powers that be on Capitol Hill—to support the Icahn reorganization plan with the stringent limits on Carl's pension liability.

Once again Icahn had managed to maneuver through a labyrinth of issues and opposing forces to position himself as the deal maker or breaker. Even when the PBGC attempted to neutralize his leverage by offering to inject $200 million of its own funds into TWA, the creditors balked, fearing that Icahn (who, as an owner of TWA bonds, was a creditor himself) would seek revenge by employing every means available to break the deal.

"There was a fear factor at work," Burkley recalled. "The creditors worried that Carl would not give up his bonds. That he would fight all over the place against the deal with the PBGC. They worried that Carl would make their lives miserable. That they would be stuck in the bankruptcy process and that after six months the airline would die.

"The fact is, we had an answer to the TWA capital problem, but the creditors refused it. They asked, 'Why should we risk a run-in with Icahn when we can get his money and have peace with him?' "

By the late fall of 1992, the PBGC—which had entered the

negotiations assuming it had Icahn cornered—found itself in check. To placate the influential forces in favor of the Icahn deal, it would have to strike a deal with its shrewd and nimble adversary. The plan would shield Icahn's fortune and, in the best of circumstances, conceivably cost him nothing.

Under the terms of the settlement, Icahn would make the $200 million TWA loan, extending $50 million up front and the balance after the federal bankruptcy court gave its blessing to the company's reorganization plan. The carrier's two pension plans would remain in place but with no additional benefits accruing to employees.

Both Icahn and the restructured airline would be responsible for a portion of the pension funding. The new TWA would give the PBGC two fifteen-year notes for a total of $300 million, the debt being collateralized by the company's assets. Much of the note proceeds would be used to cover the pension plans' so-called minimum funding of about $35 million annually; any shortfall would be made up by Icahn. The price tag for this was projected at $80 million over five years. But even this relatively modest bill could actually disappear. Because the settlement called for Icahn to manage the pension assets, should he be able to earn in excess of the projected 9 percent, his liability could dissolve and, should the pension performance really skyrocket, he could profit on the transaction.

In the worst-case scenario, if TWA went belly-up and the pension plans were terminated, Icahn would be responsible for a maximum of $240 million payable over eight years. In present-value calculations, Icahn's liability was even less, falling closer to the $150 million mark. Considering that his $200 million loan would be collateralized, and that his darkest scenario called for relatively modest annual payments well within the means of his existing companies (primarily ACF), Icahn was walking away from the worst nightmare of his life remarkably unscathed. Although he had a continuing obligation to the PBGC, and although he would be facing a total loss on TWA junk bonds he had purchased several years before for $60 million, he had used the airline's cash flow to help finance his windfall Texaco investment and his deal with the PBGC would relieve him of all additional liabilities.*

Of all his high-stakes poker games and epic confrontations, this was Icahn's most important and, in all likelihood, his most successful. As a controversial and incompetent airline chairman, an infamous raider, and one of the few financial czars of the past decade who had yet to be toppled, Icahn had seemed a ready target. With a federal agency and influential U.S. senators aligned against him, he appeared destined for the junk heap of the eighties. But in the end, the man who had determined to control the destiny of companies had been effective in controlling his own.

It makes one think of his favorite Kipling lines:

"If you can meet with Triumph and Disaster / And treat those two imposters just the same . . . / If you can make one heap of all your winnings / And risk it on one turn of pitch-and-toss . . . / Yours is the Earth and everything that's in it / And—which is more—you'll be a Man, my son!"

---

*At the time this book went to press, the terms of the settlement were announced but yet to be signed by all parties.

SOURCE NOTES

5. House Subcommittee on Aviation hearings, June 6, 1985, p. 111.

14. Quote from "Icahn on Icahn," *Fortune*, February 29, 1988, p. 55.

17. *Ibid.*

22. *Ibid.*

24. Quote, Pinnacle/CNN.

31–32. Bayswater Acquisition Corp. hearings, Icahn testimony, March 24, 1983.

72. *MacNeil/Lehrer Report.*

76. SEC, "In the Matter of Icahn & Co.," Icahn deposition, October 8, 1980.

76–77. *Ibid.*

78. *Ibid.*

80. *Ibid.*

81. *Ibid.*

81–2. *Ibid.*

84. *Ibid.*

84. *Ibid.*

85. *Ibid.*

92. Alfred Kingsley deposition, SEC, September 23, 1980, p. 19.

92. Kingsley deposition, p. 20.

96. *Hammermill Paper Co.* v. *Carl C. Icahn, Icahn & Co.* v. *Hammermill Paper Co.*, U.S. District Court for Western Dist. of Pennsylvania, Hammermill's memorandum of law in opposition to Icahn's motion for a preliminary injunction, p. 23.

97. Hammermill, p. 29.

110. *New York Times*, July 3, 1984.

112. *Dan River* v. *Carl C. Icahn et al.*, U.S. District Court for Western Dist. of Virginia, deposition of Stanley Nortman, December 14, 1982.

115. *Marshall Field* v. *Carl Icahn et al.*, U.S. District Court, Southern Dist. of New York, deposition of Angelo Arena, February 23, 1982.

117. Skadden Arps memorandum to SEC, Division of Enforcement, March 15, 1982, p. 1.

117. *Ibid.*

122. *Dan River* v. *Carl C. Icahn et al.*, U.S. District Court for Western Dist. of Virginia, November 12, 1982, p. 97, hearing on motion for preliminary injunction.

124. *Dan River* hearing, p. 85.

126. *Dan River* hearing, p. 93.

126–7. *Wall Street Journal*, September 16, 1982.

130. Dan River proxy statement & notice of annual meeting, April 28, 1983.

131. *Barron's*, November 29, 1983.

144. *New York Times*, August 9, 1984.

149. House Subcommittee on Telecommunications, Consumer Protection and Finance, hearings on corporate takeovers, February 27, March, 12, April 23, May 22, 1985, transcript p. 56.

152. House Subcommittee hearings, p. 46.

153. Icahn deposition, SEC, "In the Matter of Phillips Petroleum Company," September 26, 1985, p. 79.

156. *Ibid.*

162. "Phillips Petroleum," Ivan Boesky deposition, p. 57.

162. *American Lawyer,* May 1985.

167. House Subcommittee hearings, p. 2.

175. House Subcommittee on Aviation hearings, June 6, 1985, p. 125.

176. "Seventeenth Annual Institute on Securities Regulation" transcript, Stephen J. Friedman, Charles M. Nathan, Harvey L. Pitt, Roland J. Santoni, eds., October 1986, p. 12.

178. "Securities Regulation" transcript, p. 151.

180. DOT hearings, p. 3.

181. House Subcommittee on Aviation hearings, June 6, 1985, p. 86.

182. House hearings, pp. 88–89.

183. House hearings, p. 101.

184. House hearings, pp. 104–105, 111–12.

184. House hearings, p. 129.

187–8. "Securities regulation" transcript, p. 159.

197. "Securities regulation" transcript, p. 161.

217. *U.S. Air Group* v. *Carl Icahn, TWA, Inc., et al.,* U.S. District Court for Western Dist. of Pennsylvania, complaint, March 8, 1987.

223–4. *IAM* v. *TWA et. al.,* Supreme Court of New York, complaint, August 24, 1988, p. 13.

224. *IAM* v. *TWA* complaint, pp. 11–12.

235. *Newsweek,* January 4, 1988.

48–9. *Wall Street Journal,* December 21, 1987.

255. *Texaco* v. *Icahn et al.,* U.S. District Court, Southern Dist. of N.Y., June 12, 1988, Carl Icahn deposition, pp. 349–50.

256. Texaco press release, May 25, 1988.

256. *Ibid.*

257. *Texaco* v. *Icahn et al.*, Icahn deposition.

260. *Ibid.*

262. *Texaco Today*, "We Won."

266–7. *Texaco* v. *Icahn et al.*, Icahn deposition, p. 237.

INDEX